No Love in War: a story of Christian nationalism

Copyright © 2023 Valerie H. Hobbs

Published by Mayfly Books. Available in paperpack and free online at www.mayflybooks.org in 2023.

This work depicts actual events in the life of the author as truthfully as recollection permits. It is a representation of memory. While all persons within are actual individuals, names have only been used in connection with public figures. All other names and various identifying characteristics have been changed. Although every precaution has been taken in the preparation of this book, the publisher and author assume no responsibility for errors or omissions. Neither is any liability assumed for damages resulting from the use of information contained herein. All quotes are included for purposes of critique. All Bible quotes are taken from the New International Version.

ISBN (Print) 978-1-3999-4048-1
ISBN (PDF) 978-1-906948-63-4
ISBN (ebook) 978-1-906948-64-1

This work is licensed under the Creative Commons Attribution-Non commercial-No Derivatives 4.0 International License (CC BY-NC-ND 4.0).
To view a copy of this license, visit http://creativecommons.org/licenses/by-nc-nd/4.0

Book design by Valerie H. Hobbs

Cover Image by Vintage Armament Illustrations,

Licensed via Envato Elements 2022

Typeset in Adobe Garamond Pro by Jess Parker

Valerie Hobbs, not to be confused with the YA author of the same name, is a linguist at the University of Sheffield, where she teaches and researches on religious language. This is her second book.

No Love in War: a story of Christian nationalism

Valerie H. Hobbs

This book is dedicated to all who suffer violence in religious communities with visions of empire, to all whose homes are sites of war.

Contents

PROLOGUE	01
LAND	08
WOMB	64
GRAVE	120
FIRE	171
EPILOGUE	249

But where can wisdom be found?
Where does understanding dwell?
No mortal comprehends its worth;
It cannot be found in the land of the living.
The deep says, "It is not in me";
the sea says, "It is not with me.

Job 28: 12-14

Prologue

As I write this essay, the Christian Reconstructionist Chalcedon Foundation is celebrating the fiftieth anniversary of its establishment by Rousas John Rushdoony. And in some ways, the movement he built is just now coming into its own.

— Julie Ingersoll [1]

I was born in a wilderness end-times cult in Alaska in the 1970s, after which I spent most of my childhood in a Christian Reconstructionist church and school and then in a conservative Christian college led by some of the key players that laid the foundation for the Christian Right in the United States, extremist politicians and religious leaders instrumental in paving the way for the election of Donald Trump and the violent, political insurrection at the US Capitol Building in 2021. To this day, I have resisted telling certain parts of my past, even to myself. Initially, traumatising events can, like corpses, sink rapidly to the deepest seabed of one's memory, until, having decomposed, they rise with sudden buoyancy, triggered sometimes by even the most innocuous or seemingly unrelated event, word, smell, sound, touch. The sight of their decay is startling. I'm old enough now to have been surprised a few times by this, by the unexpected ascent of some putrefied relic from the past I've carried around unconsciously for decades. It's astonishing, after so many years, to discover such consequential things about oneself. How quickly the world can be reshaped and we in it, and at so late an hour.

---

[1] Ingersoll, J. (2014). 'The Christian Reconstruction Movement in U.S. Politics,' *Oxford Handbook Topics in Religion* (online edn, Oxford Academic, 3 Feb. 2014), https://doi.org/10.1093/oxfordhb/9780199935420.013.25, accessed 3 Nov. 2022.

For example: Of all the artefacts from my childhood, I first threw away a certain packet of letters in the immaturity of early marriage. The oddness of this act now intrigues me. Why throw out these letters especially? I kept other things, a card from a controlling childhood friend, a blue Trinity hymnal with a personal inscription from a Christian Reconstructionist friend I regularly cycled with at university, photos of awkward dates with domineering men to Spring and Christmas Banquets at university. All these I kept, and I can't now remember a single word on the letters I threw away, only the particular curve of the handwriting and the thickness of each envelope, holding all those pages and pages. I question myself on this. I sit with curiosity among my choices. Why did I let those letters go? Why did I instead preserve other relics of past relationships?

I now look at the images I've carried with me, the objects, the notes and cards, this bulky baggage I've brought, even across the ocean. And I feel nothing. I see that perhaps keeping them facilitated a kind of desensitisation therapy, by and by I stopped involuntarily cringing at how I had again and again been treated as prey by men of war who sharpen the knives of their ascendant worldview on the most vulnerable. Perhaps if I'd discarded all these mementos of harm too soon, I'd have denied myself the time it takes to revise and rewrite their meaning, to transform my relationship to them, to empty them of their destructive power. And it does take time, so much time. I'm on the long road, feet forward, one step at a time.

Yes, those letters I discarded. I can't stop thinking about them. I have tried so many times to remember their content, even a single phrase. Nothing doing. Is this for the best? If I read them now, they'd likely turn me inside out, I'd not be able to bear up under their weightiness, all that meaning, multiplied and magnified in inverse proportion to the gradual disappearance into irrelevance of the once hurtful artefacts I still hold onto. Seeing such love across so many pages, a secret seed sown in my oblivious heart, spread out and flourishing over the years, from such a sight would spring such agonizing knowledge of all my ignorance, my complicity in so much evil, so much war along the way. This would crush me. Like grapes trodden in the great winepress of the wrath of God. And what would flow out? I don't know, only that I will no longer submit to being stunted and silent. For there is nothing worth keeping that would also hinder me from telling the truth. In telling these stories, there is nothing I might lose that I haven't already lost. And I have already lost so much.

Writing history is, after all, not simply a matter of cataloguing chronology. This happened, then after this another thing took place. We went here, when you were this old we moved to this place, someone said this and that, here are the conversations and actions that followed, some people saw it like this, others like that. A full and fully frozen, seemingly impartial account of all the facts, a self-deprecating set of statements throughout, naming all known bias, a linear presentation of every key life event, a survey of every sample, add it all up and we all cancel each other out, no one is to blame for all this violence. Anyone involved in any way — and by that of course we mean anyone of consequence — should be able to read it and agree, yes, that's what happened, that's how it was, like gods we dispassionately chronicle our collective past, these are the records of the generations of Noah, the genealogy of Jesus the Messiah, the son of David, the son of Abraham.

Yet this is what people seem to want, the illusion of a perfectly balanced zero sum equation, or at least some triumphant arc, no need to imagine the unimaginable, no pressure to bear the unbearable, no call to speak the unspeakable. "You only speak to the unhappy victims. You never speak to the happy ones," Tim Thornton, Bishop at Lambeth, once said to Andrew Graystone, author of a book on notorious paedophilic abuser John Smyth. Bishop Thornton supposedly "knew thousands of victims of abuse who were happy with the way they have been treated by the church."[2]

Popular American conservative theologian, author and pastor

---

[2] Graystone, A. (2021). *Bleeding for Jesus: John Smyth and the Cult of the Iwerne Camps.* Darton, Longman & Todd, Limited (see p. 196).

Kevin DeYoung recently recommended Crawford Gribben's scholarly book on Christian Reconstruction[3] as a "fair-minded, contemporary historical research[...] as opposed to advocacy historiography."[4] According to DeYoung, Gribben answers historical questions about Christian Reconstructionist leaders, without judging them as good or bad or something in between. A now-former Christian colleague speaks condescendingly of any biographies but these, pressures me to be more critical in my review of one woman's account of spousal abuse, without two or three man witnesses no story can be confirmed. Yet he too tells tales hinging on his own perspective when it suits, when it fits the framework he desires to preserve, oh do you remember that time, doesn't this look just like, funny you should mention, have I told you about the time I – prompted by the sight of some familiar place, some suggestive scent, an expression, a flavour, the sight of someone doing this or that. This is his privilege, as man, as religious leader, to speak with authority about the way things were and are, to weigh in, to select which versions of which stories to record and pass on and deem universally true.

The histories written about the movements I have been involved in proclaim to me that its voices like his which take priority. They subtly or even overtly erase the voices of women, of the marginalised and of the violence done to us. I've read their accounts, and I know what is missing. I know what hides in the cracks. I know. Whether accidentally or on purpose, the gaps they leave gape at me like wounds that are never sewn up, they are crying out to be seen, to be wept over, to be soothed and healed. In the absence of this telling, this listening, this learning, the past follows us, its desperate fingers hold the hem of our garments, it will not let us go.

What sense is there in withholding a life-saving story until after the death of its characters? What kindness can there possibly be in refusing restorative medicine to the dying? I must give heed to

---

3 Gribben, C. (2021). *Survival and Resistance in Evangelical America: Christian Reconstruction in the Pacific Northwest*. Oxford University Press.
4 DeYoung, K. (2021, December 14). *Top 10 Books of 2021*. The Gospel Coalition. https://www.thegospelcoalition.org/blogs/kevin-deyoung/top-10-books-of-2021/

myself and keep my soul diligently, so that I do not forget the things my eyes have seen, so they do not depart from me all the days of my life. I will make them known to my children and grandchildren, to my friends, to anyone who asks. Telling stories is, in any case, one way we signal our suppressed citizenship. Our words plant our feet in the substance of the planet just so. My history is a part of its history, I too belong here, I have eyes and ears and a mouth, I was there in those places. What happens to me matters. I matter. The scholar Cheryl Glenn wrote in 2000, that,

> Writing women (or any other traditionally disenfranchised group) into the history of rhetoric… can be an ethically and intellectually responsible gesture that disrupts those frozen memories in order to address silences, challenge absences, and assert women's contributions to public life.[5]

This book is one such gesture, deliberately disruptive of other work, like that of Gribben and DeYoung, on the subject of Christian Reconstructionism and Dominionist theology, in that it is unapologetically focused on a woman's voice and perspective, backgrounding the recorded macro history of religious-political events and foregrounding women's personal history. The wars religious supremacists wage against the world read against the wars at home. For the uninitiated into Christian Reconstructionism and other arms of the Christian Dominionist movement in the United States and beyond, Julie Ingersoll accurately summarises the central goal of this cluster of political ideologies[6] as,

> establishing the kingdom on earth to prepare for Christ's return required Christians to transform the world, or take dominion, a view that became an article of faith for the religious right,

---

5 Glenn, C. (2000). Truth, lies, and method: Revisiting feminist historiography. *College English*, 62(3), 387-389.
6 Clarkson, F. (2005). The Rise of Dominionism. *Political Research Associates*, 5 December. Available at: https://politicalresearch.org/2005/12/05/the-rise-of-dominionismremaking-america-as-a-christian-nation (accessed 30 January 2023).

which popularized versions of post-millennialism as dominion or "kingdom now" theology.⁷

Christian Dominionism runs across the theological spectrum, from the intellectually high-minded Calvinist Christian Reconstructionism still popular in orthodox branches of conservative Christianity to the more "Spirit-led" Charismatic and Pentecostal Kingdom Now and New Apostolic Reformation movements currently sweeping the world via such institutions as Brian Houston's Hillsong Church.⁸ Recently, Ruth Braunstein has devastatingly captured the pivotal role of the cultivation of a white evangelical myth of Christians-under-siege by a godless-pluralistic-culture in radicalising this wide range of (mostly white) evangelical Christians to a Dominionist mindset.⁹ This myth has been immensely effective in fostering communal commitment and extremist values and lifestyle, writes Braunstein, and "despite public infighting, white evangelicals appear to be extremely unified and mobilized, and at the center of conservative power structures."¹⁰ Yet, we must acknowledge that underneath this façade of cooperation lies a pattern of exploitation, enacted through violence, not just of

---

7 Ingersoll, J. (2011). Dominion Theology, Christian Reconstructionism, and the New Apostolic Reformation. *Religion Dispatches*, 11 August. Available at: https://religiondispatches.org/dominion-theology-christian-reconstructionism-and-the-new-apostolic-reformation/ (accessed 29 January 2023).
See also Stewart, K. (2022). Christian Nationalists Are Excited About What Comes Next. *The New York Times*, 5 July. Available at: https://www.nytimes.com/2022/07/05/opinion/dobbs-christian-nationalism.html (accessed 29 January 2023).

8 See Martí, G. (2017). The global phenomenon of Hillsong Church: An initial assessment. *Sociology of Religion*, 78(4), 377-386.

9 For example, my well-known Christian Reconstructionist childhood pastor Joseph Morecraft said, following the violent insurrection at the US Capitol in 2021, "you have the socialists and their evil solutions. We've got to unite now. We've got to unite and reconcile. Now when they say that they mean … We want the Christians to unite with the anti-Christians so the anti-Christians can dominate and the Christians can be the waterboys." Morecraft III, J. (2021). How Do We Know God is Judging America? *Heritage Presbyterian Church – Sermons*, 10 January. Available at: *https://www.sermonaudio.com/solo/heritagerpchanove/sermons/110211321451092/* (accessed 20 January 2023).

10 Braunstein, R. (n.d.). Embattled and Radicalizing: How perceived repression shapes white evangelicalism. In: Sokhey A and Djupe P (eds) *Trump and the Transformation of Religion and Politics*. Temple University Press.

Christian Dominionists' perceived enemies but of the very base that they claim to serve. It is the everyday stories of this hidden warfare that this book documents.

The book is organised into four main sections—Land, Grave, Fire and Womb—themes derived from the Bible's book of Proverbs 30:15-16, which illustrate that insatiable attitude, that greedy, demanding desire for more and more that dominates and destroys the earth and all it contains. Where Christian Dominionists live by gluttony for power, imagining themselves as soldiers in a war between the righteous and the evil ones, between believers and unbelievers, this book exposes the underbelly of such a narrative, the perpetuation of intergenerational violence between aggressors and survivors and everyone in-between within Dominionists' very own communities. Key to the telling of this story is the deliberately crude use of the Biblical text to demonstrate its weaponization in the mouths of abusers.

And what do I hope will come about by means of this book? As we inscribe all such suppressed stories into the public memory, over time links appear across each known encounter with the world, then pathways, possible shapes, we thread them into constellations, a map of our life written in stars. Catching sight of the matrix we've modelled, aha! Other weary travellers now thread a line between their points across the night sky, join my constellations with yours, adding detail to each shape, a fuller map of what it is to be human, a guide for ourselves and others after us, chock full of all the mess and mistakes, all the contradictions common to this chaotic life under the sun. Together we find ourselves, we find others, now we are less alone. In the future the next generation will ask, "What do these constellations mean?" Then we can tell them, this is how war begins, this is where we lost our way, these are the moments I knew love. Now you too can locate yourself here, there, now you can become one who has found peace.

LAND

*There are three things that will not be satisfied,
Four that will not say, "Enough":
… land that is never satisfied with water"*

Proverbs 30:15-16

1

We help our students understand that no area of life can be separated from God, that no fact can be understood apart from God, and that truth and knowledge cannot be acquired except under the direction of God's written revelation ... As our students learn how to build a Christian culture in home, school, church, state, and society, they will guarantee for themselves and their children the prosperity, strength, and peace that God brings to his faithful people (Deuteronomy 28).

– 'Chalcedon Christian School,' *Counsel of Chalcedon*, 1987, Issue 1.

My parents used to tell us of one day in a long winter in our wilderness commune, one of the few stories they share about those years in the cold, in the dark, in the cult. A pack of starving wolves circled our cabin in the night, hunting a way in, my brother heard them howl, lifted the latch of our cabin door to go out and see. He would've been dragged away, dog's dinner, except that one parent snatched him back quickly and the other slammed the door. This story they elect to tell, the one where only animals are predators, never humans.

I was six years old when I began to be hunted. Or at least, this is when I began to perceive that killers lived, moved and had their being around me, squinting, spying, dissecting and determining my uses in their inherited kingdoms. By then we'd left our commune behind, traded a remote wilderness in the Pacific Northwest for an urban one in the Atlantic Southeast, arriving to this new semblance of civilisation with little but the clothes on our backs, the only worldly possessions that humans banished from paradise could personally claim.

Members of our extended family paid for our flights, took us in, no one spoke of where we'd been, here we are now, finally they're here, safely back home. My brother and I discovered television at our aunt's house and began watching episodes of *Little House on the Prairie*. It seems curious now, in a sense we were watching ourselves, peering through the window of the black and white television into an idealised pastoral scene of the place we'd only just come from, the jolly Ingalls family in their snug cabin, a subtle and almost immediate early rewrite of our history. Not long ago a niece described my parents as homesteaders, brave pioneers who embraced harmony with nature, the simple, sustainable life. How rosy and romantic it all seemed now, viewed admiringly, enviously, translated into the nostalgic fantasy of cottagecore.

After our exodus from that place I knew then only as "The Land," my father was gone day and night until we had enough savings for a small apartment with shag carpet, my bed bunked below my brother's, my grandmother bringing caramel candies, coming to spend nights on the sofa when my sister was born, until my father said he'd rather she went back to her own home. Alongside a few other refugees who'd likewise fled the brutal northwest, we attended charismatic church meetings where spirit-filled men and women spontaneously danced in the aisles, cried and laughed, made a holy racket all together. I saw one woman fling off her shoes in excitement, so eager was she to praise her God's name with dancing.

While there, I made a friend. Until one evening when she jostled a pot of boiling water from the stove, scalding most of her body. I heard then of a special kind of pool for third-degree burn victims, naively I imagined my friend swimming happily round and round in circles several times a day in her private pool, so lucky.

CHAPTER ONE

My brother and I played with the other children in our apartment complex, kicked a ball around a plot of grass in the square, threw a frisbee, ran races. It snowed heavily one year, and our dad built an igloo, his impulse always to erect structures around us. We walked with our mother to the Food Lion for canned fruit cocktail, jarred Vienna sausages and Campbell's chicken noodle soup, the epitome of luxury. I cut out images from newspapers and coupon catalogues to fill in hand-made paper books, one for each letter of the alphabet. A is for apple. B is for beans, 5 cans for a dollar, this week only. We got to know a man called Gary in an adjoining building who kept a pet squirrel in a closet. We acquired a spring mounted rocking horse from a nearby landfill, the holes in her ears a bank where we deposited the only cash we kids had to hand – green leaves, and water as petrol to send her bouncing on her way to nowhere, sloshing as she went.

At age four, I began attending a Baptist kindergarten a few mornings a week. My first teacher banged her scissors in anger so often and with such force it formed a small crater on the corner of her desk, melding her name within the moon of my memory of that place. Mrs. G-for-groceries-Grant, the only teacher there I can now recall. In October that year, and the next, at my mother's request and the teacher's special dispensation, I sat alone in the principal's office and played with a box of toys while my peers sang Halloween songs and assembled spooky crafts. In this and other ways my parents carried on separating us out from the world.

Out of my father's absence eventually emerged a house, the second he'd built for us himself after our little cabin in the woods. Now we moved further out from the suburbs into the countryside, where land was cheap and neighbours more distant, a situation my parents seemed still to prefer. My sister and I arranged our belongings in a pink room next door to my brother's, twin beds, matching chenille bedspreads from my grandmother's house, an angled walk-in closet, a box fan in the window, a dolls house, a Fisher Price record player likewise rescued from the local landfill.

Now it was my first year in full-time education, the first grade at a small Christian school several exits down the state highway, heading south towards the city from our house. The headmaster had told my mother that his was a high achieving, strict school, so I spent the summer before in a makeshift classroom in my bedroom, being prepped. Perhaps my handwriting wasn't good enough. Perhaps my spelling needed work, also my reading was poor. I saw then that the business of the world was measurement. Already I had been weighed out on the scales and found deficient, all the weights of the bag were now my concern. I traced between dots to form letters, enrolled in a summer reading program at the library, free spaghetti dinner if you read 10 books. The first one I finished on my own was *Benjamin in the Woods*, the story of a boy's adventures with animals as he grows up in his pioneer family's cabin in the forest.

Each morning, around 30 pupils came, "in vans, car-pools and family automobiles, from miles in every direction," a zealous trek our church-school magazine *The Counsel of Chalcedon* would later boast over in its inaugural issue.[11] We assembled in the building of a Christian Reconstructionist church we'd been required to join as a condition of my mother's employment as teacher. Our headmaster, an elder in the church, believed in typical patriarchal fashion that fathers were ultimately responsible for children's education. He said as much, more than once and clearly. But our school had been founded by a "sponsoring church," and so we were all, teachers and students, under another higher authority, that of the church's governmental structure, principally the pastor patriarch. This was part of the detailed advice that attorney John Whitehead – founder of the Rutherford Institute – had given our pastor and others intending to start kingdom schools without scrutiny from the state, to protect them from legal attack by "clever prosecutors."[12] Among the points of his advice were, that,

---

11 "Chalcedon Christian School," *Counsel of Chalcedon*, 1987, Issue 1.
12 Whitehead, J. (1981). 'God Versus Caesar: Taking Steps to Protect Church Schools,' *The Journal of Christian Reconstruction*, VIII(1), p. 196.

CHAPTER ONE

1. The Christian school should never be separately incorporated from the church.

2. The financial statements of the day school should show the day school as a ministry on the same level as other ministries of the church.

3. The church treasurer should write the checks and control the funds that flow in and out of all ministries of the church (including the day school).

4. If at all possible, it is advisable that all ministries use the same physical plant facilities.

5. If a church holds to a particular belief that is liable to be contested by the state, then it should be codified with supporting Scripture in the church constitution.

6. The school name should be virtually the same as the church name and should include the doctrine, if possible, taught in the church.

7. The governing board of the church should govern all ministries, including the day school.

8. Teacher contracts present a unique problem. If the church treats the day school teacher as a minister of the gospel, then it may be inconsistent to have the teacher under contract.

9. There is a problem with church leaders who have their children in the public schools.

We kids didn't know anything of the strategies at work here, but we certainly sensed the structure of say-so, tacitly taught to us when the pastor emerged from his study to use the restrooms he shared with us, to talk down to some teacher, to rebuke us for being too loud, too quiet, too slow, not slow enough, for saying damn God will damn you to hell. Still, being employed by the school granted my mother a discount on tuition fees, so I guess you could say our church membership came by means of a bribe.

My siblings and I got baptized then, a spectacle among people that typically witnessed water sprinkled only over babies. My parents promised unreservedly to dedicate us to God, to set before us a godly example, to pray with and for us, that they would teach us the doctrines of our holy religion, and that they would strive, by all the means of God's appointment, to bring us up in the nurture and admonition of the Lord. The feeling of the pastor's hand on my head, even after he stepped away, it seemed his appendage never left, a pressure that I can recall to this day with terrible accuracy. Other kids gathered around me afterwards and felt my damp hair. There was some scandalous story here, these strangers who didn't know better before now, some failure to find out, slow learners, so much catching up to do. Until then, the spheres of home, church and school overlapped only on me. Even my siblings hadn't attended my kindergarten, granting rest from the regular squabbling that comes naturally from living and growing up in close proximity. Now, all such boundaries began to dissolve dangerously, and there was nowhere to escape.

2

Some people, entering our place of worship, are amazed at the plainness at the front of our church. Behind the pulpit is a large blank wall. A modest communion table sits on the floor in front of the pulpit. There are no pictures of Jesus, certainly, but also no crosses, no flags, nothing. We do not even have flowers regularly at the front of the sanctuary.

– 'Editor's Note,' *The Counsel of Chalcedon*, 1988, Issue 9.

Then they said to each other, "Come, let's make bricks and bake them thoroughly. They used brick instead of stone, and tar for mortar.

– Genesis 11:3

The corridors and corners of the church-school are still in my dreams. Below an excessive church sanctuary, a foyer at the front with stairs to the balcony, at the side a church kitchen and restrooms, underneath these lay a collection of small classrooms, concrete block walls painted white. Fibre glass drop ceilings, also white, enclosed the roof. Thin, stained carpet of some unmemorable shade covered a cement floor. Flickering fluorescent tubes created pockets of insensitive light and shadow. Perhaps there were some images on the walls at times in certain rooms – teachers at that time created seasonal bulletin boards, and Christian schools sanctified them with aspirational Bible verses. "I can do all things through Christ who strengthens me," inscribed in a teacher's precise hand on construction paper leaves to mark autumn's return. "Behold, I make all things new," for spring. But I can remember nothing much of colour, only that the rooms seemed perpetually dismal, the corridors even more so. After all, one's memory of spaces is largely shaped by how we felt in them. The foggiest morning can fix vividly in our minds in every shade of the rainbow, just as the wildest of pinks, the most brilliant of blues can store mentally in a spectrum of greyscale, filtered through the lens of despair.

Even the outdoor space surrounding the two-story brick building seemed to take on its demeanour. I now embellish my home with colour, every empty space with some rare houseplant, every spare cent garnishes my garden. From then I can't recall a single flower or glossy leaf, only the thorniest and most persistent weeds and brambles, a wood of pine trees typical of the area, the only living things undeterred by the impenetrable red clay that lay heavy and undisturbed around the ambitiously wide asphalt parking lot. Such ugliness sprung from so much arrogance. I've held on to one of my favourite children's books from that time, bought for pennies in a library sale. *The Plant Sitter*, a story about a boy called Tommy who looks after a host of plants one summer, so many they fill his house to bursting. "Oh my," groans his mother. "How terrible." "What's this nonsense," Tommy's father roars. "This can't go on!" He frowns these words over his breakfast, surrounded by a dense kitchen forest as Tommy sits beaming. On one memorable page Tommy falls asleep in the bath, now a pool in a tropical foliage jungle. On another he runs on his own to the library, then a garden centre, grows cuttings of every plant then gives them away to all his neighbours. Tommy thought it was wonderful. All this I treasured, I pondered it in my heart.

The stairwell connecting the school below with the church above was a particularly menacing place, windowless and joined at the ends by cheap fire doors with panic bars that clapped loudly when pushed. I rarely walked the stairs, only dashed up and down instinctively when I had occasion to travel alone, fearing that

CHAPTER TWO

someone sat waiting for me in the hunting blind, that sinister void underneath the stairs' middle turn. The sound of my steps echoed and chased me as I ran, confusing and merging my fear of the hunter with a growing unease of myself.

The bathrooms were conveniently and inconveniently located just outside the top and bottom of the stairwell. If after emerging I saw someone I wanted to avoid, I could quickly burrow into the girls' bathroom. But I had to be quick. Some boys took to pouncing on passing girls and pushing them through the swinging door to the boy's bathroom. "Did you see anything you liked?" they'd hoot when she emerged. A quick dose of humiliation. One time one of the kinder boys surprised me with his presence just outside the stairwell, his arm outstretched to push ajar the now open door. This posture was too ambiguous to disarm my defences. My hand sprung out and slapped him, hard, our faces fixed into the same sad, startled expression, gazing at each other as if in a mirror. Another time a boy got his hand caught in the hinge of the heavy, self-closing door to the men's bathroom. He screamed and held it up urgently in the air for us all to witness, angry and weeping red lines now traversing each finger below the nail.

There were four or five classrooms only in those early years, two year-groups combined in each. K4 and K5. 1 and 2. 3 and 4. 5 and 6. When it rained, all classes would assemble together in a central common room and play chess on white boards painted onto long folding tables with dingy wood veneer tops. Our headmaster for some time developed aspirations of discovering the next Bobby Fischer, but with a difference. Through the coercive power of chess, surely one of us would conquer the communist Soviets for Christ. We had no one to teach us really, yet we played at it until his attention turned. These ambitious tables were also our lunch space, a study hall space, cleared away after school for martial arts instruction for boys, ballet for girls. When not even a single desk more could be squeezed into the narrow classrooms, a cheap partition appeared, separating off a portion of this central room to create a new, equally pinched teaching space for grades 3 and 4, now enclosing the entrance to a separate office space. The convenience of this room-within-a-room facilitated an increase in corporal punishment. Here was where I received my first school smacking for the gravest of sins: being "disrespectful". I'd dared to declare my distaste for mayonnaise on Burger King whoppers, as our teacher took our order for lunch on some class trip. Other teachers without access to such private penal spaces sent most errant children out into the hallway to be verbally vanquished with a Bible verse, though repeat offenders would be sent to the headmaster's office for a smack. Or even sometimes to the church office, a suite of rooms leading to the pastor's study, also accessed via the common area. I never knew what happened then.

The spaces between the immovable concrete walls seemed always to be changing shape and character unpredictably. We were rodents in a maze, test subjects in some psychological experiment. The headmaster dragged in a stained carpet he'd found by the side of the road, only discarding it once we complained of fleas crawling up our legs during lessons. He regularly paused lessons for "class fieldtrips" to the local DIY store. We wandered the aisles while he purchased supplies for some school building project. Another particularly memorable school trip was an all-day recording session for a Christian music album, for the sister-in-law of our pastor. "Why Can't I See God?", we warbled obediently. "Is he watching me?"[13] The children of the most important church families sang solos and duets while the rest of us with bit parts sat in a corridor most of the day, late into the afternoon and evening, our day dissolved into child labour for the kingdom coming.

My first desk at school was in the far corner of the first and second grade classroom, and I recall a view out of the facing windows, towards the swings that held me up to the sky on rainless days.

---

13 "*Why Can't I See God?* was recorded at Twelve Oaks Studio, Atlanta, GA, Judy Rogers – Vocals and Guitar… Children of Chalcedon Presbyterian Church –… Valerie Howard", Raymond, J. (n.d.). Welcome to Judy Lyrics! – Thanks & Info. Available at: http://judylyrics.klsoaps.com/T_and_I.html (accessed 29 January 2023).

CHAPTER TWO

At break times, I pumped my legs harder and faster until up and down swapped places, and my legs now dangled over a canyon of clouds. My peers pumped alongside me, some jumped at the top of their arc. If they landed without falling over, everyone would cheer. The most skilled knew how to propel their bodies forward just so, to hit the ground ready to run. I never joined in. I imagined if I leapt I'd fall into a void, plunge endlessly toward heaven's blue and bottomless pit beneath the fixed roof of the earth where my classmates now moved about upside down. Almost every day, I terrified myself in this way.

I loved the outdoors, especially its impartial hiding places. The precious hours between schooldays I spent playing in the creek and the deep woods around our house, cycling around the loop of our small neighbourhood, pedalling desperately alongside my older brother and a neighbour boy, I'd keep up with them, I would, I would. My thoughts didn't linger yet on matters of identity or bodies or how the two might be related. A few curious incidents had happened already here and there but none that unsettled me memorably beyond the joys of play and discovery. Such was our happy genderless existence.

Until one morning. The event was this: A boy wrote, "Valerie is a foxy lady" on the outside of his notebook, in big, bold letters. To my tiny body on that day, there was no physical violence, nor even the sound of an unkind or ambivalent voice. Just a bit of cheeky fun. No harm done. A friend even pointed the easily visible words out to me eagerly, as if I'd be pleased. My name enshrined with boyish desire for all to see. My first conquest. Except I wasn't grateful. Some secret alarm began to ring in my ears. Enraged, I marched confidently to the boy's desk and belted out that he'd better rub out my name or else I'd squeeze him till he shrivelled up, like a hotdog in a bun. My hands fleshed out my meaning, menacingly forming the shape of his neck. I remember his face, so blank. This reaction, this rejection, perhaps, was new. This memory is mapped on my mind mainly because of what happened next, the sound of the teacher's gasp and then her cheeks, hot with disapproval and something else I couldn't then comprehend. She pointed to the door, and I exited in front of her in confusion and fear, the boy now smirking in his seat.

"Don't talk about hotdogs and buns. You sound like you are threatening to perform a lewd act. Don't you know your body parts are like a bun and his a sausage? You have behaved so inappropriately. You must be more ladylike in future."

"Yes, ma'am."

I said nothing more in reply. The look on her face, I now know its name, a dense and clumsy baggage she promptly deposited over me in hushed urgency in the narrow hallway outside the classroom that morning. I received it upon my head as a millstone, it bullied its way into my heart, feasted on my flesh and took root. The undead seed of women's plight in this place, perhaps joining other similar contaminants I'd not known were already there. Beacons for all trackers. I remember only that shame and its lesson, nothing else after. I can't recall ever speaking to that boy again, as small as our school was. I could never have articulated the meaning of all this then, but any child can grasp the lesson. No hunter would be blamed for tracking me. All resistance would be condemned. She is an animal and will be treated as animals are, little foxes are ruining the vineyards, catch the foxes for us, while our vineyards are in blossom, break them in, kill and swallow them whole.

3

The central area of dominion is thus not politics nor economics but the family under God... The family as a social organization is the prime area of dominion. It has far more than personal significance.

– R. J. Rushdoony, 'Marriage and the Family,' The Counsel of Chalcedon, 1989, Issue 7.

All things considered, my home wasn't the best of homes, but neither was it the worst. That house that dad built. We had rooms to sleep in, we had plenty to eat, we had books and toys, a treehouse, the freedom to explore the creek and the woods around our house. We went weekly to the library, we visited the playground in the local park. We had well-meaning parents, of that generation that emphasized tough love, independence, being seen and not heard, working within the system rather than calling attention to it, keep your head down and get on with it, don't make a fuss. In some ways, then, perhaps our home was somewhat typical.

Still, we had some strangeness, which sometimes I became painfully aware of when spending time with extended family or when out and about. There was always some distance there, some separation. I sensed this space from pursed lips, glances, there were things certain family members didn't say, maybe our cousins had been instructed on how to interact with us. "If they mention something about such and such, here are three neutral things you can say." In the summer, thanks to my grandmother's generosity, we shared a house with our extended family at the beach for a week, our family always occupying the furthest basement rooms, our father nearly always insisting we set off somewhere on our own some days instead of joining in with the group. Sometimes he stayed home to work, and the rest of us went alone to reaffirm our blood connections. Too much time spent with others, especially with family, this seemed to unsettle my dad.

Yet this perpetual gap that yawned between any one of us and any other person existed within the walls of our home as well. For years, my dad made us scrambled eggs in the morning, we ate thrifty meals around a kitchen table in the evenings. But as the years went by, we ate together less and less often, didn't talk about anything much, didn't really know one another, like most people who carry the weight of untold stories. To open our mouths too widely or too often was to risk talking about something unmentionable, embarrassing. Better to avert our eyes, go about our days and our duties with minimal contact, keep conversation light, keep it infrequent. We passed the time together always busy with some task, pulling weeds or housecleaning, pursuing some hobby, the frenzy of our hands using up every ounce of our energy, sapping all our focus. In the moments between, at breakfast for instance, we seemed incessantly to be searching for some text to hold our gaze, to disrupt any overly lengthy eye contact, a cereal box, a pamphlet, a book, a Christian newsletter. I read so many dull papers in those days, so many fundamentalist film and book reviews. In all this, our violence simmered passive aggressively, always lurking just beneath a veneer of supreme outward Miss Manners politeness. We were opposing forces, living alongside one another in tension, the stresses within and between us building internally, until, occasionally, they exploded unexpectedly. Here a chair thrown across the room, there a voice yelling, a household item rapidly repurposed as a paddle, leaving me and my siblings deeply insecure, mistrusted and mistrusting, generally tight-lipped. We maneuvered our everyday life like water bugs traversing the delicate viscosity of a murky pond's surface.

In the early months of life in our country neighbourhood, a little brown crossbreed dog called Smiley bit my stomach badly, and my father swore—something he didn't often do in our presence—and threatened to go round and shoot the dog with the shotgun he kept under his bed, though he cooled down and the gun stayed put. After that, we interacted very little with our neighbours, apart from one boy, Michael, who came round nearly every day with his dog Bear. Michael's dad took us hunting for squirrels and treated us to a fried chicken lunch at PoFolks Restaurant some Sundays. In winter, he pulled our sleds wildly around the neighbourhood behind his truck when it snowed. He earned his money driving around all day collecting rent from his numerous tenants, my first encounter with the concept of "landlord," an occupation we learned about by listening at doors. He was a tempestuous man, prone to outbursts and dramatic mood swings. He'd give Michael permission to go with us to the beach, to a theme park, to the city pool, then change his mind minutes before our departure. This was familiar territory, and dodging all his deceptive changes of direction kept me sharp for home life. With Michael we practised keeping our emotions in check, holding our faces straight as we rode the peaks and troughs of men's fragile moods.

Michael had a younger stepsister, but we rarely saw her, and Michael had nothing good to say about his stepmother, in the few times he spoke about her. At Christmas, she would send him over to deliver a tin of beautifully handmade cakes and candies. "She can't cook anything else, she's really a terrible cook," Michael would say, if we kids made even the tiniest show of awe or gratitude as he handed it over. If it happened to be me at the door, I took the parcel from him silently, solemnly, in the same sombre way returning to Michael or to his mailbox a handwritten thank you note from my mother. Instinctively, I deferred to Michael's lack of enthusiasm by mirroring it. We never heard anything of his biological mom, nothing I can remember now anyway, it was as if she'd never existed, perhaps she was dead or merely living nearby, either or neither, we never knew. Michael, my brother and I would often meet early in the morning and be gone all day, until Michael's father whistled to call him home. We could hear that sharp signal for miles – wherever we were, Michael would start running. "Bear, come on boy!" he said urgently. He often wrestled and sometimes punched Bear, for reasons I couldn't then grasp. The mutt was altogether loyal and bore his companion's beatings without complaint, receiving onto his furry flesh the punishment for whatever aggression that day, that week had recently inflicted.

Our home of mostly beige walls and carpet was nearly always tidy, systematically cleaned weekly from top to bottom, smelling of nothing. By then we had a yellow dog which my parents finally purchased from a local farmer, after the dog stubbornly adopted us by escaping her fence at every chance and coming to find us kids. I'm not sure what she saw in us, what canine knowledge did she possess that pulled her to our animal-unfriendly home. She was rarely allowed in the house and especially not in the living room, though once my father said we could call her in for a family photo. Her whole body trembled then at his confusing violation of rules, I recall the picture now, my dad's hand around her neck, that unsettling flash of the whites of her eyes, glancing nervously to the side as dogs do when stressed. Occasionally, I snuck her in to sleep under my bed, until her fleas established themselves in the carpet, and we were found out. When the temperature dipped below a certain level, she was allowed in the basement. One evening, my dad arrived home before the rest of us and tried to enter the house through the basement door as he often did – his work equipment was stored there – only the dog refused to let him pass. She growled and barked at him until the rest of us returned, then lay down, reassured, and went to sleep. My sister and I took her on long walks all around the surrounding streets, but most of her life she spent tied to a dog run between two trees, some distance from the house. There, she'd purposely tangle her lead around one tree or the other, desperate for a visit, a pat, a kind word, the repetition of her name. Eventually, she began to display signs of regret for placing her hopes in us, escaping from our backyard, at every opportunity sniffing and searching the neighbourhood for someone worthy of her devotion. We'd roam the neighbourhood calling her name, carrying bread to tempt her home, hoping she was hungry enough to be enticed back again to us one more time.

Growing up in this orderly, uneasy set of spaces, each of us began displaying signs of obsessive compulsiveness. My brother and sister developed a habit of placing one hand, palm up, under a ceiling fan pull, then giving it a slight bump towards the ceiling, whenever either of them entered the room. For years, I never saw them move from one part of the house to another without performing this ritual. My sister and I became fixated on tidying our play kitchen just so after every game, in this way all our play teetered anxiously on the horizon of the inevitable clean-up. The inclusion of each piece of plastic food we removed for our game was carefully calculated against the effort to replace it. Any mess seemed deeply out of place, unsettling. Once my sister set up all our stuffed toys for a game while I was at a friend's house, and upon seeing it, I berated her cruelly. I hadn't wanted to play and now look at all this work.

4

Israel was fighting their oppressors. In this case the bad guys were the Philistines. Deciding that they preferred to risk dying to serving a tyrannical civil government, the Israelites went to battle. But they were at a distinct disadvantage. The Philistines had their own "Hand Gun Control Inc."

– Rich Jefferson, 'Guns and the Bible,' *The Counsel of Chalcedon*, 1989, Issue 6.

Yet many Christians do not seem to understand the relationship between their values, beliefs and behaviors, and their economic situation. Some Christians seem to believe that wealth and prosperity are just an accident of situation; ... Even those called to the working class should expect, over time, monetary and career advancement by God's blessing. They should still expect to be, over time, ahead of their worldly counterparts through a combination of financial reward from their satisfied employers and Godly frugality in their lifestyles.

– Brian Abshire, 'Restoring Christian Wealth,' *The Counsel of Chalcedon*, 2003, Issue 2.

My first friend at church-school was Sofia, and the contrast of her home with mine set up a situation of extremes, another early signal of the push and pull that would figure so powerfully in our eat-or-be-eaten childhood. Sofia's family were loud, crass, stunning human specimens, exhibitionists and lovers of pleasure, to whom it seemed no one said no. They ate well and argued openly, sometimes coming to blows. Her house had things from faraway places, terracotta tiles in the kitchen, long fur coats, a mink stole, thick oriental rugs, a bidet. Sofia had a pet hamster in her bedroom, dogs and cats that came and went as they pleased. Two puppies appeared one day, one of whom drowned in Sofia's swimming pool, the other eventually executed after mauling a postal worker. One night, Sofia and I sat reading, and my fingers played with a rubber band they'd found. "If you fall asleep with that in your bed, the cat will stretch it around your neck and steal your breath," Sofia warned solemnly. I believed everything she told me, already acquainted as she was with so many worlds beyond my experience, she of the future and I always stuck stumbling behind in the past. She and her siblings tore at the corners of the wrapping paper to identify their Christmas presents in advance and watched violent and sexually explicit films and television. "How bad was the language?" Sofia's mother asked us when we'd come back from the cinema, shrugging at Sofia's matter-of-fact reply.

Sofia's father was a powerful figure on our small planet, which to me seemed somehow related to the hallowed matter of money. Whenever our pastor found occasion to preach on tithing, he would hold up certain men in the congregation as examples. The kingdom of God is like one wealthy man who closed a business deal to the tune of a multi-million-dollar profit, then promptly put his gifts into the treasury, out of his surplus into the offering. To such men as these, who supplied some form of social or economic capital, our pastor awarded sacred prowess and near carte blanche. Their offspring were now children of the covenant, declared so by the power of preaching, through the seal of the pulpit. This was another law of our hunting preserve. Every relationship was transactional.

Some Sundays, after the endless sermon, Sofia invited me to go to lunch with her family at a Japanese restaurant. The pastor and his family were often guests as well — such was their privilege. Perhaps my parents were invited once or twice — likely not. We rarely went out for a meal, except for the occasional fast food. My father felt awkward in social settings involving wealth and unknown food, places where no one comforted the uncomfortable, unease being one of rich men's finest delicacies. Sofia and I perched next to an enormous tropical fish tank, drank Shirley Temples and dared each other to eat pieces of pickled ginger, while the men drank heavily and gorged themselves on slippery noodles and enormous platters of meat and vegetables. Consumption and dyspepsia. Such was the Sabbath scene.

Having only ever seen my parents drink tiny glasses of chilled pink wine at Thanksgiving and Christmas, I had my first taste of alcohol at Sofia's house, aged 6 or 7. After a table of taunting Christian men goaded us toward an inch of vodka (maybe it was two), my head spun and ached as we lay on sleeping bags in the formal living room. Light and shadows fell across our faces from the room next door, where some other featureless man-faces from church—I can't remember who—and Sofia's chummy pagan uncle smoked cigars, gulped and guffawed loudly into the early hours of the morning. At some ungodly time, we were roused by unfamiliar noise. We stumbled sleepily towards the bottom of the stairs, where Sofia's older sister awkwardly leaned, nearly passed out. Sofia's mother placed her between us and instructed us, once upstairs, to lay her sideways in bed to keep her from choking on her own vomit in the night. Did I sleep after that? This detail my mind didn't see fit to collect.

Some summers I joined them on family trips, where Sofia and I drove recreational vehicles across cow pastures, our wheels flinging cow pats into the air, onto our clothing, our hair, our skin, roaring out to the creek where we swam and played all day. At night we ate dehydrated army rations all together at a long, loud table, packets of chicken a la king alongside freshly fried okra, desiccated ice cream after. Sofia's dad's hunting expertise and apocalypse readiness were another significant source of renown in our church. He was ex-military and owned an impressive arsenal of weapons, stocked in a concealed room below the garage, along with who knows what else.

CHAPTER FOUR

Nearly everyone I knew owned guns, but his arsenal could've armed a small militia. Perhaps it did. Once, in a field, he placed an automatic weapon into my clumsy hands, along with a single word set of instructions. *Shoot.*

These instruments of death were significant fixtures in the wildlife preserve I was learning to survive. One afternoon Sofia's older brother and a friend appeared with pistols and waved them towards her and me as we played on a balcony above the garage. They'd been shooting squirrels and birds in the wood behind the house. Why not now these birds too, perched similarly as we were? We cried out. Sofia's father emerged and matched their idiotic aggression with his own, whipping them both with curses and what object he could get quickest to hand, a metal bar. Months later, Sofia's older brother chose his moment, surprised her and me in our sleeping bags, metal bar in hand. We were as defenceless as worms, and he duly squashed us. Another time Sofia's dad took a similar implement to her legs while I stood by watching, bracing motionless and mute against the wall. I can't recall the reason for this round of retribution, set off erratically as he was. One Saturday after I'd stayed the night, he drove away early and came back with take-out breakfast for all of us, for me a ham and egg bagel in a yellow carton. This was new food to me, and I had an overactive gag reflex and couldn't make myself eat it. I instead closed the lid and said "yes, sir" quietly and quickly when Sofia's father asked if I'd eaten it, his steely look signalling the singular possibility of only one admissible answer. He stared at me silently for a moment – Where, when and what had this animal eaten? I was as an open book to this trained hunter who possessed the skill to identify and analyse every available sign. "Open it," he challenged. I obeyed and he, upon spying the uneaten food, said only, "Give it to the dog then." Take the children's bread and toss it to the dog, for even the dogs under the table eat the children's rejected crumbs.

Sofia and I never spoke at any length about all this turbulence in the flight of our childhood. The grammar of our shared language we constructed from books, treks in the woods, talk about fairies, games with plastic farm animals, songs to cows. In all this we created and occupied our own habitat, the woods our sanctuary, the streams our dwelling place. I can still smell that deep scent of the forest, the creek, the thrilling fragrance of cool and wet and green. Anything could happen there. Once, we caught a mole and imprisoned it for an afternoon in an empty hermit crab aquarium, its sad star nose searching for hours for the soil. At last we had compassion, we inclined to it and heard its cry, we delivered it from its bondage.

Yet the agency that Sofia lost at home, she reclaimed at times in our friendship, often cruelly. One day of swimming in the creek, I stood on a massive rock I'd paddled to and climbed, she on the bank. She studied me up and down and dispassionately declared, "You're fat." Another day she pushed me in rapid circles on the tire swing in her front yard until I was sick, stood laughing at the sight of the circle my open mouth drew around me in vomit as I spun. She developed a particular habit of pointing out a set of items, any in the vicinity. "Which do you like best?" she'd ask. Whichever I chose was wrong, and she'd wryly explain why. "It's so funny you would choose that one. I'd never have picked it." I took to trying to divine which one she was likely to select, but I was never successful. That was the whole game of it.

5

Salvation (healing) is not simply ethical regeneration and the transformation of human character. It involves restoration of the whole cosmos (the Greek word for "world"). Salvation, in short, is comprehensive. Not everyone will go to heaven, but not all sinners will be sent straight to hell this evening, either. As Christians, we have tasks of dominion assigned to us by God. We are told to be healers. We are to impose biblical law on society, which will begin to heal the institutions of society. Biblical civil law protects life, property, and morality, so that Christians, working individually and in voluntary association, can begin to serve as agents of healing in the world.

– Gary North, Editor's Introduction, Symposium on Social Action. Journal of Christian Reconstruction, 1981, Vol. VIII, No. 1.

Diseases and problems do not "exist" unless the Marxist state allows them an official existence or recognition. Medical training is controlled; doctors and psychiatrists are controlled; hospitals are controlled; drugs, like all medical practice, are a state monopoly. The medical profession serves the state, not the patient. Doctors are a part of a bureaucracy which has a state-controlled life and conscience.

– R. J. Rushdoony, 'Statist Medicine,' in Roots of Reconstruction, p. 499, Chalcedon Medical Report No. 8.

Christian Reconstructionists don't always like to be called Dominionists. They can perceive this as denigration, a word coined by those who misunderstand them and lump them in with groups and beliefs they disavow. But Dominionists are what they are. They believe that through the blessing of God on their own political, social and economic efforts, the kingdom of God will grow until the earth is as full of the knowledge of the Lord as the waters cover the sea. What distinguishes Reconstructionists from other Dominionists is their belief that the Old Testament provides a model of that righteous supremacy, its judicial laws applying to all peoples, all nations, all governments. These laws must of course be properly interpreted by the proper people—men, almost never women—who prove themselves through a show of theological expertise and argumentation, a concert of clanging gongs, those who pose in front of cases full of books for photographs, who revel in the precision of their ecclesiastical procedures, their recitation of precise propositions, who, when visiting other homes assess its occupants by the volumes (or lack thereof) on display, packed in, filling up, running over, pouring out into the laps of everyone in every room, all their paginated intellectual gravitas. Bonus points for antique editions of certain theological texts, authored by men, always by men. The particulars of interpreting the law lead to many quarrels and the end of many relationships.

Other Dominionists look similarly to certain forceful personalities to lead them in the path towards victory, though such leaders identify themselves other ways, such as signalling their especially intimate and charismatic communion with the Spirit of God. Such leaders often mark their worthiness with a story of God's personal word to them, the moment the Spirit appeared to them, in a vision, in a crisis, while in prison or plagued by demons during a near death experience, and declared them set aside for special use. For all Dominionists, though, the goal is the same: a theocratic state or some version of Christian occupation of all secular institutions, the reclaiming of the land, the cosmos, for Jesus Christ, whether by violence or by some other coercion. Whosoever yields themselves to those with sacred authority—and by extension, God—will together claim control of every mountain: government, education, media, the arts, business, religion and family. Within the ideology of hard-core Dominionists, those who do not yield will be executed or enslaved. This reclamation of a lost Christian nation is the central unifying ideology of the Christian Right.

Spurred on by such lofty goals, Dominionism in all its forms attracts a lofty-minded sort of people. They may not all be entirely committed to the cause, they may not even wholly understand it, but what they share is a hunger for the recovery of something squandered or stolen, some unrecognised intelligence, the re-affirmation of personal potential, the justification of socially anomalous behaviour, in all, some acknowledgement of previously unacknowledged worthiness. Predictably, then, most in our church-school membership were escaping something or someone elsewhere – we drew in society's white detritus, wounders and wounded, people of privilege who identified as tyrannized, people of intergenerational trauma, anger, arrogance, secret corruption, those born to agricultural poverty, people of conspiracy, tax fraud, suspicion, violence and other abuse, anti-immigration, pro-segregation, people who spanked their children in supermarket aisles, who prayed loudly before meals in restaurants, people of malcontent, families ostracized for objecting to liberalism and inclusion somewhere in some way, now seeking a vessel to weather the coming storm. Two by two according to their own lost kind. The shadows of our enclosed community enveloped them all, lifted them up over the rising waters of the condemned world, made them heirs of the self-righteousness which was according to faith in ourselves, more so in the fearless men we followed.

One memorable family joined us with stories of how they'd fled Germany under threat of the state seizing custody of their children, perhaps even imprisoning the parents, since they'd refused to enrol their offspring in a local school. These were our home-schooling heroes, the sort on whose behalf the father of Christian

Reconstructionism and of home education—Rousas Rushdoony—argued vehemently in courtrooms across the United States. Others came with harrowing stories of being fired from their jobs simply for being vocal against communism, the gay rights movement and, of course, feminism. Nearly anyone with a story offering persecution porn was welcomed, the more they made themselves a public nuisance the better.

Such were we, our everyday lives mapped onto the unnatural habitat of incarcerated canines and their prey, a complex social unit orbiting around two spiritual alphas and their offspring, jostling for position, continuously controlled and controlling, supressing and being suppressed, eating and being eaten. It turns out that most of what we think we know about wolf behaviour is misconception. Wolves that roam freely tend to live in peace with each other, each family operating as an independent unit, working together for the best interests of their young and any other wolves in their care. All wild breeding wolves are alphas, and contests for dominance with other wolves are rare. Family packs may work together at times to hunt, especially in desperation. But wolves in captivity are a rather different matter. In confinement, in a zoo, what matters is what every animal can offer the captain, the kingpin, the head, and what place in the dominance hierarchy each will occupy as a result.

My family lacked the correct social and economic capital to be much of anything to anyone in those early days – even the possible glamour of our mysterious previous outpost meant little in the hierarchy of holiness. An elder's wife rebuked my mother for her shabby clothes our first Sunday in attendance, labelling us foreign instead of fascinating, a slight my mother's already faltering confidence never recovered from. Neither was my father suitably assured or even devoted enough to be selected for the dirty work that made the community go round. One Sunday service he was asked to assist in serving the bread and wine for weekly communion, then rebuked publicly and sent back to his seat since he wasn't wearing a suit jacket, an item of clothing he didn't own. We were perpetually low-ranking, outer circle, a place where different rules applied. One of the elders hosted annual New Year's Eve parties, and each year a small sub-set of our congregation, including our pastor, would leave early after a brief appearance, bound for the more exclusive event at a certain deacon's house. One banquet for thee and another for me.

When I was with Sofia I could claim some semblance of citizenship in these inner circles. But in our small world, in our struggle to raise heaven from the dust of earth, alliances were always moving, changing, now I'm your friend, now I'm not. Occasionally new families would join our church and then their children would appear at the school one morning. Their arrival jostled all our relationships, and as the dust settled we eagerly abandoned one another for the possibility of new friendships, new techniques for rebellion, word from the outside world, something, anything. A good proportion of these newcomers were people looking for fresh blood for their business empires. Men and women in expensive suits and dresses travelled the kitchens and living rooms of our church-school, dropping tablets in glasses of tap water to reveal the toxins the city was using to poison us, quizzing us about all our physical frailties, just look at the deal I can offer you now with this NSA under-sink filter, I can give you these nutritional supplements for free if you spend this much, this spirulina formula healed me body and soul, it'll change your life too. They cunningly tapped into and soothed our deeply rooted paranoia about the bogeyman of postmodern culture, its science, its psychology, its medicine, its steady diet of "nutritionally void food" which had "released an epidemic of neurological inefficiencies on its young."[14] They gave our overworked, exhausted and lonely housewives hope for earning extra cash within the sanctified walls of their domestic sphere, of ascending to the pinnacles of (other)worldly success we were undoubtedly worthy of. Did we think our child had a learning difficulty? Did we suffer from a chronic illness of some kind? If only

---

14 Educational Philosophy, Goals, and Emphasis of the Reformed Presbyterian Church in the United States, *The Counsel of Chalcedon*, 1999, Issue 4.

we were willing to free our minds from government brainwashing, to seek alternative solutions from so-called experts ahead of their time, unrecognised voices operating outside the profane establishment, people as misunderstood as we. If only we would, we could be transformed body and soul, cleansed from the sin of the surrounding culture, return to our tents with great riches and honour. It's difficult to say when our community and others like it began to more radically reject modern medicine, dental treatment, vaccinations. But for decades, pyramid schemes affirmed and exacerbated an already growing mistrust in science, modern medicine and, above all, the state. This would become even more glaringly evident in 2020 when Georgia Right-to-Life, closely linked to my church-school, voiced opposition to a Covid-19 vaccine on the misguided assumption that it was developed using aborted foetal cells.[15]

Eventually, most of these opportunistic nomads would tap out the market of our small community and move on to despoil the green pastures of other congregations, though not before recruiting certain members of the church as loyal sub-contractors to mop up any reserves left behind. One couple stands out in my mind, she a fashion model and he a silver salesman of unknown age. They owned a private jet, appeared at church events in five-minute increments in their Porsche, by instinct they knew who to flatter, who to incentivise, who to ignore. Our pastor and his wife seemed to perceive their presence as another feather in their cap. Look what glamour and success we can attract. After this couple moved on, my mother and I were visiting a larger church in the area for a baptism or some such occasion. We passed them with their kids in the hallway, they gazed through us as if we were ghosts, the sight of us failing to register in their profitability scanner.

Occasionally, some naïve exception would find their way to our church or school, rarely both, some generally well-meaning set,

---

15 Szilagyi, J. (2020, December 13). *GA Pro-Life Group Says It Opposes COVID-19 Vaccine Development, Production*. All On Georgia. https://allongeorgia.com/georgia-state-politics/ga-pro-life-group-says-it-opposes-covid-19-vaccine-development-production/.

CHAPTER FIVE

people of milder interest and commitment, attracted by a particular issue, unaware of or possibly disinterested in the whole package. Don't ask, don't tell. Such times were my only true Christmases, the advent of the loveliest friendships of my childhood. One girl living with her grandparents was assigned a desk near mine, and we quickly formed an attachment. "My parents are jewellers," Marie said proudly. She saw them only during summers, told me confidently that they travelled every other month of the year to source gems. I imagined them as enviously cosmopolitan, an enigmatic duo with special access to the world's back rooms and locked boxes. I knew too little to doubt Marie. It was like something from a book, and through her I sensed the possibility of other places, other people. One summer she invited me to come and stay with her and her parents for a whole week. The postcard invitation spelled out Wisconsin in pieces of clapboard, overtop a lake scene with a red and white striped umbrella shading an ice cream cart, too wonderful to be real. My mother said no – children roamed too freely in waterside towns in the north, and Marie's parents couldn't guarantee I'd always be within sight. Marie left our school a few short years after. Anyone who was kind or good or lovely did not stay.

6

Obedience is the most necessary ingredient to be required from the child. This is especially true for a girl, for she must be obedient all her life. The boy who is obedient to his mother and father will someday become the head of a home; not so for the girl. Whereas the boy is being trained to be a leader, the girl is being trained to be a follower.

– Reverend Jack Hyles, How to Rear Children. (Hammond, IN: Hyles-Anderson, 1972), p. 158.

"Better whipt, than damn'd.

– *Cotton Mather, quoted by B.M. Palmer, in 'The Family in its Offices of Instruction and Worship,' The Counsel of Chalcedon, 1989, Issue 7.*

God was everywhere and altogether absent. His name thundered down on us every Sunday, God spake all these words saying, I am the Lord your God, who brought you out of Egypt, out of the house of slavery. And so spake we all these words every Sunday, we had come out of the world, out of other churches. We had all come out and now we were all in. A people of naught, defined by what we didn't do, who we weren't, not like them, a people of opposition, distinction, antithesis, our yeses yes and our noes no. Whatever you're like, I'm nothing like you. Whatever you say, I'll find the flaws, slice them out, carry on carving until nothing remains. We waited each day for the cut, who would be next, which one of us had erred and how. Only the abysmal, the vacant, the empty vessels could stay. We were a people of no substance. Thou shalt not.

Following the example of his mentor Rousas J. Rushdoony, our pastor was the mouthpiece of God, the spirit of truth, guiding us into all not-incorrect precepts of men, speaking on his own initiative. Introducing any other Christian writer, any other leader, he always began with caveats, warnings, we could trust almost no one completely apart from him. The same stories perpetually flowed from his mouth on refrain to illustrate. He visited a man who lay dying, who dared to voice his desperate, feeble faith. "Pastor, I don't think I can believe in a god like yours." At this crucial juncture, our pastor would pause dramatically before telling us the answer he stooped to offer. "There is no other God!" he blasted, his face quivering from all that drama, and then the hand, slapping the pulpit and us by extension into submission, leaving us to stew again briefly, until the judgement. "The man turned his face to the wall and died." Our pastor often wept in the pulpit, moving himself to tears at the wonder of his own words. As a teenager, I took a Black friend from an after-school job to our white church with me. "Something's off here," she said. "Your pastor shifts so quickly from hot to cold. He starts crying, then suddenly he's smiling. I don't feel right here." Her outsider eyes unsettled me. I quickly dismissed her insights, but they stayed with me.

I sat, I heard, I believed our pastor had power over life and death, blessings and curses, could send me straight to the lake of fire as I deserved. He relished telling the story of the first meal his wife had prepared him, his favourite. But she'd burned it, then burst into tears at the thought of telling him of her domestic failure. "She rightly feared the one she loved," our pastor explained. "Such is our fear for the Lord." As Sarah called Abraham lord, every word that proceeded out of our pastor's mouth his wife absorbed, endured, praised, she the perfect puppet. Once she related a time she'd burnt some sausages for his dinner. "Unfortunately not the only time I've over-burnt his offering," she joked. On such occasions she'd catch all our eyes with hers as she spoke, whatever feeling we saw there we were to imitate. This technique she also performed during sermons, rotating her head to find someone's face in the room, holding their expression with the intensity of her own until it reshaped itself into a likeness that mirrored hers. Isn't he so funny. Isn't he so insightful. Isn't that point he just made so profound.

Another regular sermon illustration involved a child who, perhaps seeing some divine quality in his massive girth, gazed up at our pastor as if to heaven and asked innocently, "Are you God?" One Sunday service, my parents happened to choose a section of chairs that positioned me in the angled path of the sun. Its rays penetrated the clear glass from an octagonal window high above the pulpit and, from where I sat, illuminated our pastor from behind. I imagined that glowing, he might rise up in the air, I wondered whether others might join him and who. Not me, I'd be left behind, rooted uselessly in the damned clay, everyone would at last see my true nature, a worthless sinner. Our pastor alone was the way, the truth and the light. No one could come to the father except by him.

Why would anyone consent to subject themselves to such tyrannical governance? This is the puzzle of communities defined by domination, violence and consumption. My father regularly complained bitterly about our environment, and he made a point of rebelling in various ways, nearly all trivial but which nevertheless dangled us all over the cliff of disapproval. He often darted straight to the refuge of our car after services and remained hidden there until the rest of us were socially exhausted. I wondered what cost I'd pay for these infractions and when. Certain years, our church asked members to pledge an amount they'd tithe in total in the coming year, and my father would commit and later back out, citing a bad fiscal year. By making and breaking promises, he clawed back some semblance of control. He did the same to us kids, in ways like those of our neighbour Michael's dad, always citing some ironclad reason for his sudden change of plans, based on variables we had no way of

CHAPTER SIX

examining or questioning. We had a roof over our heads, we had our basic needs met, what else did we want.

But skipping Sunday evening service was my father's most common tactic of subtly disrupting the church status quo. Our pastor glorified legalistic Sabbath keeping, his stories on the subject casting moulds of perfect obedience which only the privileged few could set aside. The rest of us must melt ourselves into complacent pools of resignation, submit our shape to our pastor's every command. "This is not Mother's Day. This is the Lord's Day!" he would annually remind us, before piling into the car with his family for a post-service celebratory meal, a feast for hypocrites. Neither was it ever Christmas, at least on certain calendar years. The kingdom of God is like a certain quiet and gentle woman with stage four cancer, who nevertheless wrapped her hairless head in a towel and, dearly beloved gathered here together, she got herself to church.

My brother acquired the skill of sleeping in the service while sitting up perfectly straight. I endured each tedious sermon—each accompanied with a tome of pastor's notes—by concealing a tiny treasure in my pocket and tracing its every bump and corner. As I got older, during the service I passed the time doing the only thing I could get away with: reading and rereading certain books of the Bible our pastor rarely if ever preached on. Esther, Ruth, Song of Solomon, Ecclesiastes. Proverbs was an absolute no-go-area, as was any part of the Pentateuch. And the books of Paul. I absolutely could not stand to read anything written by the Apostle Paul. For many years, though, no matter which section of the Bible I had occasion to read—and I read it by choice only rarely—I heard only the voices of my pastor and other men who shouted us down from the pulpit, who rebuked and minimised us, who rejoiced in the privilege of our special status as dominion warriors then proclaimed we were entirely unworthy of it, whose stale enunciations sealed me off from the Spirit. All God's messages were never mine, only theirs.

We kids were further indoctrinated at school in the particulars of our weekly plight of rigid rest, writing a yearly essay for a certain

Sabbatarian organisation, intellectual display the principal engine of our warfare.

What does observing the Sabbath mean to me?

- Morning and evening worship, always on time. Those who are late are not welcome – Remember the story of Stonewall Jackson's noble refusal to "disturb the worship of the Lord" with his tardiness.

- Never leave the service for any reason other than to discipline a child.

- Children who don't empty their bladders before the service deserve the resulting public rebuke, either from the pulpit or upon leaving.

- No hair covering your face and especially your eyes during worship, this shows a spirit of rebellion.

- No use of images of any kind in the service.

- No being distracted, no being a distraction, we who are above all distraction.

- No work of any kind, no swimming pools, no cinema, no shopping mall.

- A restaurant meal is lawful since the Israelites at times used pagan labour.

Such is our joy, for God is coming to judge the earth.

All this and more we learned during regular sermons and illustrative stories, regularly appearing in the many pages of the

CHAPTER SIX

church's regular magazine publication. In the company of the blandness of our church sanctuary's empty walls and drab chairs, our thoughts were sure to ascend to heaven, which appeared in my mind equally plain as the miserable earth. At the end of every service, our pastor planted himself at the church's front entrance. There he could catalogue our attendance, our attire, he looked on all our outward appearance, his point of access to our hearts. Even visitors weren't immune. And of course, there were the drawn out "Ask the Pastor" sessions after the Sunday evening service. Only men and boys as young as four could speak in church, even then. One evening a quiet and gentle elderly widow forgot herself, raised her hand to make some query and was admonished by the pastor with a single, overly familiar word: her first name. Let the women keep silent. Special dispensation was claimed without explanation by the pastor's wife, who ascended regularly to the balcony and belted out some psalm, hymn or spiritual song. On her soprano singing voice hung all the law and the prophets.

Even my father's meagre insurrection, mostly unnoticed by anyone important, was simply an exercise in flexing dominance, in shoring up his broken sense of self, shattered before any of us ever knew him. Some people are attracted to tyrants, they themselves might also become tyrants, often because it's all they know. By replicating and perpetuating this dynamic they further normalise it, avoid the searing pain of confronting it. But there is also the pull of proximity to perceived power and to the opportunities followers might have to bask in that power, to be recognised by or perhaps even to resist it, to topple and take it. For the particularly ambitious, every rebellious act of non-compliance offers a glorious climax, every pack participant confined to prison probes their place in the hierarchy of the hunt, feels the secret thrill of identifying those below them, maybe even gaming the system. All such acts constitute a venomous cycle of destruction. No one can survive by staying.

We all jostled for toxic oxygen, girls and women absorbing all offenses from Men in quietness, in all submissiveness, redirecting each negative atmospheric charge towards each other. An eye for an eye. We couldn't conquer except over one another. We couldn't live except another died. The American Southern woman is perhaps queen of killing by sweetness, but in this microcosm, almost any form of violence could be sugared with a self-righteous smile, with the proper grooming. Adults as always led the way. During my first year of school, a new teacher was introduced with this brief biography: "She spanks with her hand." That same year, we girls began ballet lessons. Our instructor was married to a member of the founding family of one of the first major pro-life lobbying groups in the country. She marched and protested abortion, picketed and campaigned with all her heart, soul, strength and mind, then punished us girls for the transgression of being born, screamed at us in the central common room after school, exiled any girl who forgot her shoes or whose hair was not adequately knotted in a bun.

Into the janitor's closet each errant girl went. From there the seemingly ceaseless whacks of a wooden board against her silent body sounded out, reverberated all around us. These sonic vibrations inflicted their own vicious violence, each thwack clapped the air, pummelled our eardrums, permeated our bowels. We stood still as statues, all we little girls in two straight lines. Talking was strictly forbidden during the class – even when occupied by her fervent thrashing she might hear us. The pastor's multi-room office was steps away. I recall also a teacher, sitting steadily at her desk in an adjoining room. He never came, nor she, no one came. Sometimes our sadistic teacher moved our class upstairs to the church sanctuary, carrying out her cruelty boldly in the presence of the Lord our God. After one recital—some rendition of the parable of the 10 virgins— she showed a graphic "pro-life" video of blood and butchered body parts to our audience of family members and other loved ones. We were oppressed and afflicted, yet each girl did not open her mouth. Like a lamb led to slaughter, and like a sheep that is silent before its shearers, so we did not open our mouths.

Brutal encounters like these polluted every relationship, beginning

CHAPTER SIX

with my own body, my closest and by now most hated friend. It alone believed and answered the urgency of my need. In those early times of torment, I often feigned stomach pain so my mother might allow me to miss ballet class, speaking a lifelong digestive disorder into the world, such was my commitment to self-preservation. In the second grade, a classmate and I buried our daily grievances in the tomb of a closely guarded notebook. We met covertly in the woods during playtime to carry out the necessary documentation. We discovered a wispy weed which to us resembled tobacco, and we chewed this as we discussed and argued, spun stories and moved names back and forth across columns at our whim, girls we hate, girls we consider friends, boys we like, mean boys whose direction we agree never to look in. We absolutely promised each other, solely on the testimony of a hunch, not to speak to nor even to look at the new boy Luke and his brother. Keep your eyes on the ground, avoid their eyes. A teacher finally spotted and confiscated our handiwork. "Girls, what is wrong with you?"

Then there were the oddly cruel games my sister and I created, I suspect they were all my idea, one involving coloured wooden blocks under a basket. We'd take it in turns to reach under and pull one out – if the block was blue, we were safe. If, however, one sister pulled out a block of another colour, the other sister would punish her by smashing her hand with it. The angles of certain shapes were particularly painful, and we showed each other no mercy. I sat at my desk at school and daydreamed about shaving off the beautifully crimped blonde hair of a girl whose recent arrival had disturbed the delicate and dismal ecosystem I was still discerning. Having been subjugated, I too longed for a subordinate. In the absence of one, I would create her for myself, shave her head and make her suffer as I had. This is how sociopaths form. They walk freely among Christians, among children.

7

The Coalition on Revival (COR) views itself as a "Bible obedience, holiness movement" that crosses denominational and theological lines. The next step on its agenda [involves] the vision of mobilizing their people to "Get God's will done in their city as it is in heaven" to whatever degree that is possible before the return of Christ. We believe America can be turned around and once again function as a Christian nation as it did in its earlier years. We believe that wherever the pastors of any city in the world join together in unity to make Christ Lord of every sphere of life, and, with Spirit led strategy, mobilize their people into a unified spiritual army; that city can and will become "a city set upon a hill" and be "a place where righteousness dwells."

— A Manifesto for the Christian Church, The Coalition on Revival, Inc., July 4, 1986.[16]

But does God require us to tell the truth at all times? Such a proposition is highly questionable ... This truth-telling means, not the exposure of our privacy, but bearing a true witness in relation to our neighbor. It does not apply to acts of war.

— R. J. Rushdoony, The Institutes of Biblical Law, A Chalcedon Study with Three Appendices by Gary North, 1972, p. 543-544.

CHAPTER SEVEN

The year before my tenth birthday, money somehow materialised and funded a large extension to our church-school. Even more of the grounds were now covered over with concrete and asphalt, more parking to accommodate our pastor's vision of an expanding infantry of kingdom soldiers. A two-story brick wing of new classrooms, a dedicated church nursery, a lunchroom auditorium, a science lab – these were our training ground. My fourth-grade year was my first in this imperial expansion. As in the previous year we were taught by the headmaster-elder, a gregarious man who put equal amounts of energy into loud laughter and ballroom dancing as he did into strict student discipline. He installed a mirror above the blackboard, his eyes now followed us, glaring, even when his back was turned. One day without a word he drew a crude picture of a bare bottom (whose?) below a splintered paddle on the chalkboard, threatening vertical lines around and between the two to represent repeated strikes from which emanated heat and pain. In later years he drilled us on the catechism, installed a camera in a corner of a classroom, switched on one day without our knowledge, its lens another male gaze to fill any remaining gap in his probing vision, inspect us continually when he turned around or left the room to deal with some school duty.

Our church-school hosted our first annual Reformation Day Fair, strategically labelled "Arts & Crafts Fair" on public signage facing the street on the corner of our property, more likely to get bodies through the door and facilitate fundraising. These sideways methods were a notable feature of our overall strategy. No historian would ever be able to trace the tracks by which we amassed righteous influence – we would conceal our path, come in through the side door, omit certain details, lie outright if necessary.[17] So began our annual tradition marking the

---

16 Signed by 460 "National Christian Leaders," including Mr. Cal Beisner (Covenant College), Dr. Tim Lahaye (President of American Coalition for Traditional Values), R. J. Rushdoony, Dr. J.I. Packer, Rev. Joe Morecraft, Gary Demar, Randall Terry (Operation Rescue), Edith Schaeffer (author, lecturer and wife of Francis Schaeffer) and Dr. Raymond Ortlund.

17 "As Gary North once noted, "No historian will ever be able to go back and identify in terms of the primary source documents [the history of the Christian Reconstruction movement] because we can't possibly do it." McVicar, M. (2010, November 9). *The Lord Will Perfect That Which Concerneth Me: The Work of Rousas John Rushdoony. Chalcedon Magazine.* https://chalcedon.edu/magazine/the-lord-will-perfect-that-which-concerneth-me-the-work-of-rousas-john-rushdoony

launch of Martin Luther's Protestant Reformation, in his honour setting up various children's games and selling hot dogs, candy and various odds and ends in a massive flea market set up in our sanctuary. That first year my dad ran a booth where, for a small fee, attendees could hammer a nail on a makeshift Noah's Ark, imagine themselves fleeing the judgement of the world. Another game of archery guided our eyes and our arrows to a target outlining the seven circles of sin, one of them homosexuality, a word I heard often yet whose meaning I didn't understand. Encouraged to wear costumes, Sofia and I came dressed as a bunny and a cheerleader. The following year, to encourage more explicitly Christian costumes, a prize was given for best Biblical character, and Sofia and I adopted the personas of Mary and Martha, though we didn't win. That first honour went to my brother, for his cardboard-clad rendition of a Roman soldier. The elders, deacons and their wives dressed as various church fathers and their helpmeets, the women cooked and served at Zwingli's Café while the men walked around in full costume ensuring we were all carrying out our duties. In the evening, after the fair was finished, though our pastor annually preached against the celebration of Halloween, warning us often about the trouble that happens after the sun goes down, his son Matthew—a boy my age—donned some disguise of rebellion. Together with friends on the margins of our church-school, he threw eggs at parked cars, toilet roll at the trees, and sprayed lines of shaving cream around his neighbourhood.

As time went on, our fundraising expanded. Like our peers at other schools, we kids began selling chocolate bars and coupon books door-to-door. Sofia and I committed ourselves to this unreservedly, marching around her neighbourhood for hours upon hours, growing ever more defeated and enraged by the reluctance of her neighbours to pay premium prices for overpriced candy and vouchers they'd likely never use. Maybe the next door. Maybe the next. The thought of winning the prize bicycle held up in the school chapel service as incentive propelled us on. We worked and worked to gain entry to the pyramid's pinnacle. But unlike at other schools, there was as always a spiritual element stirred into the mix, sacred pressure spiked with guilt, the headmaster's urgent reminder that the school really depended on us, we all needed this money, God himself required this money. His words heaved the immense burden of kingdom building onto our tiny shoulders. Another set of events was the church-school's annual themed dinner auction, in service of which we kids were of course recruited again as volunteer wait staff, dishwashers, greeters, cleaners. One was based on a Hawaiian theme, and elder's daughters Leah, Jenny and I began the evening by greeting guests with a flower lei, dressed in our botanic sarongs and t-shirts, fielding more than one father's boringly predictable paedophilic sexual innuendoes as they entered. "Now I can tell everyone I got laid tonight."

Our pastor announced he was going to run for U.S. Congress, even secured a personal endorsement from President Ronald Reagan. The New York Times briefly profiled our pastor's Congressional candidacy, picking up on two peculiarities, first that he advocated a government based on Old Testament law, including the stoning of those who practice adultery, blasphemy and witchcraft.[18] And second, that our Christian nationalist pastor refused to withdraw a campaign advertisement containing unfounded claims against his opponent, even after the Republican campaign committee acknowledged the inaccuracy. What cared our pastor for such insignificant details—like the truth—when there were such enemies to be battled, such worlds to be won. What mattered was the fervency of our belief in the corruption of the current establishment, in the predatory threat that loomed large around us. After all, Christians have "no obligation to speak truthfully to those who have forfeited the right to hear the truth."[19] This was war, and our opponents mere footstools beneath our feet.

---

18 Gailey, P. (1986, November 2). Talking Politics; Finally, an Issue! *The New York Times*. https://www.nytimes.com/1986/11/02/us/talking-politics-finally-an-issue.html

19 West, J. (1983). Rahab's Justifiable Lie. In J. B. Jordan & G. North (Eds.), *The Theology of Christian Resistance: Christianity and Civilization* (Vol. 2, pp. 66–74). Geneva Divinity School Press. https://epdf.tips/the-theology-of-christian-resistance-christianity-and-civilization-2.html (see p. 73)

That same year, our pastor joined a crowd of like-minded Christians on the steps of the Lincoln Memorial in Washington, D.C. for a three-day coalition, at the end of which, close to 500 Christian leaders signed a Christian manifesto for revival.[20] Among them were Christian Reconstructionists, members of the Latter Rain movement, the New Apostolic Reformation and followers of Bill Bright's, Loren Cunningham's and Francis Schaeffer's Seven Mountains Mandate—the seven "mountains" being government, education, media, arts and entertainment, religion, family and business—mostly men and a few key women united in their ideals of a Dominionist mandate.[21] Together, they forged a plan for implementing God's kingdom on earth, casting out demons and bringing "judicial and legal systems in as close approximation to the laws and commandments of the Bible" as possible.

In the weeks before the election, our pastor's wife presented her husband with a painting created in honour of his candidacy as well as the man whose seat he was trying to fill, Larry McDonald. McDonald was one of our pastor's dearest friends, a notorious leader in the far-right extremist John Birch Society, and recently martyred – so it was said. He had died in 1983, going the way of all the earth when his plane, Korean Air Lines Flight 007, was shot down, having strayed into USSR airspace. Our pastor presided at his famous funeral, and the *Washington Post* later quoted our pastor in a report on Kathy McDonald's failed attempt to claim her husband's now empty congressional seat. "The devil is one up on us for the time being," our pastor lamented, his politics and the mission of his god always and completely overlapping.[22]

---

20 *Background of the COR Documents*. (n.d.). Retrieved January 20, 2023, from https://www.reformation.net/background-of-the-cor-documents.html

21 "One of those Seven Mountain adherents, Paula White, became arguably Trump's closest spiritual advisor, chair of his Evangelical Advisory Board, and a special advisor to the White House Faith and Opportunity Initiative… Seven Mountain dominionism joins with other forms of Protestant Christian dominionism, Christian nationalism, and newly emergent strains of Catholic integralism (which seeks to integrate Catholic "religious authority with political power") to place an immense amount of spiritual importance on political leadership." French, D. (2021, February 28). *How a Rising Religious Movement Rationalizes the Christian Grasp for Power*. The Dispatch. https://thedispatch.com/newsletter/frenchpress/how-a-rising-religious-movement-rationalizes/

CHAPTER SEVEN

Forty years later, the magazine *Politico* would consider the legacy of Larry McDonald, calling him "a militant cold warrior and talented zealot who built his own mini-deep state."[23] It detailed his paranoid practice of stocking purified drinking water and dehydrated food, his love of alternative medicine that led to at least one major lawsuit, his arsenal of around 200 firearms. At least one senator, Jesse Helms of North Carolina, believed for many years after McDonald's death, that he had survived the crash and was being secretly held by the Soviets. Whether our pastor was convinced by that conspiracy theory or not wasn't then clear, but McDonald was frequently held up to us as an example of Mighty Men who lived out the principles to which all our lives were devoted. The painting our pastor's wife gifted to her husband depicted campaign signs in support of our pastor and his pal McDonald, on the front wall of a rural general store. This event was covered in the local paper, and the painting's inscription contains a code immediately recognisable to all devoted to the trifecta of Christian white male supremacy, neo-confederacy and Reconstructionism: "names of men who promise to take us into the uncertain future by preserving the things from our past – men who will honor history. This is America – at her best."[24]

The day of the congressional election, we stood all together in campaign hats, young and old, in a hotel conference room too large for our number, fully prepared for certain celebration. A television in the corner broadcasted the vote tally as it became available. Finally, the results were in. Everyone stared in silence as the reporter announced that our pastor's opponent had won in spades, 2 to 1. My eyes followed our pastor as he walked to the screen, glanced and squinted at his defeat, his face stamped itself onto my consciousness,

---

22 Harris, A. (1983, November 9). Mrs. McDonald Is Stoic in Defeat. *The Washington Post*. https://www.washingtonpost.com/archive/politics/1983/11/09/mrs-mcdonald-is-stoic-in-defeat/d4b043bc-c145-4d6f-b170-8c1552fa8fad/

23 Dorfman, Z. (2018, December 2). The Congressman Who Created His Own Deep State. Really. *POLITICO Magazine*. https://www.politico.com/magazine/story/2018/12/02/larry-mcdonald-communists-deep-state-222726/

24 Becky Morecraft Presents Painting to Husband Joe, and Announces Contest. *Counsel of Chalcedon*, 1987, Issue 3.

stern and unmoving, full of hubris, a loser concealing his loss.

Still, our pastor had courted some attention. Capitalising on this, he and his pals launched the first issue of our church-school magazine, *The Counsel of Chalcedon*,[25] its lead article directing readers to *The Manifesto of the Christian Church* that our pastor had signed the previous year.[26] A national documentary series by Bill Moyers covered the anomaly that was our sect. Among his Reconstructionist brothers and Pentecostal compatriots, our pastor was triumphant, proud, prophetic, his brazen words laid bare his expectations of all his children.[27] The lone father, narrating a staged clip of some of us involved in some contrived game in the expansive church-school parking lot, our primary play area, he proclaimed his vision. In mere decades, kids in Christian schools like ours will graduate and take their positions, move into places of influence and power. Equipped with his teaching, his unbending example rooted in our consciousness, we would reconstruct America, the world. We would make for ourselves a name, no longer scattered over the face of the earth. "Children in the Christian schools of America are the Army that is going to take the future," he said. Our school was nothing more than a scam. Onward, white Christian soldiers.

Perhaps attracted to this and other publicity of the promise of a utopian future, yet more families joined our church, our school. The early days, months and years of every community like this are exactly the same, a band of hopeless people grasping again after some ancient set of broken promises, now repackaged, rebranded by another dear leader. These are the early days of eagerness, a façade of jolly communal meals and battle anthem singing, happy hands working together, shushing and slapping any early misgivings. Surely this will

---

[25] See *Chalcedon Presbyterian Church | Scribd*. (n.d.). Retrieved February 6, 2023, from https://www.scribd.com/user/258651949/Chalcedon-Presbyterian-Church

[26] Goodrum, D. E. (1987, January). From the Editor's Desk. *The Counsel of Chalcedon*. https://www.scribd.com/document/235453629/1987-Issue-1-From-the-Editors-Desk-Counsel-of-Chalcedon

[27] Moyers, B. (1987, December 23). *On Earth As It Is In Heaven*. Acorn Media. https://billmoyers.com/content/earth-heaven/

be it, we will make ourselves to be a kingdom and priests to our God. We will reign upon this earth.

Yet we kids were by now already growing weary of one another, of little lives so like our own. The taste of monotony was nothing to me but bitter – I knew little of earth's reassuring rhythm. Everything was known and despised, because it was known. Time passed speedily along in its sameness – what was one day, one week, even one year but the same as all the days, the years before? I had no sense of any future beyond more of the present. Time moved on, yet we went nowhere, nothing much changed, we stood still, each day the hours went by, the date on the calendar changed but there we were, fixed and frozen. I went with Sofia to a water park in the summertime and we circled for hours in the artificial river, its current pushed us along, round and round, we were in constant motion yet passed the same scenery over and over. It was like that. Everything was like that.

While each new family brought the potential of something novel, here and there a taste of fresh, liberating worldliness, some semblance of something approximating normal, this too was only façade. Still, Sofia embraced these newcomers, grew crueller and more distant, left me behind to fend for myself in the new awkwardness of puberty. Though maybe I was the one leaving her behind in our trip to nowhere, dressed to the nines in my stuffy mask of piety, instinctively the safest option for a girl like me, from a family like mine. I learned my stubborn body was decent at foursquare and kickball, games we were often required to play in school. Where I could locate and harness the physical force of my flesh, Sofia's willowy, otherworldly arms and legs seemed disinterested in acknowledging the physics of an object's movement. Her strength emanated from elsewhere. The divide between us grew and grew. She and a new friend laughed callously at the homemade bow clip I wore in my hair, my home-sewn uniform, things I'd always donned. She announced one day she was going to have an exclusive birthday party, only one guest could be invited, sorry, Valerie, I could only invite one.

8

I see a serious defeat before us if we do not seize the moment and rescue the children from the bondage of Pharaoh's schools and lead them to the Promised Land of Christian schools and home schooling... Church history will not be kind in the remembrance of this disaster should it happen. ... Similarly, Christian families will one day ask, "Why did our pastors and Christian leaders fail to lead our families and children out of danger and into the safe pastures of Christian schools and home schooling?"

– E. Ray Moore, quoted in a book review by James A. Boyes, *The Counsel of Chalcedon*, 2002, Issue 2.

In the fifth grade, I was taught by another long-time member of the church, a woman who cried when we girls stood at her desk and obediently recited Proverbs 31 from memory, who sternly sent us out to the expanded headmaster's office across the hall for rolling our eyes, talking and talking back, smirking, being loud, having the audacity to be children. Corporal punishment carried on. We grabbed our ankles and hung on through the humiliation.

My main friend that year was Emily, the daughter of a water filtration system salesman. Her family seemed just awkward enough to allow me to blend in, yet they too were somehow transcendent, another set of angular, ageless beings for whom mass-produced supermarket food was unpalatable, unclean. Her grey-suited dad performed his solemn duty one afternoon in our kitchen, warning us about the local government's death wish against all of us, the poison we were all ingesting in city water. Were we so dull? Didn't we understand that we are defiled by what we eat, that all these chemicals go not only into your stomach but also into your heart? He offered my mother a special, one-time only deal on a whole house filtration system, which my dad experienced as a challenge to his manhood. He could do better, he'd install his own system which he'd find by himself at a home improvement store, no man who claimed to know better than he ever got his money. At Emily's house I saw my first Apple computer, ate cereal that tasted of cardboard soaked in some non-dairy, non-Newtonian fluid, snacked on carob-covered nuts and raisins and went swimming in her neighbourhood pool. One Christmas her mother invited a small group of us girls round to sew buttons and sequins on felt Christmas trees, surrounded by wholesome wheat-free holiday treats.

As one of the older girls in my set, I ripened first, and my longsuffering flesh gradually began to betray me. Certain boys began more assertively testing my vulnerabilities, commenting on my mutinous chest. "Do you have something in your shirt pocket, Valerie?" one elder's son asked nearly every morning. Emily's mother gently suggested I might ask my mother to take me bra shopping, but this too I experienced as shaming, as I did all talk of bodies. Sofia gave me a much-coveted Banana Republic safari t-shirt for my birthday, two sizes too small, then asked me why I didn't wear it, her expression made me feel her wrong choice was intentional. A few weeks later, on impulse I pulled and stretched this solitary piece of trendy clothing over my head for a church picnic, its stiffly printed image of a lion enclosed me as in a cylinder, a rigid casing, armour. I felt nearly invincible, from then on I donned this shield underneath my school uniform until one sad day when the seams finally gave way.

This too was the year eagle-eyed boys spied my bulky handbag I'd begun bringing to school one week in every month. They squeezed it for any sign of crinkly, feminine contents. I sensed their eyes scanning and appraising me. How could they know about things I'd only just learned about, been startled by one morning? When the teacher was out of the room, the headmaster's son Timothy told the whole class of a science experiment he suggested we try: drop a tampon in a glass of red Kool-Aid, see what happens, it's hilarious. He nodded in my direction as he said this, anticipating some reaction to prolong his joke. One girl in our school, unprepared for her period, bled all over the bathroom floor, on her desk chair, on the carpet, to the abject horror of all the teachers. Inspired, I too inscribed my humiliation and hopelessness into the indifferent architecture, thick sanitary pads flushed down into the building's bowels, my menstrual blood the pigment for vengeful feminine graffiti. I stared blankly, without remorse, as the headmaster sent all the boys out of the classroom one afternoon, then soberly reported the clogged plumbing, the exact, itemised cost to the school. Please, girls, this has to stop. Whoever is doing this, please stop. I command you to stop. I didn't stop, there was no stopping in a place like this, no one was stopping anything.

My aunt started taking me in for several days each month. I lay on my cousin's bed, reading books, watching TV, my aunt made me banana muffins, brought me tea. Otherwise, she left me alone. How did she know to offer such hours of stillness I'd not known till now, a peace that passed all understanding, a rest that only earth's primordial molecules, which, having fused and formed my flesh at my conception, could recognise and respond to. Still, as my body singled me out, separated me, I suffered even more anxious stomach aches. I began to press a thermometer against the warm bulb of a lamp, a ceiling light, insist I was sick. Again, I'm sick again. My mother took me to various doctors, perhaps I had a milk allergy, was bulimic, had an ulcer, had a leaky gut. In desperation, she employed the services of an alternative healer recommended by a woman in our church who performed colonic irrigations in her home on the clogged and unclean bodies of other women in the church. As I lay on her examining table, the healer positioned her hands in various places over my body, bent my hands and fingers this way and that, in and through the energy fields she

CHAPTER EIGHT

said surrounded my body. She seemed to be listening for something, straining to sense with merely the hovering of her hands some hostile presence, some malignancy. Afterward she prescribed a combination of various herbs and tinctures, black walnut hulls, lungwort, star anise, fennel, cinnamon. This pricey potpourri I obediently swallowed for months after, accustomed as I was to sprinkling sweetness and spice over the rancid stench of my distress.

9

The difference between a Christian and a Christian Reconstructionist, at its extreme, can be described this way: There are people who as a result of war or accident are basket cases. They are missing their hands or feet. They are individual human beings, but they are seriously incapacitated. There are many people in the church who are basket cases. A Christian Reconstructionist is someone who is alive, healthy and active in the Lord's service... We are in the midst now of the earliest stages of worldwide judgment that will begin with an economic collapse. So God is shattering all those who are trying to live outside of His law... It could be four or five years before we see the full effects of it, but it's already underway.

– R. J. Rushdoony, *Counsel of Chalcedon*, 1988, Issue 2.

At the end of my fifth-grade year, our school celebrated its first graduating class. "Providentially, all three students were from families in our church body," our church magazine proudly reported, alluding to our pastor's dual decree, first, that no child is safe in the hands of state schooling and, second, that our school was both a worthy and righteous substitute for our atonement.[28] This edict we kids of course internalized. A group of boys, including the pastor's son

---

28 'Chalcedon Christian School Graduates First Class; Awards Special Honors', *The Counsel of Chalcedon*, 1989, Issue 6.

CHAPTER NINE

Matthew, ascended a tree overhanging the street next to our school and threw rocks at a passing yellow school bus. "Pagans," they crowed. Thus they prevailed over the Philistines with the strength of their arms and a handful of stones.

A picture of our church-school's first three graduates posed on the porch of an antebellum mansion accompanied the joyful article, proclaiming our school's "legacy of quiet strength," drawn from the Old South. So our school sent them forth, to "conquer for Christ and His Kingdom." A group of us made our church-school presence known at an anti-abortion march that attracted a crowd of around 3,000, the largest rally for the cause our city had seen. A carefully selected group of we children, myself not included, accompanied a solo written and performed by our pastor's niece on the steps of the state capital building, a banner advertising our school hanging next to them on the steps. Their words were pure propaganda, harnessing all the racialised power of the pure little white girl in service of white masculinity, her angelic voice pleading with her mother not to kill her baby brother.[29]

This too was the year I began winning the Cornelius Van Til Scholarship for Academic Excellence, this first time for science, history and overall average in the elementary school. I was also awarded a certificate for exemplifying the ultimate Christian trait of obedience. I wrote a sanctimonious essay for the school newspaper on friendship. Be a good friend, and you'll soon attract good friends. So easy, it's as simple as the sun. I memorised and recited vacuous phrases like these, performed them, was publicly rewarded, words and behaviour that denoted nothing I knew of, values I had never seen. There was no goodness, there were no good friends, no good people, no not even one, all had turned aside, together we had become useless.

The following academic year, my first in middle school, the headmaster decreed that our school would form teams and compete

---

[29] Rogers, J. (n.d.). *Dear Jesus – Little Brother*. Retrieved February 6, 2023, from https://judyrogers.bandcamp.com/track/dear-jesus-little-brother

with other schools of a similar size in our area. We were now the Crusaders, our uniforms bearing the image of a knight trampling a serpent underfoot. We kids were completely ignorant then of our pastor's likely ulterior motive for this title. Biblical scholar Meredith Kline had, some years prior, referred to our pastor and his compatriots as "crusaders" with "cult-like fanaticism."[30] Ignorant of our strategic branding in these Man Wars, a small group of us committed enthusiastically to this new opportunity and travelled together that summer for preparation at a basketball camp at Bob Jones University. Our eager band included me and two girlfriends, Jenny and Leah. One sect of Christian fundamentalism met another, creating a conflict of laws.

We were given a rigid and unfamiliar list of rules beforehand to adhere to: no shorts, skirts or dresses above knee length, no sleeveless tops, no mixed bathing, and no swimsuits should be seen outside of the shielded pool area. No music, books or magazines could be brought unless explicitly Christian, best to bring none at all. No walking around campus alongside or meeting up either on or off campus with people of another gender. At mealtimes we were likewise instructed to segregate strictly by gender. That week I ate rehydrated scrambled eggs and drank off-brand Sunny Delight for breakfast, an assortment of questionable casseroles, overcooked vegetables and unidentifiable meats for lunch and dinner, separated from my older brother across the room. There were mandatory services morning and evening in a darkened, dismal chapel with no visible windows. The chaplain said he hoped we'd all respond to at least one altar call by the end of the week. Anyone who broke any rule, skipped chapel even once, would be confined to their room until their parents could collect them. Included in the girls' timetable was daily choral singing, likely a subtle correction to any disruptions that the basketball sessions might cause to our training up in ladylikeness.

---

30 Kline, M. G. (1978). Comments on an old-new error: A review article. *The Westminster Theological Journal*, 41(1), 172-189. https://meredithkline.com/klines-works/articles-and-essays/comments-on-an-old-new-error/

CHAPTER NINE

That first night the college student assigned to supervise us girls announced excitedly she was going to meet a boy, safely supervised of course in an on-campus, dedicated courtship space called the dating parlour. Her friends arrived in anxious anticipation to help her prepare in a dorm room similar to the one my two friends and I had been assigned, its walls decorated with posters of Disney cartoon films, Bible verses written in bubbly script, Precious Moments figurines. Someone pressed play on a cassette tape player, and the sound of The Little Mermaid soundtrack started up. Hands moved rapidly around the blessed young woman's head, curling her hair, then spraying it, while others held up one voluminous dress for possible approval, then another. Finally, she was ready and exited the building, a thousand eager eyes watching her jealously from the windows above the exit.

Years later, I encountered the echoes of this environment during a summer of Bible translation training after university. There, an elderly, retired staff member invited us women to her room in the halls of residence once a week, to gorge ourselves on mounds of cookies, masses of chocolates and sweets, while she, a woman no doubt full of fascinating stories and wisdom, conducted a dramatic reading of the Winnie-the-Pooh books. Other times we women students gathered in one of our rooms to watch a children's film and met up with the men in our cohort at a local water park. Even now an older conservative pastor's wife I know talks about getting a group of women together to see the latest Paddington Bear film. When would we graduate from this school of the infantile, infantilised and infantilising? When can women put away these childish things?

The Bob Jones University gymnasium was an oven by mid-day, and we girls took turns standing next to the industrial fans that stood in each corner, circulating the sweltering, humid South Carolina air. Many of the exercises involved individual dribbling and shooting drills or one-on-one challenges with a BJU varsity team player eager to put us in our place. In my billowing khaki culottes, I felt altogether awkward, faint and crabby, yet my two girlfriends seemed to enjoy themselves, chatted easily with the other campers, joined in enthusiastically with other girls in other rooms before lights out, to eat sweets, tell stories and read Christian novels. What was wrong with me, why couldn't I make the best of all this, as my friends had? What filtering mechanism did they possess that I didn't? What tool allowed them to transform all the many horrors that stared at me, that slapped me in the face, into nothing more than minor inconveniences? All that made me miserable they shrugged off. But how?

I felt ill every day that week, crushed under the weight of yet more conflicting standards. Eventually I confined myself to my room, missing the last few sessions where we were divided into teams for playoffs to be held the final day. I managed to pack my things and leave the residential hall without saying goodbye to anyone, I sat on the bleachers next to the soccer pitch with the families of other boys, waiting for my parents. I was no longer a camper, just a sister watching her brother now, as if none of this had ever happened, I'd never met any of these people, I'd never see them again. If I closed my eyes, maybe I'd disappear.

Despite such setbacks from my week at fundamentalist basketball camp, I carried on with sport. My childhood ritual of riding bikes with friends around the block turned into daily, solitary, long treks up and down country roads. I exchanged secrets with my body then, learned to listen, respond to pain's cues. I pounded out my despair on the road, every hill I climbed I was heaving my hate of myself, these people, this place, this world, up, up, up, out and over. No one could ever reach me here. This precious time with myself was the happiest of my youth. Then track and field, basketball, volleyball, I participated in every opportunity available to push myself further physically. When I passed, when I threw, when I jumped, when I rode, when I ran, when my muscles ached and hardened, I felt strong, I felt able, I felt worthy. I worshiped and blasphemed at the temple of my body, the only sacred space I knew.

Still, there was interference. Any moment of conquest or

CHAPTER NINE

achievement could be sabotaged, claimed, re-appropriated. One month I became determined to win the President's Challenge, a physical fitness award that came with a cash prize, which I learned, all too late, didn't even come close to making up for one of the stipulations: our Bible-teacher-slash-athletics coach requiring all us girls to step on a scale in front of the whole school. Oblivious to this, I began lifting dumbbells in the weight-room-cum-utility-closet after school, when boys abandoned it for other scheduled activities. Sofia's older brother caught me in there one unlucky day, and I heard about little else for weeks, my arms squeezed and joked about, my every movement interpreted as coyness, repurposed in the service of men. Even adults joined in. I often played basketball with some of the boys after school, and for a time our pastor was their coach. Once, he came out of his office to watch us, commenting on this boy's passing form, that one's missed shot. "And oh just look at how lovely Valerie looks with her flushed cheeks. Everyone look." I didn't know what to do, awkwardly I carried on playing, unsuccessfully ignoring all the eyes our pastor had trained towards me. Whether attempting the same passes, the same shots, whether I ran in this way or that, whatever move my body made, the benchmark was always Man-desire. Look at her, disciplining her body, making it our slave, so that after she has toned her body, we will not disqualify her from our lust.

Perhaps one of the most humiliating episodes of this was after one of my high school triumphs – a winning shot in the last second of the finals of a basketball game in our small private school league. At the sound of the buzzer, a boy called Luke ran onto the court and lifted me up into the air, parading me around in glory, my win was his win, his friends' victory too, look at our girl, now look at me, look what we did. I think of this now when I hear of a man proposing to his girlfriend as she graduates from university or bestowing on her some expensive public gift of jewellery in front of a crowd when she finishes medical school, achieves something, anything for herself. Her special moment is his, you are mine, everyone now witness me claiming her, see what I have, see what she can do when she's with me.

WOMB

*There are three things that will not be satisfied,
Four that will not say, "Enough":
… the barren womb*

Proverbs 30:15-16

10

"It has been a conscious policy of government to liberate the wife from the leadership of the husband and thus break up the family as a unit of government." First, [Howard Phillips] said, in the 1800s, legislation was passed that gave women property rights. "Second, we saw how women were liberated from the leadership of their husbands politically. You know, it used to be that in recognition of the family as a basic unit of society, we had one family, one vote. And we have seen the trend instead toward one person, one vote. The ultimate extension of this philosophy has been the sexual liberation of the woman from her husband," said Phillips, and hence, he said, we got adultery, promiscuity and so forth.

— Judy Mann, 'Listening in on Speech by "Pro-Family" Orator, *The Washington Post*, October 31, 1980.

Little Billy now wants to get his ears pierced, and little Sally now dresses like a prostitute... parents who allow their teenage daughters to wear short skirts and bikinis are another problem.

— Brian Abshire, Dealing with Rebellious Christian Teenagers, *The Counsel of Chalcedon*, 2002, Issue 2.

"Today we will be talking about the ladder of promiscuity."

Our small school sat in rows of padded chairs in the immense church sanctuary, youngest in front. One of our church-school's Bible teachers, also an elder of course, stood at the front, as always at his most passionate when talking about personal piety. Each act of obedience to the law was a seed planted in the grassroots movement by which we holy white people would raise heaven from our earthly efforts. When preaching, when teaching, this man's whole zealous body boiled and bubbled over, eventually producing pale globules of spit at the corners of his mouth which occasionally dropped away. Today, we were gathered together in part because our church-school magazine had published an article on teenage promiscuity. If parents fail in their responsibility to deal with wantonness among children, the church must step in. And to our Bible teacher's disgust and delight, indistinguishable as they were, there had been reports of another debaucherous high school party. I was 14.

Parties like these often took place at the behest of church leaders' kids, though adults never discussed the relevance of this in front of mere children. Here was where the repressed exercised liberation, and the most reckless kids from the most untouchable families led the way. I saw them exchange knowing glances at school, recite jokes only they understood, hinting at experiences only they shared, mocking the blank faces of the absent and uninvolved. The youngest of our pastor's sons, Matthew, reported snippets of the older crowd's revelry to me, all disapprovingly, though he too had joined in, by rights bestowed on him by birth. Our phone calls almost always operated as his confession booth and I his priest of sorts. For hours sometimes he heaved upon me all his emotional baggage, the click of the receiver returning to its cradle signalling his absolution and my further idealisation.

"The first rung of the ladder of promiscuity is dressing to attract attention. Girls, you might do this by wearing tight or low-cut blouses."

I sat lower in my seat, not daring to catch anyone's eye, my cheeks

CHAPTER TEN

growing hot. I didn't own any tight or low-cut clothing, yet I was suddenly hyperaware of the pressure of my buttocks against the seat, the heft of the half-moons on my chest, presently concealed by my bulky, crested school sweatshirt. It was a hot, humid day, and tendrils of my thin, reddish blonde hair curled around my face. This somehow seemed now irreverent too. I pushed my legs together tightly and positioned my feet under the chair, crossing my arms over my stomach. An instinctive tool in every shrinking woman's repertoire. I'd recall this moment, years later, when a roommate at university showed me a Sabbath trick her mother taught her, of positioning a Bible strategically against her body, its blessed angularity concealing sacrilegious softness, a full chest or rounded stomach. Men would see only the Word and none of our flesh. My mother too disapproved of the existence of both girls' and women's bodies. We pretended they didn't exist, speaking about them rarely and only in coded whispers.

This was how. We imagined ourselves as ephemeral spirits in disguise, occupying tented clothing, ghosts under a sheet, collapsing at the touch. We lived not in the realm of the flesh but in the realm of the spirit, if indeed God lived in us. And did he? To wear revealing clothing was to tell a lie, to fail to put to death the misdeeds of the body, to communicate the existence of things that shouldn't exist. Fitted jeans might reveal the curve of a thigh. The visible strap of a bra might suggest a possible reality of breasts, might blaspheme them into being. Let there be boobs. Let there be legs. And there were boobs and legs and Men saw that they were very bad. Perhaps Men's bodies would resurrect at the final day of judgement, but girls'? Women's? Such straw, such stuffing would surely be burned away, had come from the discarded dust of Men's more original bodies and to the dust they would return. Who could blame Men for their response to any unsettling of this sacred order our feminine forms committed? They were unwitting recipients of any such deceitful, immodest lessons, innocent of whatever our flesh enticed their hands to do. The woman whom you gave to be with me, she gave me her body, and I ate.

Adults talked perpetually in front of us about girls whose bodies were too visible, too robust, too substantial, too sickly, too weak. The so-and-so girls' butts are too big. If only so-and-so disciplined her diet, she might find a husband. If she were thinner, she'd be happier. So-and-so puts on too much eyeliner for church. I saw so-and-so wearing bodysuits in worship, can you even imagine. Every gathering was an opportunity to scan and judge, to accumulate information, to recalibrate one's position by trampling another. Nothing was off limits. Yet like all our rules, our version of purity culture was riddled with hypocrisy. The elder's wife most openly critical of other girls' clothes and makeup was also the most lenient with her own daughters' wardrobe choices. The elder who initiated a bulk purchase of the book *Christian Courtship vs. The Dating Game*, he was also the most permissive about makeup. Our pastor was adamant that piercings of any kind were ungodly, yet his children smoked and drank underage and listened to whatever music they fancied. Hot and cold, here and there, up and down, everyone had opinions and arguments, everyone made it their daily profession to outdo themselves in drawing and redrawing definitive lines, in dishonouring one another and honouring themselves.

Yet even according to the almighty adults, adorning ourselves with proper clothing, modestly and discreetly according to our fickle and self-contradictory system, this was only a short-term solution to the problem that is women. A stop gap. The long-term answer was of course marriage. Whew, marriage. Finally, marriage. We thought it'd never happen for her, but at long last, it has. The pastor's wife once listed her children's names in an announcement, complete with a blank line and question mark after the daughter who wasn't yet married. To be completed. To be determined. Work in progress.

In the beginning, Men created the universe. Women were fulsome and void, and obscurity was over the surface of their bodies. The spirit of Men hovered over their shape. Then Men said, "Let her be mine." And then, as if by magic, babies appeared, their lives

CHAPTER TEN

birthed into our commune triumphantly via the most sacred of information delivery devices, the pulpit, usually in the form of an elaborate poem written by the father-to-be and read dramatically by our pastor. Breaking news headline: Woman finally saved through childbearing. Parents sighed with hope and relief at the thought and then finally the reality. Audible gasps of rejoicing accompanied these announcements, to mark that brief period of celebration in a woman's limited life, lasting between the moment of conception and a year, maybe two, after her baby was born. Until the risk of wickedness sets in again. Time for another pregnancy.

A man I know moved from England to Arizona a few years ago and was unprepared for another conservative evangelical church's similar elation, their chorus of cheers, once because a woman and her daughter were *simultaneously* found to be with child. According to my incredulous friend, the minister had even pumped his fist in excitement as he proclaimed such glad tidings. I shrugged when my friend reported this to me. I wouldn't have been surprised if the whole congregation had jumped to their feet and run seven laps around the room, shouting and blasting their trumpets to mark the collapse of the wall that was another woman's hymen. So everyone charged straight in, and they took her uterus.

As a child, listening to these elaborate announcements, I recall watching certain women quietly slip out of the room weeping, the memory of their reproductive loss unnoticed and unmourned, trampled under the eager boasts of the holy mob, zealous to win the world through the wombs of women. And what of the women who never satisfied our community's demands over our reproductive systems? Years after I left my church-school, I visited my friend Leah in her parents' home, her sisters dropped in, no time to waste, haven't you heard, our eldest sister's husband had a vasectomy, what use is she now, their sharp words like knives eagerly cutting even the bonds of blood, reinforcing our savage sisterhood.

The concept of asexuality was of course absolutely foreign to us. Any single woman was seen as exceptionally unnatural, stuck as she was in purgatory with purposeless breasts, vagina and womb. Men and women frequently deliberated with one another on that undesirable state of being useless, unleashed or, worse, unwanted, heaven help the undesired because there's nothing more we can do for her. These messages were always delivered loudly, always loudly, and often in the presence of the offending girl-woman. In these moments, we were 'she,' 'her,' and almost never 'you,' in this way required to listen, included by force yet simultaneously excluded, both the subject of the conversation and its object.

"She looks so pretty today. When will someone snatch her up?"

"What she really needs is a husband."

"Her education is important up to a point, so her husband doesn't get bored with her."

Promiscuity was not just being sexually uninhibited. It was to be unrestrained. Unrestricted. Unbridled. Unconventional. Uncontrolled. Daring to exist, to distract, and even worse, to prosper, without the rightful oversight and exploitation of Men. Loose. Wild. Many of us internalised this compulsion to be securely positioned under close supervision, to be chewed up and swallowed, digested by manly desire. "I can't wait to submit to my husband," Leah whispered to me excitedly one Sunday, expecting shortly to be engaged. At a church picnic, her church elder father snuck up behind her mother as she played horseshoes and pinched her ass, grinning as he displayed before all our eyes what he was in a position to take, what he and his hands alone could grab and whenever. There were many among us who could imagine freedom and fulfilment only as marriage, the only mechanism to leave the family home, away from the suffocating control of patriarchal parents, trading one despot for another, maybe this one would be better. This theme of ownership followed me relentlessly to university and beyond. "Why isn't anyone dating you?" a college study partner puzzled, he surprised by the fact of my unclaimed intelligence.

CHAPTER TEN

"Holding hands, kissing on the cheek, then the lips. Fondling each other's genitals over top of clothing."

Here was my high school Bible teacher again, each rung in his ladder of promiscuity growing more and more explicit, blending into a single, horrifying climax. We had never heard such talk from our teachers before. It was impossible to mask so much collective mortification, yet every child was trying, bodies turned to stone in every seat. Each squirm was an admission of immorality. We'd surely turn to salt if our eyes moved even half an inch. My mother, as a teacher also in attendance, could stand this mockery of her carefully honed modesty no more. "We're leaving," she announced to the room. "This is inappropriate." Her catch-all word for whatever was false, whatever was ignoble, whatever was wrong, impure, unlovely, abominable, whatever was worthy of condemnation, we were never to think on such things, she washed our mouths out with soap when we did. She tapped me on the shoulder, and I joined my siblings in the corridor. Somehow, our exit was even worse than staying for whatever licentious level was next, camouflaged in the herd as I had managed to remain until then. We drove home in silence, the only known cure for the falsehoods we'd heard.

Such mixed messages were profoundly confusing. Language about sex, about bodies, all this was implicitly (and sometimes explicitly) labelled as forbidden, coarse, unwholesome. Sexual immorality and all impurity must not even be named among us girls. Yet those with self-appointed authority established all our rules, made rigid decisions, then broke them, changed them at whim, demonstrating the location of the law as internal to themselves. These men, in their bodies, their words, their actions, they were the commandments, the statutes and the laws. They the word fashioned into Man-flesh. The summer before I turned 15, I began attending our church youth group, led by a young man under the singular ministerial tutelage of our pastor. Most meetings we played sexually awkward games – one where we girls sat in a circle, instructed to remain absolutely straight-faced while boys whispered the phrase "Honey, I love you" in our ears, another where in pairs, we boys and girls maneuvered an orange between our two bodies pressed together, from abdomens to mouths, without the use of our hands. Afterwards we listened to moralistic sermons about the faithfulness and unfaithfulness of various Biblical figures. One time, as part of a service initiative, we painted the walls of a room in a church member's house – the pastor's eldest son and his friends dipped their hands in paint, pressed them on the backs of girls' t-shirts, then cajoled them until they rotated their shirts to position these painted hands atop their breasts.

I both wanted the attention of others and dreaded it, just as I'd learned to loathe my body yet instinctively shield it. I longed for love, though I'd rarely felt it. Respect though I'd never known it. Belonging though I'd never experienced it. I wanted to be seen and understood yet could imagine nothing worse. I couldn't fathom such gifts without their cost, the hunter, the possessor, the eater, the devourer, the eraser. In 1990, our church hosted 'The Christian Vision of Victory Seminar,' featuring an array of men including R. J. Rushdoony, Walter Bowie, Dan Jordan and Gary Demar, alongside our pastor.[31] Each spoke on some vision of the future. The future of world missions, of politics, of medical ethics, of Christian activism. But what was my future? Where could I go, who would I be, apart from the dictates of all these men? I developed a habit of writing letters to my future self, to speak her into existence, to ensure her survival. To Valerie at 18. To Valerie at 21. To Valerie at 25. Dear Valerie, are you there? Dear Valerie, where are you now?

---

31 The Christian Vision of Victory: ACTS Seminar Review. (1990). *The Counsel of Chalcedon*, 7. https://www.scribd.com/document/235689076/1990-Issue-7-The-Christian-Vision-of-Victory-ACTS-Seminar-Review-Counsel-of-Chalcedon#

11

Women's liberation has become a topic of cocktail party conversations, college campus debates, laundry room fantasizings, and General Assembly headaches. Even the most naive of persons cannot plead ignorance of this present controversy; for, besides the deluge of publicity, it is one which hits home. A husband cannot ignore a once-contented wife who is suddenly driven to "find herself," drop the dishes, and pick up a career. Nor is it likely that an ordained woman behind the pulpit will be accepted without so much as a raised eyebrow, a clenched fist, or perhaps even a letter of transfer.

— Rita Mancha, The Woman's Authority: Calvin to Edwards, Journal of Christian Reconstruction, Winter, 1979-1980, Vol. VI, No. 2.

One reason for the abundance of sexual offenses was the number of men in the colonies who were unable to gratify their sexual desires in marriage.

— Edmund S. Morgan, The Puritans and Sex, Journal of Christian Reconstruction, Winter 1978-80, Vol. VI, No. 2.

In those years, I became whatever version of myself I needed to become to escape the unsafe eyes, mouths and hands around me. In a community which could not be trusted to respect its members' true selves, I was to every person what would preserve me. An effortless liar, claiming to be here when I was there, right when I was wrong, this kind of person when I was that kind, yes, I like that too, yes, I too have heard and seen this or that. Version 2.0, 3.0, I clothed my entire self in camouflage, they would never own me or know me. Half-truths and untruths, all these were my truth. As my pastor and his pals lied to us and to all their enemies, so I lied to them, straight to their very faces. A teacher asked me to tell the class my pattern of studying, since my scores were always high. I fabricated some tantalising fable about putting my class notes on the piano and playing a tune while reading. I invented friendships from outside our church-school, turned down invitations to go here or there, no, I'm sorry I already have plans with my other friends, those other people from other places always so eager to spend time with me, people who understand me. Wishful thinking. Flat-out lies. Our headmaster's son Timothy told his father I was the only happy girl he knew in our group. Upon hearing this from the headmaster's own lips one afternoon after school, I nearly choked in the effort it took not to expose my surprise by laughing. I was a living web of contradictions, a shapeshifter, I embraced all possible unsteadiness. I hid from everyone, even from myself, and I knew all the best hiding places.

For this pattern of self-protection, I paid a terrible cost. At night, I cried all my tangled anger and hopelessness down the shower drain, my stomach protesting with acidic insistence, any and all food was objectionable, eventually most nights I'd vomit and go to sleep. My teeth kept the score, why does she suddenly need so many fillings, my mother asked, her teeth were always so good. Sometimes I'd hold a hand or a foot under the hottest tap setting, practising my deceit on my own skin, sensing cold not heat, such was my skill. I crushed various medications, squeezed out the contents of multiple creams, mixed them all together in warm water in a paper Dixie cup, sent this toxic mixture to my stomach, apathetic as to what might happen, unaware even of why I'd ever do such a thing. Ignorant of anyone's similar practice before me, I began binding my chest, first in the summer, when pool parties forced the full embodiment of otherwise godly Christian girls' intangible spirits. I tied the straps of my one-piece swimsuit together in the back with a shoelace, a waterproof watch band, dental floss. One time I forgot any such tightening tool. The host of the party, an elder's daughter, was by now liberated in her bikini, she who could do so since a ruling church elder ordained it. She held the centre; I could skirt the sides. So I thought, until, leaning over to dry my legs, the pastor's son Matthew caught a glimpse of that perilous valley of death between my breasts. "Valerie!" Practically naked and unashamed, how dare you, without my permission no one shall expose even a hand or foot in all the land of Egypt.

His rebuke reminded me of my place. Some of us were somehow selected as those who would bide our time in chastity, wait in the wings, hands folded patiently like carefully preserved meat. Bodies trussed for the taking. One friend's church-elder-father elected to give his daughters a promise ring and a tiny gold lock on a chain to enclose their ring fingers and their necks securely until marriage. The key to this lock would then be passed, father to husband, by transfer of authority, sealed in condescending public ritual at her wedding. A bridesmaid in her wedding years later, I stood in my gown before an assembly of witnesses, as my friend's father took the lock in his fingers, now drawing the key like a knife across her exposed neck, unbinding her briefly, then legally transferring the custody of her collar to a man whom I'd never once seen smile. The following year, after my university graduation ceremony, her husband agreed to allow his wife to attend the celebratory lunch, though he himself would not be joining us for reasons deliberately unspoken and unknown. Through the window I watched him drive circles around the restaurant for the duration, each iteration encircling, tightening around her as with loops of a rope. By the meal's end my friend emerged to meet her master's impatient eye, suitably cinched for transport. "It's a relief when he's away on a trip," she told me sometime later, straight-faced, no indulgence in further explanation. Matter of fact. Dispassionate. The way of so many women I knew.

This was what awaited we schoolgirls in reserve. This was our future.

As for girls who rebelled and lived as they wanted to, boys could treat them accordingly, so long as their parents attended another church, beyond the pastor's circle of protection. Fair's fair. They're not really our people. Hey ho, this is how it goes. Such girls would become fodder for future jokes. Haha, remember how wild those girls were. It was all so funny, so much fun fun fun. Weren't those the days. Wasn't she something.

While the boys sowed their wild oats in anticipation of the prison of marriage they'd soon oversee, I felt certain eyes intensify on me each year. Yet the more I dodged, the more reluctant and elusive I seemed positioned as prey, the stronger the self-determined hunter's desire to capture and consume me, to parade my dominated body, trophy-like, to his lusty band. I meant nothing more to them. Every day seemed a test of my resolve, would I be taken now or later. I could never be the one who takes. I could never be not taken. Inner circle, outer circle, there were no safe circles.

In ninth grade, several new boys joined our class, and I discovered that one lived just up the road from me, had attended the same summer basketball camp I had. I located Thomas's address from the school directory and walked over to say hello. We practised free throws and layups for a few hours, struck up a sort of friendship I thought. One day he invited me to a party at the house of another boy at school, Benjamin, who, when someone dropped a heavy textbook one day in biology class, immediately dove under the desk as if preparing for an air raid. He told some of us that his father struck his and his sister's heads if they didn't do their schoolwork, if they talked back, didn't do their chores. "This is probably why my sister is a bit funny in the head," he reasoned.

"Come on up, I'll show you my room," Benjamin said when we arrived. His house was enormous, his parents were hosting some event downstairs, there was champagne, finger food arranged artfully on silver platters, a room full of adults in fancy evening clothes. I followed the rest of our small group up the winding stairs, to a bedroom at the end of the hall. Once there, someone closed the door, I don't know who, the boys suddenly combined forces, they pushed me down on the bed, I bumped my head, hands jostled me, held me down whenever I tried to get up. A disposable camera appeared in someone's hand, flashes that confused me and recorded my violent humiliation. I never saw whatever images they stole from me, whether they preserved them, what they did with them. I remember nothing else in the house after that.

I do recall this, though, that Thomas left without telling me, and another boy in our group, Lucas, was somehow my only ride home. He tried to hold my hand in the back seat of his mother's jeep as she drove towards my house. I was dazed and could not find the words to refuse, though my body conveyed its own messages. "Your hand is so sweaty," I recall him saying. "Why is it so sweaty?" I managed to relocate some language the next day and told him plainly and briefly that No, I was not interested in a relationship of any kind with him. He looked surprised, then angry. "Bitch." He left school early that day, telling everyone he was sick, no one must ever witness any boy's humiliation at the hands of any girl. Though that night I reflected, perhaps he really was sick, perhaps the Angel of the Lord struck him, perhaps he was eaten by worms, perhaps he might die. Resting on such hope, these thoughts made me to lie down on my bed that night, led me beside the still waters of sleep.

We didn't speak again about any of this. Lucas transferred his intentions quickly to another girl. But one afternoon some months after, he stopped in to where I was again playing basketball at Thomas's house down the road. The two boys chatted a minute as I carried on shooting, then said there was something of mine in his car, a book of mine I'd left somewhere, I could retrieve it if I still wanted it. As I leaned in, looking, the two rushed over and gave me a push, held the doors shut so I couldn't get out, their faces jeering and laughing at me through the glass, again I was a prisoner. I sank again into the mire of my own stupidity. So naïve. Not again, I promised myself. Never again. I swore and swore to myself too many times to remember, cried tears of rage and shame into my pillow. Now this boy Lucas is a man, now I too am grown, he has found me on social media, he sends me a direct message, "Hey, Valerie, it's you! How are you? Been such a long time. Are you still in touch with anyone else?" This unexpected contact propels me suddenly backwards, now again I can't locate the words I need, again I am a tongue-tied child. My awkward abruptness sends him on his way, he is gone but again without penalty. Again.

This is the tension that pulled me here and there. Survive yet submit to slaughter, maybe just get it all over with, these two impulses continually at war. All power in heaven and on earth belonged to Men, and women in the proximity of such power could find some measure of protection and approval only if we pleased Men, did their bidding, recruited, corrected and punished one another and anyone lower than we. All this our pastor blessed with his preaching and teaching, that the Men who direct the affairs of the church are worthy of double honour. As for women, our meaning lay in the lives and choices of men. This was the true north of my moral compass, internalised from childhood. Yet, like all living creatures under the sun, I instinctively sought to shield myself from harm. Every awkward and abrupt word, my sweaty hands, even my silence, these were each one a form of resistance, sabotage, mighty acts of rebellion, thundering refusal to submit. All such subtleties were my striking back, my crying out.

"That doesn't sound like you," a friend said to me once, when I spoke up sharply and directly in defence of myself. It's likely she meant it as aspiration. "I expect better of you" maybe summarised her rebuke of my forthrightness. A colleague tells me, "You are so quiet and reserved." This too surprises me, privy as I am to my volatile internal wars. This is simply how others experience me, how I am with them. I'm this way and that way, I'm not like this, then suddenly one day I am. At university, a boy condescendingly criticized my bland style, I look like everyone else, fleece vest, baggy cargos, why not express myself, live a little. What privilege! To be a peacock instead of a sparrow or a factory chicken, parading and displaying my unique personality instead of scrambling to hide among my sisters, to escape the butcher's knife. Was I not a genuine life form? Was I not living? Was I not grasping after survival, chasing it, claiming and choosing it, fighting for it, every decision a desperate act of self-preservation?

Which one of me is real, all, some, none? Our selves are a series of reactions, accommodations, impressions of every point of contact, held not just within our mortal coil, but also without, in the recollection of other humans, other animals, even the very inorganic elements of the earth. I am whoever I am right now, who I was back then, tomorrow I'll still be me. Good and evil, weak and invincible, fixed and flexible, full of rage and turmoil and altogether calm and completely content. I want to walk with my rucksack towards the sun, I want to sit by the warmth of a fire and see no one for days, I want the mundane and the thrilling, I want to choose between things in ways that only make sense to me. I could've done this, I could've been that, except for them, except for him. What a waste of all these years of my life, all these currents carrying me along, pulling me here and there, without even a crumb of concern for the glaring absence of my conviction. So many of my friends now lament the loss of past possibilities. I too wonder about all that was stolen from me, what might've been, in the absence of all their roadblocks. I have no answers for all our painful questions. It's unjust to measure the repressed and oppressed against people of greater privilege and liberty – courage and victory take many forms. Who can make sense of such unruly and mismatched fabric as we are truly except our creator, there before the world began.

12

Making sexual harassment a crime is dangerous to our liberties in several respects. First, it opens the door to a great deal of subjectivity as to what constitutes behaviour which is 'unwanted,' 'persistent,' and 'abusive.' This is a 'crime' that is difficult to prove and is open to interpretation as to what exactly happened.

– Rev. Steve Schlei, 'Sexual Harassment,' *The Counsel of Chalcedon*, 1994, Issue 6.

In this cruel community of my childhood, there seemed to be no rest between episodes of conflict. To be sure, we were no different than any other school in many respects—in our drug use, sexual assault, teenage pregnancy, abuse of alcohol—yet the additional spiritual burden we carried, our façade of sacred exceptionalism, this was something else. This moral veneer required endless polishing and repairing, and we worked at mimicking the adults, hiding from each other and from ourselves our true nature and impulses. At 16, I was at elder's daughter Jenny's house along with the headmaster's son Timothy. The three of us, along with Jenny's sister, had set out to climb up into a decaying treehouse left behind by some previous inhabitants of Jenny's family farm. Over the years, various animals passed through their barn and fields – chickens, a horse that died after eating some barbed wire, buried afterwards in an enormous pit dug in the family's

CHAPTER TWELVE

back pasture. Other odd things happened there. Someone locked a cat in the bathroom on another of my visits, the creature unravelled an entire toilet roll across the room, its footprints documenting its vengeful steps first in its own faeces then across every inch of tissue. Jenny's mother came out yelling, demanding to know who'd made this mess, and without hesitation Jenny and her sister blamed me. "Don't worry, we're only saying it's you because she wouldn't hit you." I wasn't following. "But wasn't it the cat?" They shrugged – "Just pretend it was you, Valerie." I said nothing, still their mother marched me in there to bag up all that mess.

Now on this particular afternoon, we took turns finding our way up into the treehouse, discovering nothing of interest, then, as I was climbing back down, my body dangling to reach the branch below, my shirt got caught on a nail. My hands were fully occupied with holding myself up, and so it seemed I had little choice but to continue the drop down and temporarily leave my shirt behind, exposing my fully blossomed chest to the group, tightly encased in a sports bra as usual but nevertheless there it was. Apparently, this brief revelation was just long enough to hatch a plan in Timothy's mind. That afternoon, before we left Jenny's house, he told me he admired me, liked me even, let's walk together tonight around your neighbourhood and talk, I'll come by.

I felt again that hidden hindrance, the muddled set of memories of what boys could and probably would very well do. Still, I said only that I liked him too, words that formed robotically in my mouth without any measurable feeling or coherent cognition. It's more than a little difficult to explain the complex yes and no that mingles and quarrels in the heads of repressed girls and women. The pull for power was by now intuitive, that much I have moderate certainty of. I sensed that Timothy was closer to the centre than other boys who'd expressed interest in me, why not see where I could get with this particular tether. But who's to say, this is only what I suspect are the likely mechanics that produced the set of articulations that came unbidden and unrehearsed from my mouth. Words I almost immediately regretted and wished to take back. He showed up, we walked around the single block of my neighbourhood, and as we went, I was again at war within myself, my defensive impulse again took the reins, and I somehow dodged his quick and clumsy efforts at embracing. "Let's save it," I said, wary of the possible penalties of outright refusal.

Over the next few days he seemed distant, I saw him share an odd, knowing glance at school with a girl who thought as little of me as I did her. Something wasn't sitting well. Not trusting myself or him with in-person contact, I wrote Timothy a letter expressing my desire to disassociate with him, just before my family left for our yearly extended family beach trip, and, on the assumption I'd return to a sorted situation, I relaxed into the sun and sand. Until my mother took me aside and handed me the letter, which she'd spied and removed from the mailbox before we left, inappropriate as she believed my initiative to be. Matthew the pastor's son finally called me up a few evenings later, revealed that Timothy had told everyone he'd French-kissed me for hours in my basement, now claiming a bounty on my head only boys were privy to, interactions which decided each girl's fate, her station, without her access, her input, her consent. Matthew reported this to me as a matter of established fact and very disapprovingly – I saw then he'd called to berate me and to probe the damage to the stability of my particular use to him. Was I still pure for his purposes? I immediately denied everything, but what use was this, nothing I said meant anything in the face of Tim's claims. No woman can ever come as her own witness. From then on, I saw I had fallen in Matthew's eyes, his star from heaven had sunk to the earth, she who had made Tim drink of the wine of the passion of woman's immorality.

I couldn't face Timothy again, and we never spoke again about these events. Yet all this had consequences which I alone had to pay for. Not long after, Sofia's brother convinced our Spanish teacher to let him occupy the seat next to me so he could improve his grades by following her good example." The teacher was only too pleased

CHAPTER TWELVE

to see such a misbehaving boy express willingness to be transformed into Biblical manhood by the right righteous girl. The challenge began promptly. "How do you say 'sexy' in Spanish?" he whispered in my ear. I ignored him, shot him cold looks, finally fired a frigid warning shot from my water bottle across his bow. Every response only encouraged, escalated, excited. The headmaster required me to write a two-page essay on the ways spraying water from my drinking bottle showed blatant disrespect for the building and, by extension, the whole school and, by further extension, God Almighty and all the angels of heaven. Sofia's brother showed up suddenly at the door of another class one afternoon after that, bucket of water in tow, he dashed over to deposit its contents over my head. I sat in shock and shame in the expanding puddle as he ran out, victorious, rewarded by so much laughter. The teacher's face was expressionless. "Get changed," she said, before carrying on briskly with the lesson.

Sofia's brother wasn't finished with me even then. One evening he told a girl who'd offered me a lift home from youth group that he'd arranged to take me instead, she could head off home now, no need to wait for me. On the way, he veered into ongoing traffic, hydroplaned in the flooded streets, ran red lights, turned the wrong direction. We ended our journey at his house instead of mine, all was unlit, no one was there, he grinned and laughed at my predicament, another opportunity to frighten, break down, tranquilise, neutralise, humiliate, dominate. I called home from Sofia's kitchen, please can you come get me, yes I know I didn't have permission to do anything like this, no I won't do it again.

All this escalating attention alerted others to my scent, attracted all those keen to stretch and flex. That boy called Luke openly stared and grinned at me in classes, until finally the teacher commented on it. "Is there something you want to ask Valerie, Luke?" He lingered in rooms I occupied until everyone else had left, he located me leaning against a wall in the cafeteria and pressed his palms against it beside my face, one on either side of me. He snuck up behind me as I stood at my locker and bit my earlobe. I ducked and dodged, yet he enjoyed the energy of all my unease, like fuel to get him through the day, subjugation of women the breakfast of champions. I saw his friends, my friends, watching and laughing at the show he put on at regular intervals at my expense. Another elder's son, Joel, told me after Bible class that my outraged retorts to his claims about the limits of women's intelligence had given him a hard-on. Such was I, a feast for the famished, upon me boys erected and tested the sturdiness of their manhood.

And then perhaps the worst. At my friend Leah's family's housewarming party, our pastor arrived to say a prayer of blessing. I was rushing about here and there, recruited to ensure a steady supply of clean dishes and cutlery. After the formal events of the evening, a certain church leader leaned against a particular corner in the kitchen, just next to the doorway leading to the front hall. I remember the deep cherry wood of the cabinets, popular then at that time, he just next to a unit operating as a desk. There he stuck out his arm and stopped me as I passed by, then pointed at his cheek with a wink, his inaudible way of indicating I should kiss it. To such a man I could never even contemplate saying no, and besides, no words had been offered to which I might reply. His head lowered, and as I leaned up and forward, he strategically adjusted the angle of his face, our lips brushed, I ducked, I ran, the sound of his chuckles penetrated my ear canals, an aural assault to finish off the physical. Kiss the Man, lest he be angry, and you perish in the way, for his wrath is quickly kindled. This was my first kiss.

13

The destiny of your very soul is at stake. It is possible to be deluded. It is possible to have a false security. It would be tragic to go through life living a lie. Every professing Christian should ask himself, 'Am I really a genuine Christian?' Do I manifest the traits of a true disciple?'

– Rev. John Otis, 'Who is the Genuine Christian?,' in *The Counsel of Chalcedon*, 1988, Issue 8.

Comply, resist or hide – whichever I chose, the outcome seemed the same. More than once I retreated to the woods, rubbed my face, my arm with poison ivy, my eyelids swelled and shut, my arm oozed. I would render myself repulsive to any such gaze. I could not get away. Oh God, where is my refuge, do not leave me defenceless. In and amongst so much vicious noise, as I sank into the pit of myself, I early on began to look around for other neglected and unknown things. Like so much other coping behaviour, I did this instinctively, another means for me to connect with some world beyond the boundaries of our cold community. When I was very young, it was as simple as pocketing a glass button I found in the street, an unusual leaf, an acorn, a colourful string or even a paperclip. Wherever I went, I carried one or more of these treasures in a coat pocket or zipped into the inner compartment of a thrifted white leather clutch I sometimes carried.

The items I found were never relics of home – crucially, they were things that seemed to me wholly disconnected from any space I inhabited. For this reason, I learned I had to keep them hidden since, once an item entered the public eye of my family or certain members of my church-school, it could be seized. This lesson came after a period collecting kittens and puppies that seemed to me abandoned. As soon as they became aware of each animal, my parents made the journey to the local pound in my father's work van, delivering whichever homeless creature I'd adopted to an uncertain fate. Each time I felt again a surge of searing separation from life somewhere out there, from some semblance of hope.

So what I found could be seized and lost again. What was worse, it could be ridiculed or admired – the latter was equally as bad as the former, deposited as each item would then be into the repertoire of some church-school person, now no longer my sacred thing but ours. Theirs. Our pastor's eldest daughter Diana would often publicly claim things she especially liked, telling a detailed, personal story demonstrating why she alone had the most special, the closest connection to some tree, some musical artist, some food, some author, some location. "When you were driving that way, did you pass my tree? That's my special tree, you know." Anyone else who expressed any appreciation at all for anything she earmarked was somehow participating in her family's curated collection, their ancestral brand – We declared it to be good, so of course you like it too. Doesn't everyone want to be just like us.

For all these reasons, I kept all things I treasured to myself. All my genuine joy I squirreled away. As I got older, as experience taught me to trust in each new day's potential, I looked beyond just the concrete, things I could touch and handle and carry, to the abstract, even the fleeting, the reassuring touch of soap and warm water on my face, the hectic push of wind against my back, the resolution of my breath as I climbed a hill on my bike, the susurration of the wind moving across leaves, a hug of hot soup in my stomach. One day I discovered a grove of pitcher orchids in the woods behind my house. Our science teacher didn't believe my joyful account and this I took as a sign that this too must be kept secret, protected as sacred. Gradually, I let go of any compulsion to hold in my hands the things I found – I could leave behind an unblemished acorn in the woods since another would certainly come or something like it, perhaps something even better. In this way, I began slowly to place some trust in the world. All such items, all these moments I gave the same name: secret presents.

Initially, I had no conscious idea of who might be the giver of these gifts, the universe maybe, or perhaps they came to me through the power of my own summoning. This thought thrilled me for quite some time. But as the years went by, I came to think that maybe, after all, it was God, who, as he travelled in and amongst the hills and valleys of heaven and earth, came to where I was. And when he saw me, he took pity on me, and wrote my name upon the artefacts of the earth, storing them in stealth for me alone to spy and hold in my desperate hands. This was the comfort of my childhood, that perhaps the god we worshipped weekly was, in truth, a false god, and not this God of small things who met me in the woods, in a tree or in a gutter, a God I'd come to look for, wonder about and expect. My God of the lost and found. All these secret presents were his trail of breadcrumbs, they'd lead me somewhere, only I had to watch, gather and wait, and tell no one. In and amongst all these lost and neglected things, perhaps I could one day locate myself, perhaps in finding I too would be found.

14

She does her daily chores cheerfully and not grudgingly or bitterly, as many women do today.

— Rev. Joseph Morecraft, 'A Full-Length Portrait of a Virtuous Woman,' *The Counsel of Chalcedon*, 1999, Issue 1.

The principle of tabula rasa is this: the human mind at birth has no innate ideas, is rather a scraped tablet ready for the world's writing. Our entire internal mental state comes through experience, perception, being situated in some environment. Its counterpart is innatism, the belief that a human infant is born with an inborn structure, placed there by God or some other supernatural being, or perhaps nothing but our biology. Upon birth, this structure is activated by every encounter with the earth, shaped and filled further by it. So the thinking goes.

The fundamentalist Christian version eclipses these, beyond the doctrine of original sin, which speaks of the universal fallen state of all human beings, our natural proclivity to sin that lingers since our first parents fell from paradise. More than this, some Christians believe women to be particularly and principally wicked, from infancy eyeing the forbidden fruit, one foot always inclining towards the gloom. This is the unofficial doctrine of woman's special depravity. Malum rasa. The evil slate. Left to herself or in a hive of corrupt and rebellious Jezebels, she will infect the church, just as she has already ruined the world. But, kept perpetually virginal, infantile, sequestered, educated principally by the wisdom of her father and then one day her husband, men whose hands hold up the universe, perhaps she can be scraped clean again, emptied out and filled by men, perhaps all may be well.

But this is only the short version. Training up a girl in the way she should go involves a careful division and hierarchy of labour. Men carry out the holy work of breadwinning and of formal Bible instruction. After marriage, husbands are to instruct their uneducated wives in the discovery and mechanics of their own foreign, female bodies for the purposes of Man-centred sex. And as for the rest of our tutelage? This is women's work, a team of devoted matriarchs propping up the patriarchy, weaponised against one another, in service of our own destruction. If a man appears to assist in any feminine duty, his help and his discipline is a last resort, a sign of some female failure. Even worse is when Man must by duty materialise in order to stand in the gap of an inadequate brother. Unprompted and nearly always unwanted, such a Hero will appear, Captain Conqueror, to set aright all floundering men who thus embarrass their fathers and brothers, those who listen to or learn from women, emasculated as all such men are assumed to be, to rebuke them and set the world back in its proper order. If the errant man in question does not respond well to this macho display of correction, does not take up the mantle of his domination duties, the Hero must escalate and put the offender's woman back in her rightful place by whatever means necessary, as a matter of urgency. "Does he know you are wearing that?" my father once said to me, rebuking me via my boyfriend's presumed oversight, during one of my weekend visits. "Where is your husband?" is another one I've heard, as elders of the city we shall summon this woman's True Head, and speak to him. Or even, in one particularly horrific incident, I was recipient of this abominable bulletin: "Your husband wasn't doing his duty, so I had to step in." Yet even in the face of all this vile and humiliating Mantitlement, and there is indeed so much of it, there is perhaps no force more threatening and formidable against women than we women ourselves, fuelled by submissive zeal and the ever-present threat of punishment from our master superiors, alongside the hope of freedom by means of their favour.

At some point, I was identified by Mrs. Pastor's Wife as a potential model of ladylike subordination in our multi-level misogynist marketing scheme. Or perhaps my threatening nature was growing painfully visible. Thus began her first stage of personalised grooming. I became vaguely aware of this one day in our whole school music lessons. Our pastor's wife began each tutorial with a display of her own prestige by means of a very loud solo warmup. Now she was instructing us in proper breathing, "Imagine a rubber ring around your waist, breathe in deeply, everyone inhale, imagine the ring expanding outward ..." We all breathed in deeply and entirely incorrectly, requiring more focus, further direction, more of her expert modelling. "No, boys and girls, see how my breathing amplifies my voice lalalaLAAAAAA!"

We couldn't see, but she saw our every move. She spotted my straying gaze, distracted as I was by a large insect crawling on the head of a kid in front of me. I tapped on the kid's shoulder to alert him, and in so doing jostled the insect down the collar of his shirt. At this I gasped, stealing the attention of the class further away from their holy focus. Mrs. Pastor's Wife was not pleased. After class, she sternly told me to stay behind, then emphasized how disappointed she was in me, how so many of my girl-peers looked to me as an example, how important it was for me to lead. in. a. godly. way. Such a notion was news to me, I didn't imagine myself leading anyone, and the possibility of more prying eyes rather unsettled me. I didn't know then what I know now, that those spying my potential were not girls but mostly women, anxious for new recruits. While we girls collected each other's faults as ammunition, as the adults around us did also, certain women scrutinised our faces, our movements, our clothing, our body shape, our families, which one

CHAPTER FOURTEEN

can I make my admirer, which can I conquer and claim, which can I possess and make my puppet, my brand ambassador, my future daughter-in-law. Let us make woman in our image, according to our likeness, let us create her in our image, in the image of ourselves we will create them, ladylike and submissive we created them.

The training escalated, bit by bit. Mrs. Pastor's Wife approached me one day after school and said she had decided I should start working certain afternoons in the church office. I was to start immediately, that very day, here, let me show you what we'll have you do. My duties included sifting through reams of church documents, coming up with some kind of suitable sorting system and filing the papers accordingly, all in an airless and windowless rectangular closet crammed to bursting. The Rev. Dr. Pastor's sermons, article drafts and random writings, old church bulletins, magazines, leaflets advertising Friday night suppers, men's meaty breakfasts, women's modest teas and Bible studies, all were priceless historical artefacts, none could be thrown out, no not even one. Occasionally Mrs. Pastor's Wife asked me to come in on a Saturday, and she was always there, chatting on the phone, making runs to the supermarket for her husband's lunch, an entire rotisserie chicken and some sort of beverage, now she was fretting she'd bought the wrong drink, now she was locating napkins for his greasy fingers, all while I thumbed miserably through a million miles of dot matrix printouts.

I could make no sense of what I was doing. "I'm sure you'll figure it out, dear!" was my only direction. I grabbed fistfuls of sermons, notes, outlines, chapters, bulletins, orders of service, all at random, stacking them into folders and boxes, whatever my hands happened to land on I threw in. As I worked, I sensed myself dissolving, disappearing, under the clutter, under this Man, my body, my mind, my time, all less important than this endless archive of minutiae, this homage to every event he had ever overseen, every word he had uttered, every thought. I never finished this pressing cataloguing of the pastor's precious papers. The $2.50 or was it $3.00 per hour Mrs. Pastor's Wife promised me never materialised, eventually somehow, I stopped coming, I don't remember why or how, likely over time she forgot I was there, stopped looking for me, talking to me, I dissolved before her eyes, what was the point, so I left. Another episode in her characteristic flightiness, from absolute urgency to utter apathy.

Eventually, she'd recall my existence and by extension, my usefulness. Not long after my stint in the church office, I was forced to follow her whims again when she decided once more what I simply must do as a matter of emergency. There was to be a poetry workshop in North Carolina and I her special companion, don't worry about the triple digit attendance fee, something about the Rev. Dr. Pastor's discretionary account, winky wink, it'll be our secret, mentor to protégée. Lickety split, the day arrived, my mother dropped me off at Mrs. Pastor's Wife's house, and I carried my bag inside where she promptly inspected its contents, determined my clothes to be wholly unsuitable and glided off to her daughter's room for more appropriate attire.

"Here is a dress Diana has decided doesn't suit her. Why don't you try it on and we'll see if it works."

She sauntered from the room, having set things to right, and so I pulled the floral Laura Ashley dress with its massive white collar over my head, tried in vain to squeeze it across my hips. Nothing doing. I sheepishly emerged from the room as I'd entered it. "It's too small," I said simply. "Oh, hmmm," she replied. "That's strange as it was too big on my Diana. Who knew she was slenderer than you? Oh well, we probably won't attend church services on Sunday anyway, since they'll likely all be Episcopalian." In her eyes there was nearly nothing worse, that cursed community of false believers – which my beloved grandmother and aunt happened to belong to.

The rest of the trip proceeded in a similar fashion. On the long car journey up to the retreat centre, I was treated to a lengthy account of all of Diana's love interests, so many admirers, none of which really have been able to hold her attention, you understand,

CHAPTER FOURTEEN

Valerie. Look, here I've brought some of her modelling photos. I'll let you have a look, Valerie. I was quite literally captive audience to the parable of how Mrs. Pastor's Wife had followed the Rev. Dr. Pastor to his chosen university, she had turned down a voice scholarship so she could prioritise married life, focus on her husband's needs as wives should, Valerie. You understand, Valerie, that a young woman must learn to properly express her emotions and feelings in a way that elevates everyone around her, especially her husband. You must only express emotions to magnify, to praise, to him be the glory forever and ever, this is indeed the only purpose of any womanly feeling. You are listening, Valerie, aren't you. Is there anything you wish to say or ask, Valerie.

I was listening, what choice did I have. I nervously asked if I could open my window, recline my seat and close my eyes for a while, growing more and more nauseated as I was, not only from so many severe sermons but also from some increasingly noxious fumes that Mrs. Pastor's Wife's tortured boat of a car was emitting, poisoning me as if in cahoots with its driver. I was already prone to carsickness and felt I might vomit.

That weekend was one of the longest of my life. Mrs. Pastor's Wife insisted on reading all my poems before I presented them aloud to the other poetry retreat attendees. All her own poems she performed slowly and dramatically, each on the subject of firm foundations, strong roots dug in deeply, did you get my special use of metaphor there, everyone? As I listened, again what choice did I have, my thoughts moved to the image of those most ruthless of vines that spread by runners and suckers. My mother had once tossed a few vine cuttings into the woods, hadn't even bothered to plant them. These soon swallowed up every shrub, every inch of earth. Each object, every tree these vines encounter belongs to them. They grow as tall as whatever they grow on.

Mrs. Pastor's Wife declined most of the social activities on our collective behalf, including the aforementioned Sunday service. Instead, she elected to lead me in a micro-service not inside but outside our cabin, in front of all passers-by. This she judged righteous according to the law by appeal to Old Testament judge Deborah's undesirable situation as the only available godly leader, only a last resort, you understand our unfortunate position, Valerie. Our solitary service consisted primarily of Mrs. Pastor's Wife's dramatic readings of what seemed to me the lengthiest of the Psalms, followed by her singing hymns loudly to the trees and any other service-skippers within earshot, while I mouthed along pointlessly. More than once we "took our exercise" by walking at a speed of approximately .1 miles per hour around the retreat's lake, she pointing out every leaf, every flower, every bird, every speck on every stone, quizzing me on its identity, correcting my wholly inadequate knowledge of south-eastern flora and fauna.

On the drive home, we stopped in to see Mrs. Pastor's Wife's artist friend, the woman who had painted an homage to our pastor's congressional candidacy. I sat silently and watched the clock through their discussions about the intersections of faith and art, taking every brushstroke captive for Christ. Finally, we left. Finally, I was home. Finally, the everlasting weekend was over, forever and ever Amen. Only now that Mrs. Pastor's Wife had begun absorbing me into her substance, she also started inching towards the next stage of her scheme. A suitable period having apparently passed, she announced to me the wonderful news, "Oh just wait till I tell you, Valerie." I would be leading a group which she named "The King's Daughters," a combination of Bible studies on feminine personal holiness and free housecleaning available to anyone in the church. Sign up here, families, if you'd like your every household chore attended to by these young women, all glorious within. My companions who followed me, fair virgins, these were three elders' daughters and one elder's niece, all younger than I, and so began our free, compulsory labour, starting with a deep clean of the pastor's house and a few bouts of free babysitting. On one occasion, I arrived obediently to look after Mrs. Pastor's Wife's youngest daughter, only to discover her son Matthew also there. And there

CHAPTER FOURTEEN

he stayed, all evening, playing video games and watching American Gladiators with a friend, while I looked after the baby, cleaned up after her, put her to bed, sat strangely with the two boys afterwards, the room, the world now divided between us, they in their place, I in mine.

The King's Daughters did not last long. I reached my limit, finally I found a limit. We were called to one church family's house in total shambles, inches of crumbs, an assortment of ancient spilled sauces, so many past meals accumulated and dried in layers on the dining room table, on the kitchen counters, everywhere the odour of human shit, piles of dirty diapers, soiled laundry all around us, children weeping and naked from the waist down, the toilet stained yellow with years of urine, every corner clogged with grease, slime, black mould. I saw myself then as I truly was, at the bottom of a heap, here was my situation according to her command, done to me according to her word, things she herself would not do, what she would never ask her own daughter to do, only me, only these girls younger than I. I never even told her when I ended her ambitious group, by then I knew she'd likely forgotten about us already. Yet later, I learned that two of these King's Daughters had carried on cleaning her house, carried on babysitting, carried on humbling themselves in the presence of Mrs. Pastor's Wife, that she might exalt them.

15

[Woman] must always seek to find herself, and the meaning of her life, in terms of man… When fallen woman seeks to be the equal of man, she does not attain the happiness which she thinks to find. Only in the role of wife who seeks truly to be a help to her husband does the woman properly and ordinarily fulfil her role.

– Rev. Joseph Morecraft, 'Eve: The Embodiment of Womanhood,'
  The Counsel of Chalcedon, 1989, Issue 7.

Within the cosmos of Christian fundamentalism, nothing is more unacceptable than a girl who determines or even declares her own destiny. This is the exclusive remit of men, to define what most Christians refer to as "calling." And where women's calling is pre-determined—wife-mother-servant—Men's Calling is, quite naturally, to exercise dominion over the world, in whatever sphere seems best suited to them, and then to select the right Biblical™ woman to cook their meals, birth their babies and wipe their asses so they can go about their high-ranking work unhindered. In keeping with this, most of the girls in my peer group were duly given the same set of restrictions: No calling boys. No showing special interest in any particular boy. To be eager is to be loose. No presumption of being wanted until a member of the Man-species declares formal and explicitly stated interest. To break any of these rules risked revealing that most important and

CHAPTER FIFTEEN

carefully guarded of all secrets: the existence of female desire.

Many of the boys in our church-school made full use of this prescribed inability to indicate our wishes, our interests, our disinterests, our dislikes. We were like fish on a string, hooked and gasping, waiting for the fishers of women to keep or throw us back. My strategy was to carry on blending in. As it happened, being decent at sport provided an easy mechanism for this – often boys would talk openly about this or that around me, in ways showing they'd forgotten I was even there, rendered invisible by the uselessness of my gender in such a situation. After playing basketball at my neighbour friend Thomas's house, with another friend Isaac, in the evenings sometimes we'd go to a movie or to the mall. One time, as we were driving around, they spied some girls they knew and started talking about plans to join them somehow for the evening, how could they arrange it, should they drive back around and stop casually? Isaac suddenly stopped mid-sentence and glanced back at me, my bodily presence having suddenly shifted in meaning. "Valerie, quick, lie down in the back so they don't see you." I was indignant yet I crouched down, accustomed as I was already to making myself low. I wondered then if they'd abandon me in the parking lot, maybe they'd even expect me to stay in the car all night while they followed this other group elsewhere. My brain began mapping payphones I knew were in the area, calculating other means by which I might get home. In the end, the girls didn't acknowledge my companions, so we drove on, they took me home, I felt again that sensation of being pressed down, pushed, positioned into a pedestal onto which men could stand and, suitably propped, take hold of their hearts' desires.

Most of the boys I knew were adept at annihilating any lingering vestiges of a girl's self-esteem, but perhaps no one was more skilled at this than the pastor's son Matthew. An early memory of personal interaction with him is one morning in fourth grade, when he called me "cool" for keeping silent when he cut in front of me in the four-square queue. After that, I was officially declared his best friend, and he began choosing a desk next to me in school. I couldn't believe my good luck. We worked together on school projects, one which involved constructing a map of the Biblical world, to scale. My dad built us a wooden frame into which we poured liquid plaster, then carved out the rounded shape of a cross-section of the world's surface, mountains, valleys and oceans. About an hour into our second work session, Matthew suddenly remembered another commitment and left as if racing towards some masculine emergency. After that, he stopped showing up altogether, so sorry, Valerie, he'd say later, I forgot I have this and that, you'll be fine without me, won't you, you're so much better at this than I am. Over the next few weeks, my brother helped me paint and label the model, wrapped it in old towels for transport, then carefully carried it with me into the building the morning it was due, down the hall into the Bible classroom where we hung it on the wall, to everyone's amazement. "Look what I made with Val!" Matthew was triumphant. The teacher gave us a 99, remember that no human creation is perfect, all our righteous deeds are like filthy garments, all of us wither like a leaf, our iniquities like the wind, they take us away.

Much of my time together with Matthew in high school involved me watching him do something, climb something, play some team sport. I sat and I saw, offering up my eyes and my time, a living sacrifice to our friendship. One time he asked if I'd tag along with him somewhere after school, he didn't say where exactly. We stopped for coffee at a gas station on the way, and as we sipped, as he drove, my skin reacted, I presume to some compound in the cheap coffee, and began to bubble up into a network of scarlet and swollen welts. By the time we got to our destination, some registration centre for an outdoor sport event, I could no longer bend my arms more than a fraction. While Matthew talked with some acquaintance unknown to me, I walked woodenly to the bathroom and stared in horror at my marshmallow form in the mirror. I bought a bottle of water in a machine, then stood nearby as witness to Matthew's crucial conversation, drinking frantically,

CHAPTER FIFTEEN

hoping I could flush out of my body whatever chemical I'd ingested. Eventually but with no sense of urgency, Matthew drove me back to the church-school building, where my mother, having finished her after-school work, took one look at me and drove me to the hospital where I was treated for anaphylaxis.

One year I broke my hip horse-riding, and Mrs. Pastor's Wife showed up with flowers at our door one evening, with a card signed "Love, Matthew," so inscribed with her own ostentatious handwriting. Unable to depend on me to write a note to myself, buy and deliver flowers to my own doorstep, he'd called on his mother. This was my sarcastic thought. Or maybe, more likely he'd had nothing to do with it, fickle as he was about the place of our friendship within his list of priorities. Still, I kept this card for years, treasured even the green plastic cardette that held and positioned it above Mrs. Pastor's Wife gift basket of flowers. In truth, I've only just dug it out this very minute and finally thrown it away.

This then was our arrangement. I gave and he took. He led and I followed. Periodically, there were patronising rewards to hold me on the line. At birthdays, at Christmas, on Valentine's Day, Matthew presented me with clothes, cash, cards declaring the perfection of my loyalty, he clothed me as if I was his child, the fact of my being older a matter of irrelevance. One birthday a group of us went out for a meal, and while we were all inside, he slipped away and fixed a permanent chrome decal from the Christian bookstore onto the back of my car, that one bearing the name of Jesus inside the body of a fish. He'd not sport the name of our Saviour on his car, but he'd make sure I witnessed to the world who I belonged to, wherever I went. One year he stopped by my house before Christmas, his hand behind his back, his eyes twinkled, teasing out in suspense his perfect surprise. "Are you ready for your present?" His hand emerged holding a stuffed black bear with a scarlet bow, another ubiquitous card, in his eyes a proper gift for me, his adoring fan, his infantile and obedient companion.

As Matthew and I grew older, to me we seemed to grow closer.

Then again, I see now this came about through his naming of our relationship, whatever he called the interactions between us, that was the name thereof. Let Valerie be my best friend, and that was who I was. Still, there was some semblance of substance to it. We spent hours playing table tennis at his house, air hockey and billiards at mine. We watched films in his basement, it was there I had my first beer. His sister invited me to her birthday party, "So Matthew will have a friend." He and I regularly talked on the phone for hours, Matthew confided his every crush in me, poured out his sad and lonely heart. "Please, Valerie, can you find out if she likes me? Tell me what she says." Yes, sure, Matthew, no problem, what else could I possibly be doing? Led this way by him, lacking all confidence and sense of self, I stupidly betrayed each of his crushes with my manipulative suggestions, I helped him nail up each conquest, one by one, a row of girls' heads mounted on his wall, right next to my own. Each new addition seemed to thrill then bore him. "She is just so self-centred," he said about a brief relationship with an elder's daughter. Sometimes he'd convince me to dissolve on his behalf whatever tenuous bond I had helped him construct, my loyal hand was the one that stuck the knife in, that carried the weight of rejecting and seeing someone rejected. "I'm so sorry, Matthew just doesn't think God wants you two to be together."

Occasionally Matthew pushed my loyalty too far, even for me, and cracks appeared in our friendship facade. Once I cried angry tears and yelled in outrage when he abandoned me yet again on another shared school project, set me aside according to his secret hierarchy of sacred priorities. At my seventeenth birthday party, again I was angry with him after he redirected all attention towards himself when, driving away from the roller-skating rink towards my house, he flipped another driver the bird and got punched in the face through his open window at a red light. Having arrived at my house with a broken tooth, he regaled all our friends on my front porch with his dramatic tale while I sat inside next to an untouched table of refreshments. Another time in the school cafeteria I threw

CHAPTER FIFTEEN

chocolate pudding on his white designer school shirt when he joined in on a cruel joke aimed at me. I'd warned him to stop. "I'll throw this at you if you don't. You're not a good friend, a true friend wouldn't do that, Matthew." After, he followed me to the lockers, put out his hand to lean as he reasoned with me, another casual gesture to appease me during a quarrel, look now be sensible, Valerie, no need to get so worked up. This too enraged me, and I slammed his appendage in the locker door. Another time he challenged me to a game of bloody knuckles. He had a habit of engaging girls in some physical challenge, an opportunity for close contact and a quick top-up of domination. Usually I said no, but I was in some particularly testy mood. Our knuckles cracked together over and over as our fists met, over and over and over. Eventually mine began to bleed. He laughed and asked if I'd had enough and again, have you had enough. Just say when, Valerie. No, keep going. Again. That night I filled the bathroom sink with ice and cold water, sank my bruised and bleeding hands beneath the surface. I'd not yet bandaged them. He'd not seen me flinch even once.

Each time we fought, he laughed at the thought I'd actually object, she won't really follow through, no you'd never, Valerie. And in those times I did object, when I did say no, I'm not having this, he'd somehow turn his offenses back on me, my response was too cruel, how could you ruin my shirt, how could you hurt my hand, how could you not say hello to me, how could you not smile when you saw me, Valerie, how dare you reject me, after all I've given you, all I've done. Why are you so mad at me? I expected more from you. Of all you could've done, not this unbearable rejection. Of all people, not you. I thought you were different. What a disappointment that you didn't live up to my need of you. What a shame you aren't so special after all. If I stayed angry for more than a day, he'd leave notes on my car – I don't deserve you but you know you love me, Valerie. Do you not even like me? I'm so ashamed, but after all this time, Valerie, aren't we still friends, aren't I still your favourite.

16

God has ordained the state to be an avenger of God's wrath against evil-doers... The existence of hell and the necessity of Christ's dying on the cross are insurmountable evidence that the death penalty is God's just reward for certain crimes.

– David E. Goodrum, 'God and Capital Punishment,' The Counsel of Chalcedon, 1987, Issue 2.

Controversial Georgia state Rep. Bobby Franklin is under fire again for a bill many believe could criminalize miscarriages... Franklin is a member of Chalcedon Presbyterian Church, one of the few out-and-out Christian Reconstructionist churches.

– Julie Ingersoll, 'Georgia Legislator Behind Bill Criminalizing Miscarriage is Christian Reconstructionist,' Religion Dispatches, 1 March, 2011.[32]

Violence shaded all my church-school days, each moment in between was merely time spent in a holding pen. We were pushed and smacked, threatened, whittled down with words, eyes,

---

[32] Ingersoll, J. (2011, March 1). *Georgia Legislator Behind Bill Criminalizing Miscarriage is Christian Reconstructionist | Religion Dispatches*. Religion Dispatches. https://religiondispatches.org/georgia-legislator-behind-bill-criminalizing-miscarriage-is-christian-reconstructionist/

CHAPTER SIXTEEN

pursed lips, hands, objects, singled out for adversity, all according to the curses of the covenant which were written in the law. Items were known to fly through the air from a teacher's desk, an eraser, a whiteboard marker, chalk. All such implements, a hairbrush even, repurposed in the service of sometimes spontaneous cruelty, were now infused with so much negative energy. We dared not defend ourselves. "Move your hands," "Stay still," "Be quiet": short, sharp sets of words to ensure we never did risk defiance. For years, I hated brushing my hair, couldn't bear to cook with a wooden spoon.

Most physical touch also startled me. In chapel, one teacher illustrated penal substitutionary atonement by drawing his hand back to strike a child, then prompting another teacher to step in at the last minute, children see here is God the Son bearing the blow of God the Father's wrath in place of us, see what we deserve, see how we make Jesus suffer. Our Bible teacher, also a church elder, spoke in class about the necessity of smacking infants until they learn instantaneous obedience. "You don't wait until they're old enough to understand. You spank them *until* they understand." This same teacher suspended me from school after a field trip to an anti-abortion rally, primarily for hitching a ride home in a friend's car without adequately notifying any adult. But what really sent him over the edge was another matter he raised during his rebuke of me, that I'd behaved badly throughout the day, laughing loudly with several friends as we stood outside the state capital building. I'd displayed a reckless lack of sobriety and at such a sombre event! "Don't you care about the lives of babies, Valerie? The unborn?" I had nothing to say to this, so I sat in silence, which he took as insolence. "You meant your silence as submissiveness, didn't you, Valerie?" my mother said afterwards, intending support yet once again covering over the enduring complexity of every interaction in our mixed up, messed up world.

An elder's daughter told me her older brother had pushed their sister down on the bed and threatened to rape her. This same brother eventually had a son, carried out various abusive and otherwise criminal activities, his wife eventually left him and took the boy. A friend in our church-school conspired with him to meet his son's mother at a restaurant and take the boy from her while she was in the restroom. This same co-conspirator invaded a girl's bedroom in the middle of the night and sat there in the shadows, simply watching her, staring at her sleeping. Another elder's grown son-in-law—for whom I was a regular babysitter—asked me to collaborate with him on his impulse prank one evening at a cocktail party during which I would be paid to supervise his kids. "I'm going to tell everyone I've left my wife and you're my new, younger girlfriend, just go along with it," he hurriedly told me as we walked up the path to the front door, he draping his arm casually across my shoulders. His wife was already there setting up the party, oblivious of what he'd said to me.

At some point, I began having random, uncontrollable bouts of crying in school, sometimes in front of everyone, full-blown panic attacks, once when watching some violent film in science class one afternoon, another time upon hearing one single snide word too many. "You never really laugh anymore," our basketball coach said. "Try to smile when you walk into church," my mother corrected me. "Pretty little girls when they cry and pout, look like Izzy with a ring in her snout," sang Mrs. Pastor's Wife's sister.[33] "Why didn't you look happy when you saw me," Matthew complained one Sunday, when we happened to walk into church at the same time.

This comment from Matthew followed an event just a few days before, when I'd gone to a concert with him and another friend, Jonathan. This wasn't the type of event Matthew usually included me in. But it had happened that I was with Jenny at a salon while she was having her nails done, when they rang to see if she could go. "No, but maybe Valerie wants to?" In truth, no I didn't want to go, I couldn't think of anything worse really – I hated crowds and loud noise and worried about who else might be going that I didn't know. But I also happened to be feeling particularly defiant about

---

[33] "Isabel is a Pig," from the album Go to the Ant, by Judy Rogers, 2001.

the way Matthew so often arranged my social calendar without my knowledge or say-so. Here Jenny had given me an opportunity to disrupt the established order, and I couldn't resist the chance to unsettle and test it. Oddly, my mother said nothing disagreeable when I mentioned where I was going and who I was going with, behold, the pastor's son would protect her child and keep her alive, and she shall be called blessed upon the earth.

That night, after we found our cheap seats, Matthew spotted some of his neighbourhood friends sitting nearby, and together they formed a plan to rush past the security guards blocking the entrance to the floor near the stage. No one asked for my thoughts on the matter, but neither did I want to be left alone in an empty row of stadium seats. So together with the others, I moved without a word to stand on the stairs that led down to the more exclusive stadium floor. In no time at all, others all around saw us, word spread of what we were doing, a crowd quickly filled the stairs. Someone yelled "Go!" and I felt myself shoved, pushed, down, down, down, until finally my feet fumbled when trying to find their next step, frantically my limbs felt for something solid through the air, I tumbled and landed on the unforgiving cement at the bottom, hard, bruising my knees and my cheek. Sensing the coming crowd at my back, I had a sudden vision of being trampled, I jumped up and limped quickly toward the crowd by the stage.

I didn't see Matthew or Jonathan the rest of the concert. I hunted for them but eventually just settled into the envelope of anonymity within which the crowd enclosed me without question or judgement. After several hours of smoke and volume, it was all over, I headed back to the seats from which we'd started our evening, and the two boys were waiting there for me, chatting with Matthew's other friends. "We saw you, but you seemed fine," Matthew said, his way of making our separation out to be what was best for me, he the one who always knew best. I wondered then if he'd formed this plan as soon as he'd been forced to include me. Quick—I could see his mind moving—figure out how to get rid of Valerie, put her away, lest I look on her and see, lest she sees me. The sanctity of his own sense of self seemed always reliant on my chastity, my ignorance, on me and certain other girls not learning what he got up to, never-no-never participating in it, lest the whole world's engine freeze and fall to pieces, dependent as it is on the blessed purity and ignorance of women.

17

The Bible permits slavery. This statement will come as a shock to most people.

— *David Chilton, Productive Christians in an Age of Guilt Manipulators. Tyler, TX: Institute for Christian Economics, 1981, p. 59.*

Inequality is the rule in this life, and inequality will be the rule in heaven. Some will be wealthier than others, and even in hell some will be beaten with many stripes, some few. The teachers who want or have respect for the treasure of the Lord should study Rushdoony's Institutes of Biblical Law and learn to govern their teaching techniques by God's law.

— *Ellsworth McIntyre, 'Beware of Those Who Gush,' Chalcedon Magazine, 1 Feb 1998.*

We were anything but pure. We were disloyal, unkind, self-righteous, cold. Our teachers regularly organised us into debates on various theological questions, during which we would cruelly berate and tear each other down. One school term, coinciding with the annual Christian training seminars held in our city, the notorious Christian Reconstructionist Greg Bahnsen spent some weeks instructing a group of us in logic and presuppositionalist apologetics. He drew two pictures on the board of a stereotypically male face, one with a moustache and one without. A Christian isn't just a person with a moustache, he said. Everything about us is different from the pagan, the unbeliever. We think differently, we act differently, we are altogether different.[34] We students quickly learned that this sharp division—already seeming to exclude us women as it had—involved drawing a circle even smaller than this. This came about, when, after these sessions, our Bible teacher assigned certain students among us—notably these were kids from other churches—to contend with the shining stars of our church-school's frigid religion. We would argue not for the salvation of the soul, but for Calvinism and they for Arminianism. One debate was held publicly in front of an audience comprising the whole school along with some parents. I sat alongside my fellow Calvinists, Leah and Joel the elder's son—our debate captain—who smirked throughout and even banged his forehead on the desk in a show of pride and disdain at the perceived weakness of the opposing team. I too was full of self-righteous arrogance, covering my mouth to suppress a laugh at the other team, sharing looks. Some of the parents were deeply upset afterwards, people who "couldn't handle hearing the truth," as one of our teachers put it. We revelled in the power of our reason, we openly mocked the effects of our displays of genius on others, their foreign fragility. We gave no ground, we tore our opponents apart, performing arrogant autopsies on live bodies, we felt no regret, we felt nothing but certainty. Our critical eyes looked always out and never in, our tongues devised destruction, like sharp razors, iron sharpening iron.

As some among us, men and women, grew disillusioned, developed better sense, perhaps miraculously found the God of mercy, kindness and justice, there fell from their eyes something like scales, and they regained their sight, took their things and left. Our pastor kept careful track of this slow trickle towards the door in his own kind of folder of fates, a consecrated mental list of good and evil, his whims detailing everyone's destiny. If we walked out the

---

34 "It appears then that there are only two kinds of people in the world, non-Christians and Christians; covenant breakers and covenant keepers; these two kinds of people have mutually exclusive beliefs about everything." Van Til, C. (1982). 'What I Believe Today,' *The Journal of Christian Reconstruction*, 8(2), pp. 141-149.

CHAPTER SEVENTEEN

door, we were his enemy. If we doubted, we were never a Christian. A story circulated of someone walking into the church office unannounced and over-hearing our pastor mumbling, "I hate them. I hate them. I hate them." Our pastor joked proudly from the pulpit about rumours that he preached behind bulletproof glass. Sermons were increasingly punctuated with veiled references to some pathetic person who'd left, who was thinking of leaving, someone who'd prioritised the pursuit of romantic love and friendship over correct doctrine, some man who'd gotten married and chosen his new wife's church, someone who'd moved away for no approved reason, all people who compromised, who failed, who lacked self-control, who lacked vision. Weak people. To compromise was to depart from any of our pastor's dictated directions. To leave was to lose. To love was to conform, to control. Each message trumpeted from the pulpit, from the classroom, all these sounded down into every interaction, every friendship, every marriage, all forged in conflict.

Some who left the church also renounced all semblance of faith. A teacher told our class that she'd warned her son that if he declared one day he was no longer a Christian, he must leave her house that same day and could have no relationship with her ever again unless and until he repented and was restored. I learned then that even the seemingly sacred sanctum of The Nuclear Family had its limits. A thick cloud of desperation descended and settled – an elder after church one Sunday evening stood and asked our pastor to pray for our community's faltering young people. As needs must, our church magazine ran an article one year on excommunication in the home which laid out the principles of shunning, the ultimate aim being the shame that leads to repentance and righteousness. "It is the church's responsibility to see that he feels that shame." There were as always a few caveats, of course for women, including that "a wife cannot refuse to perform marital and domestic duties if her husband is excommunicated. She cannot refuse preparing meals, conjugal relations, etc."[35]

I saw such shunning in action more than once. For a time, our

---

[35] Rogers, W. (2008). 'Excommunication in the Home,' *The Counsel of Chalcedon*, Issue 1

family took in a man in the church who'd been excommunicated for adultery. My mother delivered his meals down to a table in our unfinished basement. We siblings looked down the length of the stairs as our mother descended with her tray, we studied the outcast in his white undershirt, his elbows resting on our card table, his collared work shirt on a clothes hangar suspended from an overhead pipe, he murmuring his thanks, so kind of you, thank you for having me, really it's so generous.

This message of control and conflict attracted more people of control and conflict, things seemed to grow stranger and more volatile by the week, even by the day. After one particular Sunday morning service, as I made my way between the two blocks of chairs towards the exit, I saw a huge human turd lying on the carpet, dead centre in the back of the central aisle. I pointed it out to my friend Leah. "Must've fallen out of a baby's diaper?" she shrugged. I wasn't so sure – I'd changed enough diapers at that point to know what we were and were not looking at. "That doesn't seem possible," I said. "But also, when – and how?" Someone discreetly removed it, replacing the carpet tile it had been deposited on, so easy, done and dusted, like it was never there.

Then one day after school, during my stint working in the church office, I was among the last to leave. An odd and perpetually solitary man from church appeared, wanting to speak to the pastor, disappointed he had already gone home. I can't remember this man's name, only that one day he'd shown up at church, during the service had slithered ever closer to the front of the sanctuary, until there he was, stood in front near the corner of the stage below the pulpit. "Excuse me, sir," he'd said and made some gesture that indicated an impending announcement. He'd no doubt have started talking just then except our pastor motioned back towards him with a raised hand, ended the service quickly, stepped down from the stage to talk to him privately. The two stood and spoke, nodded and shook hands. After that, we'd seen the man in regular attendance.

CHAPTER SEVENTEEN

Now how had I become involved in conversation here with him in the church office. There was never a moment of decision in all these times that I can recall, these things never came about by any conscious choice of my own. Predestined by others, they simply seemed only to happen, now here I was, sitting, listening without interruption to this white man's narrative of the useful institution of slavery in the American South, the genetic inferiority of people of colour, suited as they are for sport and physical labour, he insisted, perspiring as he spoke, occasionally pulling at his inconsistent beard. Their captors did them a service really, he argued, rescuing them from their savage world, bringing such unacceptably conspicuous bodies into the superior spiritual presence of the new Christian world. At some point, another adult white-man-member of the church passed by the office, joined us, sat quietly beside and said nothing. An hour passed, maybe two. I think now about his silent presence, sticking me like glue. If one can overpower she who is alone, two can hold her down.

I felt uneasy then, but what this pasty man had pressed on me in the church office was merely a more targeted version of what I'd already been taught, the ideology about race, the xenophobia I had already been tutored in, had already internalised. Sofia's brother terrorised us for years with stories of a Black man who hid under girls' beds, waiting till the cover of night to reach up and around and grab us as we lay sleeping. Our history textbooks, written by Steve Wilkins, were full not only of misogyny but of the whitewashing of human trafficking, lies about the glories of the Confederacy, the injustices perpetrated on the South by means of the "War of Northern Aggression," which we learned was above all a theological war. Nothing much really to do with slavery, a mostly peaceful institution. Some masters abused their positions, sure. Some husbands beat their wives and children, a sad reality. What mattered was that these were all unfortunate anomalies in an otherwise noble set of institutions. "Southern history is full of Christian heritage to remember, enjoy and imitate for the future," one article in our church magazine argued.³⁶ Our pastor regularly applauded from the pulpit the apologetic of—as fellow Christian Reconstructionist Doug Wilson put it—"the sticky issue of slavery" by one of our movement's heroes, Robert Lewis Dabney, Confederate chaplain and chief of staff to General Stonewall Jackson. Pictures of confederate generals in various regal poses propped up all such talk, prominently displayed in the pastor's, the elders' and other church members' homes. Yet our pastor was always careful with his words, ready always to rebut any accusations of racism, no you mistake me, I didn't mean that exactly, you've misunderstood, I preach against all racists alike,³⁷ I am not a racist I am not a patriarchist either. Years later, during a spat between our pastor and his now former friend-in-arms Douglas Wilson, our pastor wrote in to an Idaho newspaper, that

> I, too, am against all self-righteous displays of the confederate flag. Furthermore, when I visited the offices of Wilson's school in Moscow several years ago, the battle flag and pictures of confederate soldiers were prominently displayed.³⁸

Ah yes. Here is where Reconstructionists, Dominionists, theonomists, triumphalists, she-man woman haters, whatever you want to call them, whatever they call themselves, this is where they really shine, how expert they are at qualifying, omitting, letting just enough words pass through their lips—and no more—so as to give the appearance of telling the

---

36 Payne, S. (1995). Confederate Heritage Conference Review: Reviewing and Renewing Our Southern Christian Heritage. *The Counsel of Chalcedon*, 6. https://www.chalcedon.org/counsel/item/854-confederate-heritage-conference-review-reviewing-and-renewing-our-southern-christian-heritage

37 "I mean, have you watched people? Out there, ANTIFA, Black Lives Matter, the racists, all these other things? Have you seen the look on their faces? They're mad and full of hatred and bitterness, fear and frustration. You can look at their faces, if you can see it behind all the tattoos and piercings and everything. You look and you can see in their faces, they're in rebellion against God." From Morecraft III, J. (2021, January 10). How Do We Know God is Judging America? *Heritage Presbyterian Church – Sermons.* https://www.sermonaudio.com/solo/heritagerpchanove/sermons/110211321451092/

38 'Connection is in Wilson's Mind', Letters to the Editor, *Moscow-Pullman Daily News*, 23 January, 2004.

truth. If ever anyone in our church-school displayed the battle flag or pictures of confederate soldiers—and they most certainly did—it was never self-righteously, let the world understand.

This is the slavemaster's gospel. The roots of this racism, thinly veiled as it often is, of course continues to run deep, as Professor of Religion Anthea Butler has so thoroughly exposed.[39] One of the main publications of our movement, Rushdoony's *Journal of Christian Reconstruction*, had, in its winter issue of 1977-1978, published a special issue on the family. Alongside various articles emphasizing the usual importance of Man-Heads-of-Family implementing biblical law in the home and the dangers of singleness and divorce, was a reprint of a 1976 article from the *Los Angeles Times*, outlining "High Black Illegitimacy." According to various quoted experts, Black babies born out of wedlock could be linked not to systemic racism but to "educational as well as cultural differences." Also included in this journal issue was a reprint of George Gilder's 1974 article, "In Defense of Monogamy." There, Gilder argued that Black poverty can be largely explained by the unmarried status of Black men and, further, that the "central facts about crime are not racial; they are sexual." He would expand on these ideas for a book in 1979 entitled *Visible Man*, prompting 50 students to turn their backs in protest to him during a commencement address for American University in 1981.[40]

Gilder was typical of the kinds of extremists that my community ran alongside. After graduating from Harvard in the early 1960s, Gilder spent some time writing speeches for various Republican leaders, Nelson Rockefeller, George Romney and Richard Nixon. At some point in that period, he underwent some kind of conversion to right-wing extremism, which he elaborated on for an interview in 1982.[41] In the 1970s, Gilder took on the women's movement,

---

39 Butler, A. (2021). *White Evangelical Racism*. UNC Press. https://uncpress.org/book/9781469661179/white-evangelical-racism/
40 Bronson, P. (1996, March 1). George Gilder. *Wired*. https://www.wired.com/1996/03/gilder-5/
41 Gilder, G. (March 5, 1982). "Why I am not a Neo-Conservative," *National Review*, 34(4): 219-20.

including defending President Nixon's veto of a day-care bill, in a series of articles and books like *Sexual Suicide* and *Men and Marriage* that questioned feminism's fundamental tenets. Alongside R. J. Rushdoony, Jerry Falwell, Oliver North, Kenneth Starr, Phyllis Schlafly, Pat Robertson and some others, Gilder was one of the earliest members of the Council for National Policy, founded by the Rev. Tim LaHaye in 1981 to bring together various right-wing, conservative Christian leaders and wealthy funders.[42] Gilder would go on to co-found the Discovery Institute, a think tank promoting a conservative public-policy agenda, including advocating for the teaching of intelligent design in state schools. In short, Gilder was a kindred spirit, of the sort who ducked and dodged, who said hateful things while decrying hate of any sort.

One year, two Black girls started attending our school, an anomaly in our almost exclusively white community. This was the same year my friend Leah the elder's daughter decided to do her school report on Martin Luther King, Jr. She entered class the day it was due, hauling her enormous visual aid, a blown-up cheque written to the American Communist Party, purportedly signed by King himself. Together with the rest of the class, these two Black girls sat and listened as Leah detailed the FBI's surveillance of Rev. Dr. King led by J. Edgar Hoover, rumours of King's extramarital affairs, his lies, his socialist links. Afterwards, the two girls objected, what about what King did for education, he secured our right to education. We are here because of him. "Education is not a right. It is a privilege," the teacher replied curtly. We said nothing more on the matter. She too was an elder's wife. Each word from her was consecrated, to be heard and affirmed without question.

---

42 *Council for National Policy – Membership Directory*. (2014). https://www.splcentre.org/sites/default/files/cnp_redacted_final.pdf

18

Parents must recognize that in sending a child to Christian school they are surrendering to the teacher full parental authority over the child. He or she truly is en loco parentis ("in the place of a parent")... The teacher, therefore, must have full parental authority during the hours the child is under his discipleship to guide him and respond to him on all levels.

— Jay E. Adams, quoted by Robert Lester in 'Getting Involved at School,' The Counsel of Chalcedon, 1991, Issue 6.

What about an excommunicated child, son, or daughter, who is no longer a dependent, not living at home? If they are excommunicated should they not be treated as any other excommunicated person in the church? They ought to be disinherited as well. They should not, it seems to me, be included in family reunions, celebrations such as birthdays and anniversaries, or other holidays. As we have read earlier, should they not be treated as banished, dead?

— Reverend Wayne Rogers, 'Excommunication in the Home,' The Counsel of Chalcedon, 2008, Issue 1.

A deacon visited our history class to give us a lesson in economics and found us disrespectful and noncompliant, then issued an edict that he, not our usual teacher, would decide our grades. We'd now each have to phone him individually in our disgrace, prostrate ourselves and bless his name, only then would he decide our fate. A son of this deacon, my age, occasionally showed up at school with jarred baby food for lunch though no infant lived at his house. Creamed spinach, green beans, turkey, cranberry and sweet potato mush, behave like a child and you will be treated like one, spoken to like one, you will even eat like one. This too carried on for some time without comment, as did so many vile things of this sort. Oh, his family's just like that. His father's just like that. The pastor's just like that. That's just how boys are. He's just immature. This is just what we do. It was just a joke. It was just an accident. It was just a misunderstanding. Every injustice, every act of cruelty was just how things were, are, just how things will be. About what was just so, we could never inquire, never challenge, never probe. In this way we covered a multitude of sins.

We likewise camouflaged the humiliation of our mortality in odd ways. Most deaths seemed to elicit little more than shrugs, a rapid and meaningless expression of faux sympathy, yes it's so sad, hastily pasted over by some reminder, put one way or another, that our Lord did not die and return to life victorious in order to build a church of spineless whiners. In my twenties, one of my Reconstructionist friend's father died, and upon his demise, her sister-in-law rebuked her tears. This is not a sad time, it is a time for rejoicing, she said. Stop it now. I remember thinking, this is it, this glossing over of grief is why, for all those years at my church-school, I can recall only a handful of deaths, all others swallowed up in victory. One was the in-utero sibling of that deacon's son of baby food infamy, who slipped away into eternity before he was born. His brain had formed outside his skull, a sombre detail reported frigidly, factually to our class one afternoon. The deacon's son ran out of the room then, crying, I thought then this public announcement must've been the first he'd heard of it. Our church-school gathered around a tiny grave one afternoon after school, and our pastor rebuked the sting of death that had pricked the contents of the smallest wooden coffin.

What presumption to kill a baby before we could see and judge his body and soul, what right had anyone to set free his tiny spirit from every human's justly deserved prison sentence on this earth. Who dares to single him out from among his cellmates, his brutal family, our harsh and heartless faction!

Some years later I stood outside the church sanctuary, below a lit window after the evening worship service, a small set of us talking over a hushed and hurried account recently related by someone who'd overheard adults talking. This same deacon's eldest daughter had dared to name the horrors of her home, things right in front of our faces yet never given the substance of words. I remembered then the young ladies' tea I had attended at her house, hosted by her mother, with musical entertainment of course provided eagerly by the pastor's wife. I had perched miserably with the other young ladies in our hats, spring dresses and white pantyhose, eating chocolate pudding dirt cake out of a terracotta flowerpot while the adult women chatted casually in the kitchen about wife spanking, yet more talk about everyday violence which I absorbed uneasily but without understanding, sucked up without ceremony.

Only now, some final line had been crossed, some internal alarm set off, some awareness achieved that this is not just what people do. No, this. is. not. just. In talking like this, in exposing what lay beneath the thin cover of artificial goodness, this deacon's daughter posed a problem, as does anyone who names and shames bullies. Now comes the manoeuvring. Now they will make this family a scapegoat, look this family was always trouble, a few bad apples, I always knew they were, they aren't like us, they are the source of any and all sin, cast them out, now we are whole, now we are pure again, now we will no longer speak of such things. The deacon's son started breaking into the church-school buildings, stealing computers, the office's box of petty cash. See how bad he always was. What a shame that family is so dishonourable. Nothing to do with us then or now. He showed up at my after-school job one day, he confessed it was he who was the thief and vandal. I'm not sure why he chose to tell me except perhaps that same manstinct to deposit one's sins on a woman. I didn't condemn him, I told no one, one day finally he got caught in the act.

My dreams were full of threatening arms reaching out, hands to grab me, lay hold of me, pinch and possess me, rooms of thick, choking shadows that overwhelmed me, even the light around me was night. I began to believe I was going mad. I developed an odd sort of tactile processing disorder, episodes of sensations of my body being squeezed through a narrow passageway. I felt this most acutely on my tongue – I find it difficult to describe even now, as if my tongue were simultaneously engorged and suspended and stretched across a tight wire. I began to follow every scene to impending disaster in my mind. Taking a step down the stairs I'd picture myself falling, opening a window I'd envision myself plunging to my death. I gazed directly into any and every future horror, staring steadily, my careful and continuous anticipation rebuked and neutralised any element of possible surprise. This carried on for many years, into the early years of adulthood.

My life had begun in a wilderness commune, away from human civilisation. We'd left that place behind, yet here we were. Wherever you go, there you are. There and back again. I wondered sometimes if perhaps some presence had followed us, some spirit of cruelty emanating from that place, that people, that plot of ground, returning us to it, because from it we were taken, we are dust and to dust we had returned. I recited a ritual prayer without fail each evening, listing every monstrous possibility, God, please not this, nor this, nor this, please, God, anything but this.

From brutality there seemed no escape. Where could I go from these evil spirits? Where could I flee from their presence? We were a people of violence, we ate our bread with anxiety and drank water with horror. It seemed none of us would remain. A member of our church was shot several times in the face and chest, somehow surviving with bullets permanently lodged in his skull. An elder's son told Jenny and me in history class that if we travelled to certain countries, we'd certainly be raped. Sofia burned her leg badly while riding on the back of one of her dad's recreational vehicles. One of our younger teachers was assaulted in an attempted abduction by a group of men as she was getting into her car one evening. A boy in the class below mine shattered his leg in a car wreck.

The 14-year-old daughter of a family closely connected to our church-school took one of her family's guns and with it her own life with a "self-inflicted gunshot to chest."[43] And one night somehow I heard, someone called, my friend Sofia had shot herself.

---

43 Certificate of Death/State of Georgia, State File Number 003788

GRAVE

*There are three things that will not be satisfied,
Four that will not say, "Enough":
the grave…"*

Proverbs 30:15-16

19

The significance of the Reconstructionist movement is not its numbers, but the power of its ideas and their surprisingly rapid acceptance. Many on the Christian Right are unaware that they hold Reconstructionist ideas.

– Fred Clarkson, 'Christian Reconstructionism,' *The Public Eye, 1994, Vol. VIII, No. 1*

When my son was a baby, he was separated from me during a medical emergency. He'd been struggling to breathe, and seeing the pallor of his skin, we'd taken him to a 24-hour urgent care centre. The treatment they gave him there didn't work quickly enough, an ambulance couldn't arrive in time, so he and I flew by helicopter, he in the back with an emergency response team and I in the front with the pilot. I could hear his frightened cries in my headphones, each gasp I experienced as another round of torture. Our separation during this crisis was less than an hour. But time means little in these circumstances – a soul can be damaged or even crushed in less than a minute, even the whole world can be destroyed in a moment, in the twinkling of an eye.

I will never forget the look of his little face when we were reunited, when I spotted him sat on a hospital bed in the corridor, his eyes damp and searching, desperate, empty in their loneliness and despair.

I called to him while I was still far off, I held him tight and didn't let him go the rest of the night and for days after, urgently remaking for him a sense of safety, reconstructing his home in my arms. For some time after, he screamed when separated from me, even when left with the kindest of childminders. When he began walking, he kept one set of fingers firmly latched onto my coat, my skirt, my shirt, I called him my little elephant. When at a playground, a park, with friends, he'd pop his head up every few minutes, orienting himself again to me, calculating my position and his, mapping the space between us, he the roving spacecraft and I the mothership. Sometimes he'd forget, and I could see again that quick and familiar flash of relief when, having suddenly sensed the threat of separation, he was able to catch sight of me quickly. In his first year of school, we were in the tiny school garden, he playing with friends, I chatting with other parents. In his usual way, he looked up and, unable to locate me straightaway, he panicked at the possibility of another abandonment, his little legs followed the pull of gravity to safety, across streets, all the way home. My husband answered the door, startled at the stricken face that appeared, so pinched and white again, his eyes so frightened and forlorn. "Where is mummy?"

When he was old enough to understand, I told him the helicopter story. At the age of 6, he was due to go on a week-long school trip, one of his school's more ridiculous traditions. Nevertheless, I'd laid out the possible benefits of going, taken him out to preview the site, helped him pack his bag once he'd decided to go, hidden reassuring notes in the folds of his clothing. But his stomach had its own objections as stomachs sometimes do, and the night before the trip he hardly slept, waking me with a trembling lip, his fallen face. "You don't have to go," I said, something I'd said many times in the weeks before yet now was when he needed most to hear it. Again I witnessed his features immediately shift to relief. We talked that week about the possible source of his fear, the slow rebuilding of trust and safety, maybe this is why you feel this way, there's nothing wrong with you, you will be okay in time, I'll show you the way, I'll

CHAPTER NINETEEN

be with you through each and every step to surety.

Almost everything I know about the place of my birth I've found online, though I strongly suspect my brother and I were separated from our parents not long after being born. Some of this story I sense through the language of my body. One of my earliest memories is taking children's Tums tablets multiple times a day, swallowing too many chalky spoonful's of liquid Mylanta – the cure often seemed worse than the condition. Other fragments of my story are recounted in items we took when we left the Pacific Northwest: mukluks—boots made of animal skin—which we eventually stored in the attic of our first house in green, metal military chests, along with a few photographs, archived in clear, plastic pockets in several old flip albums that sat on a shelf in our living room, sometimes on our coffee table, eventually in a closet. A few pictures stand out in my mind. One of my older brother in a thick snowsuit and solemn expression next to a sled. Another shows me sitting on a bed in our cabin, grinning widely, in another I am sobbing in a group of children. "When you were a baby, I simply told you to stop crying. And so you did," my mother has often said. She sometimes alludes to further details, the structure of the community I came from, its downplaying of family life. "After having children, I felt this deeply," she says, stopping just there on the edge of a fuller telling.

In 2019, as part of their series on cults, People Magazine profiled the Movement of God, a path to salvation founded by Sam Fife in the 1960s, more often referred to by followers as "The Move."[44] The documentary contains footage of former followers reflecting on their time in the Move, prompted by Fife's vision that the world was coming to an end, that Fife alone could lead the people in righteousness because of their foes, make their way straight before God, ensure God's special protection for his most special people. "You finally found the preacher that's got the spiritual courage to

---

[44] McColl, M. (2019, July 1). *People Magazine Investigates: Cults, Season 2, Episode 4, "The Movement of God."* People Magazine. https://www.investigationdiscovery.com/tv-shows/people-magazine-investigates-cults/

stand up and call it like it is," Fife preached. One former follower summed up his message like this,

> Our family and a very limited group of people [were] to be the final people that God was going to save when the world ended and that group of people was going to be rulers of the world with God, sitting at his right hand.[45]

Fife's vision followed on from a series of post-World War II Pentecostal revivals, born out of a longing for an outpouring of the Holy Spirit onto a spiritually parched people. This became known as the Latter Rain Movement, marked by a belief in human ability to harness divine healing, including deliverance from sickness, and the appearance of the Holy Spirit via supernatural signs such as personal prophecy. Though Fife's mission was not officially recognised by other adherents of Latter Rain, he nevertheless adopted much of their hermeneutic, including their vision of a victorious and overcoming church as a mark of end times.

Fife preached elite Dominionism, a path towards sinless perfection, paved with the usual pedestrian rules about hair length, clothing and social associations. Ambitious men, such as he, are predictably uncreative, forever dull in their destruction. Yet Fife was particularly delusional in constructing a system of retribution for rule violators, perhaps we have to give him credit for that. Any disobedience, any sign of so-called worldliness Fife attributed to demon possession, which he and his carefully selected posse would expel through prolonged ritual exorcisms, often involving humiliating violence with a paddle or a whip. Those who showed no sign of releasing their demons, these they beat mercilessly. One such exorcism was recorded on a cassette tape, then passed around triumphantly among the followers, a sign of the success of their maniacal methods. Fife's voice is indescribable, though I've tried again and again to capture in words its pitch, its intensity, its

---

45 ibid.

otherworldliness. I've heard only one other voice since that brings his to mind, that of R. J. Rushdoony. Certain things defy language; we can perceive the characteristics of their substance only by employing other senses.

Some children horrifically abused in these violent episodes report that their parents not only knew about the harm they suffered, but some also stood by impassively as Fife's disciples battered their own flesh and blood. Some even joined in eagerly and viciously. One girl, 10 or 11, was raped multiple times by adult members of the Move. When another child, a boy, reported it, "She was treated like it was her fault. She was guilty and was severely beaten with the strap because she was considered as a participant rather than as a victim."[46]

This cruelty started as early as the first days after birth, since, in Fife's sadistic mind, infants possess the same nature as demons. Witnesses report that children were separated almost from their very first minutes, away from their biological siblings and parents, a purposeful undermining of any blood bonds in favour of community loyalty. A "board of education" was the name given to a wooden board used for hitting children, and a child's backside was known as the "seat of learning." About his own daughter, Fife said, "better for her to have red welts on her back end than to have scars on her soul."[47] According to witness accounts,

> If a child cried too much, they would be spanked until they were too tired to cry any longer. Any adult was permitted to beat a child if a rule was being broken… An adult was anyone who could get away with it. I remember thirteen- and fourteen-year-old girls hitting babies, covering their mouths till they stopped crying, even if it meant waiting till the baby turned blue and simply stopped crying because they had stopped breathing![48]

---

46 ibid.
47 Steel, S. (2019, November 13). *The Move*. Let's Talk About Sects. https://www.ltaspod.com/19. Transcript available here: shorturl.at/pyMR9
48 Kiers, R. A. (2019). *Swindled by Faith: A Time for Reconciliation*. Tellwell Talent.

At some of the Movement's locations, victims were tied into bed at night, put into ice baths, force fed and subjected to all manner of psychological torture. In 1979, the *New York Times* covered the story of Shari Smith, who in 1973 was sent to a Movement farm in Mississippi, where she was thrown into cold showers for running away, held there for periods of up to four and a half hours.[49] One teenage girl, sent by her parents to another Move Deliverance Farm for demon treatment, was cruelly beaten and isolated for many months, until her captors tried another tactic, recruiting her as one of their special pets. After this, she was trained as an accomplice, groomed to participate in her captors' torture of other captives. One of her duties involving tying a mentally ill woman into bed each night. "I could make my life so much easier if I would just give in," she admits in the documentary. In this and other ways, leaders of the Move manipulated its members into complicity, exploited their impulse to survive, burdened them with their own malignance, sharing that special guilt that suppresses complaint and challenge. If all are participating, if all have gone along with it, then no one person can be held to account without also toppling every individual. If the leader falls, if anyone falls, you and I fall too. We all fall.

By the 1970s, Fife had begun preaching his "Wilderness Message," prompting thousands of his followers to commit all their worldly belongings, their bodies and their souls to a number of end-times communal farms in Canada, Colombia and Alaska, with thousands more members across the globe, in Uganda, Ireland, northern Mexico and Brazil.[50] Upon arrival, all belongings were sorted into piles, and anything not deemed useful for communal use was destroyed, sometimes burned as a mandatory show of commitment.

---

49 Thomas, J. (1979, January 21). Practices of Cults Receiving New Scrutiny. *The New York Times*. https://www.nytimes.com/1979/01/21/archives/practices-of-cults-receiving-new-scrutiny-cults-in-america-first-of.html

50 Todd, D. (2003, September 22). Peace River commune awaits imminent apocalypse: Christian community of 250 shuns TV and requires year-long courtship void of physical contact. *Vancouver Sun*. https://vancouversun.com/news/staff-blogs/awaiting-apocalypse-in-the-peace-river-valley

CHAPTER NINETEEN

This included any keepsakes of the past, even baby photographs. The day of the Lord would come like a thief, and the earth and its works would be burnt up. The former things would not be remembered, nor would they come to mind.

In 1973, my parents, then unmarried, fled the coming apocalypse to Alaska with a group of fellow zealots whom they'd met at Campus Crusade and began the excruciating work of clearing the land and building shelter before winter came. That first summer they slept in tents, then moved to a nearby farm community, also part of the Move, for the long, cold winter. In the spring, they moved back, just as they'd promised, to what they called "The Land." There, they carried on in their efforts towards complete self-sufficiency, planting and harvesting their own food, building cabins from wood felled by hand, heated by wood stoves, with no electricity or running water. After a year of courtship involving no physical contact—or "walking out" as it was known[51]—my parents were married. And into this amateurish rendition of the garden of Eden, in the mid-1970s, my brother and I were born.

---

51 ibid.

20

Was [Greg Bahnsen] pushy? He could be. Was he harsh? Sometimes. Was he argumentative? That was his job. But he was not alone. If you are familiar with the biographies of our great heroes of the faith, you will know that their detractors had the very same things to say – Calvin was a "tyrant" in Geneva, Machen was a "troublemaker" at Princeton, Van Til was "unloving" toward his opponents. Spiritual gunfighters too often can't find a home in the towns they risk their lives to protect.

– Robert Wagner, 'Greg L. Bahnsen the "Churchman,"' The Counsel of Chalcedon, 1996, Issue 1.

At university, a professor heard through the grapevine that one of his students had come from a Christian Reconstructionist church. He called me in to his office one day, asked me to tell him what I had been taught, what was the philosophical and theological substance of this movement, its ideas, what motivated my pastor. "I'm so curious. I really want to understand," he said. I can't remember how I answered really, some bland recitation of basic tenets, like some factual recording in a museum audio exhibit, the non-partisan message one performs for an unpredictable, untrustworthy audience. He seemed satisfied, my curated data presentation must have been what he wanted to hear. Like so many others, he'd asked the wrong questions, sought only pointless answers that merely relate the history

CHAPTER TWENTY

as Men would tell it, as Men remember it, from Men's perspective.

"Leave no trace," we're told when hiking, camping, working outdoors. The world is in some ways better without us human pollutants, so the thinking goes. So we preserve, pick up after ourselves, show respect for the locals, leave what we find, minimise our footprint, in so doing we aim to show love and respect for our planet. In high school, a certain wilderness-loving set in my church-school put stickers broadcasting this ethic on their notebooks, guitar cases, cars. Luke was particularly sanctimonious about scrambling down a hill or into some briers to retrieve someone else's litter. His urgent display of care for the earth stamped into us his commitment to minimum impact. After all, we'd all learned it by now, there is no point of following any rule unless someone catches you doing it, praises you in the act.

There's more to this though. Leaving no trace is also troubling, since acts of erasing, of collective forgetting and moving on are also means to hide from the truth and revel in conspiracy, also to suppress acts of injustice. "Leave no trace" is, after all, also the slogan of the criminal, the human trafficker, the slave owner, the rapist, wiping his fingerprints, cleaning the crime scene, removing any identifiable fibres or cells that might link him to a particular place or person, as if he was never there. As if. An abuser may coax his victim to tell no one, to cover up her bruises, to participate in the erasure of what he did to her, now it is what has. been. done. to her. Action without agency. Crime without a perpetrator. Eventually, even he forgets, he moves on, exercises the privilege of erasing, of disremembering, that brutal form of invisible secondary violence. Someone stole from you, a person hurt you in some way, you have been stolen from, you have been hurt, it is now as if no human being but you were ever on the scene. The wounds exist without the one who wounds. They are no longer even wounds. Your wounds are just you.

This is how it happens. We who leave because someone has harmed us are often called disloyal, disruptive, destructive, divisive, unloving, uncaring, weak. We are called traitors to the cause, people playing the victim. But let's say we aren't prepared to participate in the subtle erasure of the facts, the brushing over of the who, what, when, why and how often of injustice, of our own hurt. We aren't over it. The signs of violence beaten into human flesh haven't healed because no one has bandaged them, no one has ensured the perpetrator won't re-open them. Now, in the sight of those we leave behind, we are ragged, bloody gashes, unpleasant, unpalatable.

"I see you are in a dark place," one church leader said to me, months after I left a particular church, when I still hadn't returned as some had expected. The wife of a church leader had confided in me the facts of her abusive marriage, and I'd subsequently begun to make myself a nuisance, to no avail. "Oh, she'll be back," some said after I left. This too is part of the lie. These are people who have collectively erased their tracks, now they have no memory any one of them ever did anything wrong, now their eyes have grown accustomed to seeing nothing, to living in the night. From the shadows, they sense leavers moving away to locate safety, to them it appears that we walk haphazardly, towards nowhere. Seeing, they do not see, hearing they do not hear.

In December, 1995, Reconstructionist Greg Bahnsen died at the age of 47, five years after his divorce was finalized, his wife having left him for the church youth minister. The following month, our church-school magazine published a special issue in his honour, five articles chronicling his importance in our movement, considering his significance from every angle. Greg Bahnsen as Teacher. As Discipler. His Growth in Trial. As Good and Faithful Servant. In Robert Wagner's piece on Bahnsen as Churchman, he includes this line about Bahnsen's relationship with his wife Cathie Wade: his "abandonment by his wife and a resulting divorce – and then the agonizing failure (over years) to carry out effective church discipline in the case. Life as a single parent."[52] Bahnsen's son David also, in a 2015 article in memory of his dad, similarly praises him: Greg Bahnsen, the Pastor; Greg Bahnsen, the Person; Greg Bahnsen,

---

52 Wagner, R. (1996). 'Greg L. Bahnsen the "Churchman,"' *The Counsel of Chalcedon*, Issue 1.

CHAPTER TWENTY

the Kuyperian; Greg Bahnsen the "forbearing husband, and while obviously not a perfect one, he had a threshold for pain in a relationship that exceeds beyond what mere mortals should have to endure."[53]

Reading this one-sided account of the marriage breakdown of one of our movement leaders, Bahnsen as acted upon, Bahnsen as abandoned, as "single parent," I recall one evening in the late 1980s or early 1990s, at one round of our community's Atlanta Christian Training Seminars. I found these lengthy events immensely dull, usually my friends and I would pass notes along the row of chairs, doodle on our notepads, stare at our watches. I once dropped one such note, it fell just behind my chair, and our youth leader's wife handed it back to me, along with a whispered rebuke. "Remember that it is a privilege to be here," she said. Yes, there was that P-word again, one of many in our church-school's gaslighting repertoire. We were all so lucky to be there, and don't you forget it. Hashtag blessed. But at some point during Bahnsen's seminar talk, on what topic I can't now recall, my head suddenly shot up, my ears took in every word. From the pulpit, he—one of our dear leaders—gave himself over to tears speaking suddenly off the cuff—at least it seemed so—about his divorce, confessing to us his failure to meet his wife's relational needs, he'd not prioritised his marriage, he'd been so busy with his ministry, no wonder she'd looked for love elsewhere. No wonder, he said, no wonder she left me, no one must blame her.

In the confines of our community, this was the first time I'd ever heard any man talk about spousal neglect, the first time I'd ever heard a woman's internal life acknowledged, her perspective hinted at. Still, I was suspicious of tears from any pulpit, also this woman's life was still being passed through the filtering lips of a man, again here were men talking mostly to other men about a woman. And now, thinking back, how can I possibly square

---

[53] Bahnsen, D. (2015, December 11). *In Memory of, Dr. Greg L. Bahnsen. Twenty Years Ago Today*. The Bahnsen Viewpoint. http://web.archive.org/web/20160318012845/https://davidbahnsen.com/index.php/2015/12/11/in-memory-of-dr-greg-l-bahnsen-twenty-years-ago-today/

Bahnsen's public confession with the accounts of his attempts at "church discipline" of his own wife and the youth minister, and not of himself? Who disciplines the man in charge whose own self-importance is the catalyst for the destruction of his relationships? But even so, at the time, I thought, what is this? This way of talking was something slightly different. Afterwards, I walked up to the front where Bahnsen stood. I didn't have anything to say, I cried a bit and I didn't give the reason for my grief as I myself didn't know it, I couldn't explain why I had experienced his words so viscerally. I remember he said only, "There, there, no need to cry," a man's dismissive faux comfort in the face of uncomfortable, so-called "female emotion." Dis-assurance posing as reassurance. Discouragement pretending to be encouragement. He had cried, why shouldn't I? Why were my tears wrong but not his? I said nothing more. That was all. No one around me spoke about any of this again, we talked about Bahnsen after that in terms of his theological convictions, his apologetics brilliance. The rest we deleted, we forgot, after he went the way of all the earth we then retraced, rewrote what had happened through the lens of Bahnsen's heroism, his endurance, his faithfulness, his long-suffering, his growth in trial. He was the hero we needed, the man we championed, our example soldier. As for his wife, one Bahnsen fan would later denigrate her as "emotionally and spiritually unstable," Bahnsen's marriage to her a lapse in discernment.[54] "His wife was unfaithful and eventually left him," as yet another man wrote.[55]

Yet some traces of another side of this sad story remain. In the middle of a timeline produced for the minutes of the 1993 General Assembly of Bahnsen's church denomination, are these extraordinary

---

54 *Encyclopedia: Greg Bahnsen*. (n.d.). StateMaster. Retrieved January 20, 2023, from http://web.archive.org/web/20171007105436/http://www.statemaster.com/encyclopedia/Greg-Bahnsen

55 Robinson, M. (2018, July 30). *Monday Morning Quarterbacking--"Greg Bahnsen: The Man Atheists Feared Most"* Pastor Matt's Blog. http://www.pastormattsblog.com/blog/2018/7/30/monday-morning-quarterbacking-greg-bahnsen-the-man-atheists-feared-most-by-mike-robinson

lines, from a letter written by David Arnold, the man who helped Bahnsen's wife Cathie Wade leave him:

> I do confess to having helped Cathie to leave California. I have explained to you the explanation, not excusing the choices and deeds, that I had reason to take seriously both her contemplation of suicide and her claim that she was going to depart.[56]

"Contemplation of suicide." Such words surely raise in any sensitive soul so many vital questions about Cathie's mental and physical health, the reality of her marriage and home life. Yet the recorded minutes contain no indication that anyone other than David Arnold took seriously Cathie's hopeless state. In the pages that follow the excerpt of his letter, there is no expression of concern for Cathie's well-being, nor even a comment acknowledging it, in and amongst so many details of urgent and at times extreme attempts to locate this woman who dared to leave and the man who assisted her, to rebuke them, driven by the singular desire to "help" her to return to the place from which she ran. Reading these documents we learn that in April, 1990, one year after Cathie left the Bahnsen home, "After trial in absentia (she had continued to refuse to communicate with the session), Mrs. Bahnsen was excommunicated by the session."[57] The General Assembly of the Orthodox Presbyterian Church later ruled that any disciplinary action against David Arnold—whom Cathie went on to marry—could not continue on procedural grounds, his having requested to be removed from church membership prior to being put on trial. So the two were erased from the records and from our recollections. Years later, Cathie's son would summarise his mother's desperate flight like this: "Twenty years nearly to the day later [after her marriage], she left him and

---

56 Minutes of the Sixtieth General Assembly, Meeting at Beaver Falls, PA, June 9-16, 1993, and Yearbook of the Orthodox Presbyterian Church (https://opcgaminutes.org/wp-content/uploads/2018/04/1993-GA-60-red.pdf), p. 313.
57 ibid., p. 310

his kids, yours truly included, and that was the end of that,"[58] so the enemy comes to its end in perpetual ruins, the very memory of them has perished.

There were other things like that, plenty of them, so many I can't possibly tell them all. The year following Bahnsen's death, in April, 1996, friends of Rousas Rushdoony—among them my pastor and Howard Phillips, founder of the Constitution Party—presented their mentor with a book of essays in honour of his eightieth birthday. Among the essays was a brief biography by Rushdoony's son, Mark, curious to me more because of what he left out, than what he included: any mention of his mother, Arda Rushdoony.

---

58 Bahnsen, D. (2015, December 11). *In Memory of, Dr. Greg L. Bahnsen. Twenty Years Ago Today*. The Bahnsen Viewpoint. http://web.archive.org/web/20160318012845/https://davidbahnsen.com/index.php/2015/12/11/in-memory-of-dr-greg-l-bahnsen-twenty-years-ago-today/

21

I'm going into this with my eyes open. Romanticism isn't part of my makeup. I asked [to court] her years ago, not because I was in love with her, but because I respected her. I still respect her, and I'm growing to love her... This is what I need, if I need anyone... I think we can get more accomplished together than individually.

– Gary North, about his wife Sharon (nee Rushdoony), 1979.[59]

A doctoral dissertation completed in 2010 by Michael McVicar largely confines the legacy of Arda Rushdoony to a footnote, referring in a single paragraph to the finalising of her divorce from Rousas in 1959, she citing his "extreme cruelty" and her ensuing "grievous mental suffering."[60] Likewise in this footnote is a reference to Rushdoony's silence on the matter, though McVicar notes Arda's frequent illness, according to some due to an undiagnosed thyroid problem, and her exhaustion early in her marriage during an intense period of missionary work in the Duck Valley Reservation in Owyhee, Nevada. A period that Rousas referred to as his "harsh and ruthless

---

59 McVicar, M. J. (2015). Christian Reconstruction: RJ Rushdoony and American religious conservatism. UNC Press Books, p. 153.
60 McVicar, M. J. (2010). Reconstructing America: Religion, American Conservatism, and the Political Theology of Rousas John Rushdoony (Doctoral dissertation, The Ohio State University), p. 81.

ministry."⁶¹ And then there is Rousas's 1984 journal entry which refers to Arda's "extensive fornication after the divorce," a collection of words which I've lost no small amount of sleep over, reflecting on all the meaning they carry, all this focus on the physical, on women's bodies and what we do with them, the constant objects of the male gaze.

That same year, 2010, McVicar published a summary of Rushdoony's life and work for the Chalcedon Foundation, leaving out any reference to Arda.⁶² Another of his earlier articles on Rousas's and Arda's time on the reservation, while referring to "his wife," likewise omits her name.⁶³ One reviewer of the published book version of McVicar's dissertation commented that McVicar treats Rushdoony's marriages "sparingly since this was the only part of Rushdoony's papers to which he was not granted access."⁶⁴ McVicar himself is inconsistent about the extent to which he was able to view Rushdoony's meticulous records on this particular aspect of his life, referring in one place to his "totally unfettered access" to Rushdoony's notes (p. IX), his "unique access" (p. 9), downgrading this to "largely unfettered access" by page 11.

Still, some were asking the hard questions. In 2000, scholar of the classics and former theonomist Dr. Thomas P. Roche, published a detailed account of the "theological aberrations and excesses" of the movement, including a reference to Arda Rushdoony.⁶⁵ Roche writes,

> … it is worth noting who the real first MIA is, namely the first Mrs RJ Rushdoony, who was divorced from the patriarch back in 1956. So complete has been her *damnatio memoriae* that I

---

61 Ibid., p. 39.
62 McVicar, M. (2010, November 9). The Lord Will Perfect That Which Concerneth Me: The Work of Rousas John Rushdoony. *Chalcedon Magazine*. https://chalcedon.edu/magazine/the-lord-will-perfect-that-which-concerneth-me-the-work-of-rousas-john-rushdoony
63 McVicar, M. (2008, November 1). *"First Owyhee and Then the World": The Early Ministry of R. J. Rushdoony*. Chalcedon Magzine. https://chalcedon.edu/magazine/first-owyhee-and-then-the-world-the-early-ministry-of-r-j-rushdoony
64 Gaither, M. (2018, March 19). *Christian Reconstruction: A New Biography of Rousas Rushdoony | Homeschooling Research Notes*. Homeschooling Research Notes. https://gaither.wordpress.com/2018/03/19/christian-reconstruction-a-new-biography-of-rousas-rushdoony/
65 Roche, T. P. (2000). *Meet the Theonomists*. http://theonomists.blogspot.com

have no idea what her first name is, whether she is still living, etc., *all this despite the fact that she is the birth mother of all five of Rushdooney's [sic] children*, whose apparent loyalty to their great father has meant total exile for their mother [emphasis in original].

And in 2013, a blogger called Jeri published a short piece about Arda the invisible, including biographical details about her promising life before marriage, wondering what loneliness she might have experienced in her marriage. Jeri writes, "as the 'Father of Christian Reconstructionism' and 'Father of the Homeschooling Movement,' [Rushdoony] greatly influenced my childhood. I wonder what *she* would say if she could speak to us about his character and beliefs." Below Jeri's post, one of Arda's daughters replied in the comments section, objecting to the entire line of questioning, arguing that "She is rarely mentioned because of that pain and in order not to dishonour her memory."[66]

Ah yes, how often do we see the silencing of a woman's story justified under the guise of protecting her from gossip. "Rushdoony had been divorced," as one reviewer of McVicar's book put it, "but commendably no salacious details of this episode are provided."[67] I've seen women cry when uttering words like these. "I just hate to see Christians speaking badly of each other," one elder's wife once said to me through conscripted pools of tears, how horribly it hurts them so, to be required to listen to certain truths spoken so plainly. Others similarly objected below Jeri's post, piling up their praise as protest, writing what a great Christian man Rousas was, so kind and quiet, such a nice man. So many nice men would you look at all the nice, nice men, aren't we so capital P Privileged to have such benevolent capital P Patriarchs reigning over us.

Perhaps because of rising speculation about Rushdoony's

---

66 Jeri. (2013, August 3). *Voiceless Women: Arda J. Rushdoony*. Heresy in the Heartland. https://heresyintheheartland.blogspot.com/2013/08/voiceless-women-arda-j-rushdoony.html

67 Clary, I. (2015, September 14). *Christian Reconstruction*. Reformation 21. https://www.reformation21.org/articles/christian-reconstruction.php

relationships with women, in 2016 his son Mark published a personal account of Arda's life. In his account of his parents' marriage, he says about his mother, that,

> She was very intelligent, well-educated, had some experience in domestic missions and hoped to be a missionary. She seemed to be a good helpmeet for my father's work… About two weeks after their marriage, my father awoke in the middle of the night to find Mom struggling to open their third-story window, threatening suicide. Only then did she reveal her family history of mental illness and her fears for her own sanity.

Let your eyes pass over this a few times, look at what comes first, the shining profile of a potential star of Biblical womanhood. And then here comes the hinge, preparing the pivot from one extreme to the next. "She seemed to be a good helpmeet for my father's work." "She seemed." For those of us who suffer still in the ongoing legacy of the Christian kingdom wars, this word "seemed" carries so much of the weight of women's subordination, all the expectations men pile on us, all the requirements, the assumption embedded in marriage that we as women must sacrifice ourselves at their feet, for their work, for their name, for their memory. Arda seemed altogether worthy, but she wasn't as she seemed. Arda seemed suited to support her husband's brilliance, but she wasn't so suited. Arda seemed willing to set herself aside, but then she didn't. A Christian woman in the 1950s was already expected to carry the weight of her husband's every wish. Imagine, then, a woman with mental illness in that period of history, surely doomed, met with fear and rejection by the general public, facing treatment in wards of state hospitals that were later referred to by those in the know as "snake pits."[68] This was a period when electro-convulsive therapy was commonly in use – along with Arda Rushdoony, the writer Sylvia Plath was among those subjected to this treatment in its crudest form. Some have testified

---

68 Geller, J. L. (2000). The last half-century of psychiatric services as reflected in psychiatric services. *Psychiatric Services*, 51(1), 41–67.

CHAPTER TWENTY-ONE

that men-doctors were more likely to use this treatment on women, as their minds were not valued as highly as men's.[69] Yet few options exist for women in such circles except either: 1. to accept this degradation or else 2. to mimic the Man-mind. This is how some of us have escaped, setting such a head upon our own shoulders, impressing and outdoing all men's calculations, their aggression and their arguments, their cruel and coldly logical dissections of the earth and everything in it. In the end, in this way, so many of us lose ourselves in the service of our liberation.

But who can blame us? Long is the list of women minimised and erased, airbrushed out, some replaced in time by women more willing to submit to the longsuffering support their husbands demanded. Arda's story contains many similarities to that of Dorothy (Dolly) Carey, wife to persistent, well-known missionary William Carey. Dorothy too followed her husband on to a difficult mission field in 1793, in her case having been coerced by spiritual threats against her soul.[70] And she too was later at times confined to an asylum after suffering many severe and often violent breakdowns in her mental health. Also like Arda, Dorothy was further brutalised by hateful historical accounts of her life. In his book *The Apostles of India*, the Scottish minister of Greyfriars Kirk and Moderator of the General Assembly of the Church of Scotland, James Ogilvie, wrote of Dorothy in 1915, that,

> While he was not yet twenty years of age his master had died, and Carey had taken over the business, and had married his late master's sister-in-law, a dull commonplace young woman, named Dolly Plackett. It was a rash step which laid a burden on Carey's life for many years, but of which he never complained: for poor Dolly Plackett, while quite a suitable wife for one

---

[69] Sadowsky, J. (2016). Electroconvulsive Therapy in America: The Anatomy of a Medical Controversy. Routledge.

[70] Carey's friend John Thomas told Dorothy that if she didn't go with her husband, she would "repent of it as long as she lived." See Letter from John Thomas to Andrew Fuller, quoted in Beck, J. R. (2000). *Dorothy Carey: The Tragic and Untold story of Mrs. William Carey*. Wipf and Stock Publishers, p. 82.

who was a country cobbler and nothing more, was deplorably unsuitable as a wife for one who was to be very much more. Her life had been happier had she not married an enthusiast.[71]

This cruel version of Dorothy's legacy has persisted. In a 2012 post called "Why Ann Judson didn't go crazy like Dorothy Carey," modern day missionary and Presbyterian Church in America pastor Karl Dahlfred blamed Dorothy's mental health breakdowns on her lack of faith in God's goodness.[72] How sad such men as William Carey and R. J. Rushdoony are, to be yoked to women so beneath their divine devotion, their genius, their enthusiasm, their miraculous manhood.

Arda's son Mark wrote that his mom was always at her best when she had a task, and she embraced roles in church and school programs, sport and scout meetings.[73] But as McVicar notes in his book, Arda's "social activities led Rousas to regularly lament the amount of child care and domestic work he had to do because he believed it impeded his studying and writing."[74] By way of contrast, about Rousas's second wife Dorothy, whom his children would go on to call "Mother," Rousas's son Mark wrote in 2017, that

> When he was not traveling, my father was writing constantly. My mother once chided him for doing menial, time-consuming chores, like watering trees with a garden hose, a waste of his valuable time, she said."[75]

---

71 Ogilvie, J. N. (1915). *The Apostles of India*. Hodder and Stoughton. (p. 296), accessed on 3 Feb, 2022 at https://missiology.org.uk/pdf/e-books/ogilvie_j-n/apostles-of-india_ogilvie.pdf
72 Dahlfred, K. (2012). Why Ann Judson Didn't Go Crazy Like Dorothy Carey. Available at: https://www.dahlfred.com/en/blogs/gleanings-from-the-field/557-why-ann-judson-didnt-go-crazy-like-dorothy-carey (accessed 20 January 2023).
73 https://chalcedon.edu/magazine/rousas-john-rushdoony-a-brief-history-part-iii-my-days-on-the-reservation
74 McVicar, M. J. (2015). *Christian Reconstruction: RJ Rushdoony and American Religious Conservatism*. UNC Press Books. (p. 26)
75 Rushdoony, M. (2017). 'Rousas John Rushdoony: A Brief History, Part VII "He's on the Lord's Side,"' Chalcedon Magazine, 21 February 2017 (https://chalcedon.edu/magazine/rousas-john-rushdoony-a-brief-history-part-vii-hes-on-the-lords-side)

CHAPTER TWENTY-ONE

We mustn't miss this assertion that ruthlessly diminishes women in communities like these, that a waste of a man's time is the best use of a woman's. After Dorothy's death, a friend would commend her for her emphatic reminder to wives everywhere that "when a husband returns home from the battles of life each day, a wife should have him know that as he steps over the threshold, 'in his house he is lord.'"[76]

Reading this weaponised woman's words again now, so many other stories come to mind. There was the time I brought some university friends home with me for the weekend, when my pastor had elected to preach again on Abraham's wife Sarah calling her husband 'Lord,' and so should we all. Afterwards, he walked past and shook all my friends' hands, his conscience completely unaffected by the violence of the words he had just stuck like knives in our backs, straight into our hearts. I was ashamed, I was complicit in his hate-filled words lobbed towards my friends, and after that I never took any friend to church with me again. Then there was the time shortly after Joel the elder's son got engaged, when he came round to my parents' house, stood in my parents' kitchen, said his fiancé—daughter of another well-known Reconstructionist—had agreed to quit her paid job. It's best she learns dependence and soon, since we don't want her to get used to working, he said. "We don't want her to" – yes, these were his exact words, his wife-to-be already swallowed up into the 'we' of the masculine marriage unit, already acting upon the female object 'her,' her own self already set at odds with the marriage. If you give women an inch they will claim a mile, they will ascend even unto the hill of the Lord. I was then already married, studying and working as a research assistant in graduate school, living at my parents' house on weekdays as it was closer to campus. I experienced Joel's words as a rebuke, though it was likely more of the same utter insensitivity and entitled obliviousness to the context of our conversation. Then there were all the times when various people at various churches

---

[76] Schwartz, A.G. (1999). A Woman of Faith, Dorothy Rushdoony. *Chalcedon Magazine*, 1 May. Available at: https://chalcedon.edu/magazine/a-woman-of-faith-dorothy-rushdoony (accessed 20 January 2023).

have asked me casually when I'd be giving my notice at work, now I was married, and again now I have children, oh but aren't you going part-time, oh are you still full-time, even now, have you thought of quitting, when are you going to give up, why don't you just quit now and get it over with, do you really need to carry on like that.

In his account of what he calls the "Painful Years," Mark Rushdoony concludes, with the affirmation of all but one of his siblings, that Arda's mental illness was—in his view—the source of her many problems. But more terrible was the fact—according to him—that she took "refuge in lies" about Rousas's cruelty. Any sensible critic must ask themselves to what extent Mark's opinion of his mother is heavily influenced by the views of his father, who, years after his divorce from Arda, would publicly flesh out his perspective on mental illness, writing that "insanity is an evasion of responsibility. Even more, it is a flight from reality."[77] Ironically, Rousas's motivations for writing about this were likely completely unrelated to Arda, rooted instead entirely in self-interest, his own son-in-law Gary North having suggested he was insane.[78] Train up a cold-hearted, self-centred Dominionist in the way he should go; even when he is old he will not depart from it.

In all this, though Mark cites multiple documents, he relies most heavily on his father's version of events, his father's point of view, his father's interests. He seems never to quote his mother directly nor mention the details of her complaints against her husband, telling omissions indeed. Nor does Arda's son, her own flesh and blood, fully factor into his thinking the state of psychiatric care in that period, the assumptions about women and their minds, the stigma associated with mental illness. And so, aside from Rousas's notes, summarised in his son's short series of articles documenting

---

77 Rushdoony, R. J. (2017). The Definition of Insanity. In: Rushdoony MR (ed.) *An Informed Faith: The Position Papers of R. J. Rushdoony*. Vallecito, California: Chalcedon – Ross House Books, pp. 609–612. Available at: https://www.scribd.com/document/353781396/An-Informed-Faith# (accessed 20 January 2023).

78 See McVicar, M. J. (2015). *Christian Reconstruction: RJ Rushdoony and American religious conservatism*. UNC Press Books. (p. 191)

CHAPTER TWENTY-ONE

"the subject of Mom's mental illness and the divorce,"[79] aside from McVicar's scant comments on all this, very little remains in the public record about Arda, wife to a man who considered family the bedrock of God's kingdom. And in his tribute to his father, written after his death, Mark Rushdoony once again erases his mother.

---

79 Rushdoony, M.R. (2016). Rousas John Rushdoony: A Brief History, Part IV, The "Painful Years". *Chalcedon Magazine*, 12 August. Available at: https://chalcedon.edu/magazine/rousas-john-rushdoony-a-brief-history-part-iv-the-painful-years (accessed 20 January 2023).

22

Paul declares in Corinthians that even as man was created in the image of God, so woman was created in the image of man—so that the image of God in woman is a reflected image, a second-hand image, as it were... In all of these things man today is rebelling against God. Woman, on the other hand, because she is created in the image of man—the reflected image of God—does not rebel directly against God. She can go to church and be as pious and sanctimonious as you please because she shows rebellion by her rebellion against her husband, who represents the authority of God as she is to know it. The rebellion of men is directly against God; the rebellion of women, indirectly against God and directly against the authority, the godly authority, of the husband.

– R. J. Rushdoony, The Doctrine of Marriage, 1965

Yesterday noon, I ate (as often) a cold meal, alone, because, when I sat down to eat, the phone rang. A pastor I have never met, with a weeping woman before him, called for counsel; he had called a year before in another case. For the same reason, I ate alone at night. In between, I spent a couple hours again on the phone in like matters. This goes on daily ... I will continue, only because the battle is the LORD'S...
In five and a half years, I have not been home all of any month.

– R. J. Rushdoony to James B. Jordan, March 12, 1981, RJR Library.

CHAPTER TWENTY-TWO

Yet, when it comes to Arda Rushdoony, the woman who was not what she seemed, newspaper records fill in some of the blanks. *The Eastern Colorado Times* reports that Arda's father, L. Albert Gent, a "pioneer ranchman," having been "despondent for some time," shot himself with a rifle in September, 1920. Arda was only 5 years old.[80] Considering the trauma of her early years, then, considering her later erasure, Arda's later achievements should be set before the public eye. California's *San Anselmo Record* records her completion of a Bachelor of Arts at Whitworth College in 1941.[81] In 1956, the *Santa Cruz Sentinel* records Arda's name as fourth grade room mother for Grant School.[82] In 1961, a few short years after her divorce from Rousas, her name appears again in the *Santa Cruz Sentinel*, in a report on the progress of three San Jose State college student teachers, among them Arda Rushdoony, now placed at Gault School.[83] Arda's mother Ida May died in 1964, her obituary noting her residence with her daughter in Mount Hermon and her involvement with the Royal Neighbors of America and the Presbyterian church.[84] In 1968 Arda appears twice again, both in connection to her work in schools, two years at Mountain School, where she taught singing and oversaw her fifth and sixth grade class's production of a "Charlie Brown Christmas."[85] They'd made all their own backdrops, the reporter noted, and weren't they so lovely. And later that year, there are records of her employment at a Christian school, again teaching fifth grade.[86] Whatever the state of her mental health, after her divorce Arda carried on studying, carried on working among children, many of them with developmental difficulties, as and when she was able to. Her pursuits, no matter how seemingly inconsequential, are a witness to her drive to carve out a life for herself, on her own terms – details of which were left out of her obituary upon her death in June, 1977. In his 2016

---

80 *Eastern Colorado Times*, 23 September 1920, p. 6.
81 *San Anselmo Herald*, Thu, May 4, 1944, p. 4.
82 *Santa Cruz Sentinel*, Volume 100, Number 248, 19 October 1956.
83 *Santa Cruz Sentinel*, Volume 105, Number 105, 3 May 1961.
84 *Santa Cruz Sentinel*, Thu, Apr 2, 1964.
85 *Santa Cruz Sentinel*, Volume 112, Number 70, 24 March 1968.
86 *Santa Cruz Sentinel*, Volume 112, Number 265, 10 November 1968.

summary of his mother's life, Mark Rushdoony included this heavily hedged praise of his mom's efforts, writing,

> ...she would periodically teach school, and was particularly adept at helping remedial students, though uncorrected school papers would accumulate in piles. Parents often liked her, though her employers rarely kept her for very long… she worked intermittently as either a teacher or a conference center cook.

Every achievement situated within a criticism. Every bit of praise with a caveat. Arda seemed suitable, she seemed ideal, she seemed the perfect woman, but for those intent on modelling their own chilling theocratic vision before the world, Arda wasn't enough.

Records of Rushdoony's second wife Dorothy are likewise carefully curated by those who wish to limit any visible trace of the violence and corruption of the community that shaped and damaged so many millions of lives, including my own. Dorothy was married before Rousas to a man called Thomas Kirkwood, with whom she ran several businesses, including one called Live Oak Yardage.[87] Thomas was a deacon and an elder at two churches Rushdoony pastored, his suitability for these roles significantly undermined beginning in 1960 at least, when Rousas recorded in his notes that Thomas had moved out of his home with Dorothy and was considering divorce.[88] Mark Rushdoony documents some of this but neglects to mention other relevant details, including what newspaper records indicate, that Thomas went on to marry a woman called Bertha May, who divorced him in 1966, citing—just as Arda had about Rousas—"extreme cruelty."[89] Dorothy and Thomas had one son, Tom, who periodically appeared in newspaper records, first as a victim of

---

[87] *Santa Cruz Sentinel*, Volume 100, Number 84, 8 April 1955.
[88] Rushdoony, M.R. (2016). Rousas John Rushdoony: A Brief History, Part V 'An Opportunity... Thanks Be to God!'. *Chalcedon Magazine*, 16 September. Available at: https://chalcedon.edu/magazine/rousas-john-rushdoony-a-brief-history-part-v-an-opportunity-thanks-be-to-god-by-mark-r-rushdoony (accessed 20 January 2023).
[89] *Santa Cruz Sentinel*, Volume 110, Number 291, 11 December 1966.

CHAPTER TWENTY-TWO

violent assault in 1964[90] and then in connection with cheque forgery, for which he was arrested several times and eventually incarcerated.[91]

Just as I never once heard the name Arda growing up, neither did I hear the names Ann Lawrence Sith nor Anna Tryggvadottir, the first two wives of our pastor's favourite congressman, his brother in arms. In all the praises heaped upon dear Larry McDonald, "the most principled [member of Congress],"[92] we never once heard even a whisper about how he divorced his first wife Ann after meeting the woman he'd leave her for, the Icelandic daughter of a wealthy industrialist. This second wife, Anna, would later accuse dear Larry of adultery and with "beating her with 'a garden tool' when she was pregnant."[93] At the time of their divorce, Anna told the judge that McDonald had denied her sexual intimacy for five years on the grounds that Christians are all soldiers in a Third World War and "people do not make love in wartime."[94] Lies! All were lies, according to McDonald, who of course objected, of course insisted, exclaimed, proclaimed, this was nothing but a "diabolical attempt… to assassinate his character." One Man against the devil. McDonald was later briefly jailed after his second divorce from Anna, for failing to pay child support for his three children, a sentence which according to him was only more evidence that the judge and his rivals were working together to disarm and discredit him, the communists are out to get me, it's me versus them, do you see how the world hates me, do you see now what I'm talking about, oh how alone I am in my righteousness.

---

90 *Santa Cruz Sentinel*, Volume 108, Number 262, 3 November 1964.
91 *Santa Cruz Sentinel*, Volume 111, Number 159, 7 July 1967; *Santa Cruz Sentinel*, Volume 111, Number 235, 5 October 1967; *Santa Cruz Sentinel*, Volume 116, Number 212, 12 September 1971.
92 According to US House of Representatives leader Ron Paul, quoted in Cannon CM (1983) A Congressman Recalled as a Communist-Hater. *The Philadelphia Inquirer*, 2 September.
93 Harris, A. (1983). The Widow and Her Fight for the Right. *The Washington Post*, 13 October. Available at: https://www.washingtonpost.com/archive/lifestyle/1983/10/13/the-widow-and-her-fight-for-the-right/44ca7e2d-5c50-4bea-a460-53fa1f9d3eff/ (accessed 20 January 2023).
94 Dorfman, Z. (2018). The Congressman Who Created His Own Deep State. Really. *POLITICO*, 2 December. Available at: https://www.politico.com/magazine/story/2018/12/02/larry-mcdonald-communists-deep-state-222726/ (accessed 20 January 2023).

Brother Larry went on to have two other children, a son Larry Jr. and a daughter, Lauren, with his third wife Kathy, and as far as we church-school kids knew, these were his only children, his one and only known son Larry Jr. mentioned in certain summaries of his dad's life after his death, homages which popped up in various places.[95] As for our church-school's local newspaper, it reported that principled Larry died without a will, leaving Kathy to file a petition with the court for access to his estate, $375,000 per year "to maintain a lifestyle to which [his children] are accustomed."[96] Apparently Larry was too occupied with setting the world to right to devote any of his valuable time to such common things as setting his affairs in order. Like blogger Jeri's, my church was part of a network of churches across the country that held up men like Larry McDonald, like Rousas Rushdoony, like Greg Bahnsen, as demigods in the war to reinstate God's law in the United States. Even to this day, all such men, together with my pastor, are spoken about in certain circles as men of impeccable character, men of integrity. If and when we hear any stories about them, when they have been introduced to us at conferences, in Sunday worship, all details are carefully curated, all their potentially noble qualities and acts collected and gathered together like gold jewellery, melted and cast into images for worship. And still, some continue to challenge any of us who ask questions about these heroes, they invoke their right to privacy, their personal pain at any exposure, their suffering. Don't embarrass us. Don't stir the pot. Don't distract from the mission. Stories are mostly irrelevant, lived experience is immaterial in its materiality, peripheral, beside the point. What matters is our theology, our concepts, our apologetics, our ideals.

Yet, there is hypocrisy in this too. Because of course they do tell stories, they do press upon us a certain narrative that suits their purposes, illustrations sprinkled across years of sermons, essays and

---

95 See, for example, Gomez, C. (2013). Larry's Legacy. *The New American*. Available at https://www.thefreelibrary.com/Larry%27s+legacy%3A+Larry+McDonald+was+a+doctor%2C+a+congressman%2C+and...-a0345616700 (accessed 20 January 2023).

96 *The Atlanta Constitution*, Wed, May 16, 1984, p. 11.

books honouring the lives and integrity of loyal men and women of the movement. All of the adultery, all of the abandonment, all of the cruelty, the neglect, the abuse, all those crushed under the wheels of the kingdom, they are eager to inform us of all such transgressions when smearing their enemies. But when it comes to similarly seedy stories about their friends, their family, even their own sons and daughters, about themselves – they will hush up, they will fight exposure, they will turn a blind eye as long as they can, unless and until it is exposed to such a degree they can no longer deny it. Then watch the distancing, watch the spin, see how they work quickly to position such failed fellow operatives as outsiders, see to what lengths they will go, to distract us from their own complicity. The only principle at work here is power.

The Dominionist philosophy has no use for the women who cannot, who will not sacrifice their bodies as pedestals for the prowess of men. In 1997, Rushdoony's followers would applaud another of their typical heroes, Brian Abshire, "mighty warrior for the Faith poised to do exploits for Christ the King," whose "genius transcends the intellectual."[97] What place is there for mundane faithfulness in such a community? For useless splendour? Or better yet, what place for being a woman, a minority, anyone off centre amongst all those clambering for a certain mould of excellence, hoisting onto the backs of everyone they know the impossible burden of so many expectations, nothing less than an ableist, classist, sexist, racist model of achievement. I struggle against the irony attached to my own life in all of this, that in my haste to escape, I too ran their race to the pinnacles of intellectual prestige, using the only tools to hand I had, the ones they'd pressed into my hands. This selfish sport has no winners. Whenever I have come across these people from my past, before any words pass my lips they are already eagerly informing me of my peers'—their children's—

---

[97] Sandlin, P.A. (1997). Brian Abshire: Emerging Christian Reconstructionist Leader. *Chalcedon Magazine*, 1 April. Available at: https://chalcedon.edu/magazine/brian-abshire-emerging-christian-reconstructionist-leader (accessed 20 January 2023).

accomplishments, in their eyes my every step forward is a challenge to their own worth, they imagine I'm nearing the finish line now, whatever I've done they'll say they've done better, whoever I am, they are more. Do you not know that those who run in a race all run, but only one receives the prize? Make no mistake. Among such people, this one runner is not Jesus. In this bloody battle for the crown, it's every man for himself, and every woman for every man.

I want nothing to do with this anymore. I see now the true revolutionary life is the one lived in the quiet and contented places, those which to kingdom warriors seem distastefully ordinary and unremarkable. People of compassion, people of gentleness and generosity, people who desire little else but peace on earth and amble only towards that end, good will to all humans they come across. Perhaps in writing about such rare gems, I've subverted the very wonder of their existence, perhaps I should leave them undisturbed in the revolution that is their obscurity, as a statement against the endless measurement of every human life. Let me be clear then, that I want no part in constructing monuments to them, to equal those of self-important men. I mean only to speak the names of the forgotten and what happened to them, those who sought the smallest and most tender of social circles, people of unrecognised importance, those working for wages intermittently or not at all, those whose uncorrected papers, dishes, laundry and dust pile up, the ones who do the work others think beneath them, earth's cruelly unrecognised and unrewarded, those who survive this world of Men and the ones of us who don't. All we wonderful human beings, our lives nothing more than a breath.

23

We cannot have a soulish relationship with anyone. We like these relationships where you are my buddy, and I am your friend and we can cry on each other's shoulders and we can give each other pity. Sympathy is deadly. God is never going to lay anything on anyone that is more than what is right. He is a just God. We have no room for pity parties in the kingdom of God.

— Buddy Cobb, Co-Founder with Sam Fife of "The Move" Cult [98]

Miraculously, Sofia did not die, though the bullet inflicted long-term physical damage. "It was just a cry for attention," I heard an elder's wife say, after death's door had closed, for now. This important woman talking didn't bother to concern herself with the fact of my presence, my ears could hear, but she expected my brain to slow the firing of its synapses, my mouth to stay silent. "She wouldn't have done it that way if she really wanted to die." I understood every ounce of her meaning, I watched as it bared its fangs, it bit me, it sank into my flesh, it drained me of all my blood. If someone wants to die, then, let them do it, but let them be done with it, let them commit themselves to it, none of this half-way, half-hearted business. In this way and so many others, members of the community began spinning

---

98 *FACTNet Message Board: Move, The / Sam Fife.* (2005, September 1). https://web.archive.org/web/20070930160857/http://www.factnet.org/discus/messages/3/2037.html.

tales, erasing all trace of their complicity in a child's desperate scramble to escape. Because she was lukewarm—neither hot nor cold—so they spit her out of their mouth.

The night of her attempted suicide or sometime very shortly after the ambulance hurried her away, our pastor's wife let herself into Sofia's house, made her way to Sofia's bedroom, and like some self-appointed crime scene cleaner, a reconstructionist in every sense of the word, she set about sanitising the scene to refit the sacred narrative, frantically searching Sofia's room for drugs, for any concrete, newsworthy evidence that the evening's violence had originated in this child's own errant choices, that all this had come about because she'd gone her own way, had gone away. Surely a spirit of harlotry had led this child astray. Yes, she has played the harlot, departing from all we stooped to teach her from on high.

I found this out months later, after Sofia called and asked me to help her catch up on the schoolwork she'd missed. By this point, we hadn't been close much at all, for a long time. That terrible night when I went to the hospital to be close to her, maybe even to see her, everyone was already there, all our schoolmates huddled and crying, a circle of weeping teenagers most of which I didn't much know, talking of things they'd all done together, when was the last time each one of us saw her, why did this happen to us. I went home with only one entirely selfish thought which all night walked the streets of my mind, moving in and out of every murky alley of my memory: God, please let me die instead. God, please let it be me.

Now here we were, back in her house, her room. I sat on the carpet and she on her bed. I moved my fingers through the fluffy warp and weft, her hands occupied themselves with the edge of a blanket. She told me about Mrs. Pastor's Wife's trespassing, she pointed to the chest of drawers behind me, this is what That Woman rummaged through, I found it all in disarray. I nodded, I listened, I gave her all my school workbooks, all of them already completed, just copy all my answers, what even is the point of all these rules that end only in our sadness. We had something between us which we

CHAPTER TWENTY-THREE

could pick up easily, some shared understanding which had bobbed along through all the peaks and troughs of our connection. We were near again, briefly, we laughed in our usual way about something I can't now remember. I sat still in the presence of her bandaged body and the benign spirits of all our previous times together that hovered without judgement about the room. After a short while, I left. Sofia invited me over a few times more after that, we listened to music and danced in her room a few times, just the two of us. Not long after, she started attending another school and I rarely saw her again. Through her I learned something of the comforting strata of an old friend, the cheering substance two can accumulate layer upon layer in partnership over the years, the welcoming weight of all that time together which sits quietly alongside in a crisis, which says only: I was here then, I'm here again, here I am with you.

24

We live in a humanistic age. And while spanking a 16 year-old is still within your God given rights as a parent, the State will not look kindly on it… Require children to behave. Correct them when necessary, and spank them for rebellion.

– Brian Abshire, 'Dealing with Rebellious Christian Teenagers,' *The Counsel of Chalcedon*, 2002, Issue 2.

If you want to go to the Socio-Political level, the societies that have survived have all been characterised by large strong families and comparatively weak institutions. For example, our country in its early days had very few doctors, social workers, agencies, but lots of large strong families, which is exactly the opposite of the situation today.

– Joe Morecraft, 'The Bible on Large Families.' *The Counsel of Chalcedon*, 1989, Issue 8.

For several years, I begged my parents to let me leave our church-school and enrol in the local public school. This intensified first when Sofia moved schools and then when another friend, Lydia, also transferred and wrote a short piece for her new school newspaper, extolling the virtues of her newfound access to a more diverse student body, to clubs, to teachers, to opportunities. This act our community, my parents included, considered a complete betrayal, fine if she left but no need to throw us all under the bus. So none of my pleas made any difference. My parents had always said that they'd fled Sam Fife's cult on principle. More than this, we left for you kids, they told us, so you'd have a better life. They didn't say Sam Fife or "cult"—I'm adding that now—but rather Alaska or "the Land," euphemism that tightly bound our thoughts and tongues. Things there were vaguely bad, mostly the matter was doctrinal. This is how they have consistently narrated their own leaving, instilling in me the perhaps unintended consequence of hopelessness at the situation that followed. My inability to leave this so-called improved situation, what they had faced poverty for, worked so hard, sacrificed so much. How ungrateful must I be to feel such despair while enjoying such capital P Privilege! How impossible to please was I, daring as I did to consider my thoroughly Christian education, rooted in faithfulness to the bible as it was presumed to be, to be anything close to real oppression! And now, this very minute, what disrespect to exercise my right of writing down my objections in such a way, to such an end, as if my pain is anything close to the daily hardship of so many anguished souls living with brutal violence and starvation across our sad, spinning planet! I will stop for a few minutes here and resist this false guilt again, as it's rising up to rebuke me once more, that voice that attempts to distract endlessly from the injustice within a person's immediate circle. That voice that condemns you, redirects you. "Don't look here, look over there, at those people suffering much more than you." "Things are much worse out there, so stop complaining about what's in here." Messages like these are only smoke and mirrors, curses compiled by those afraid of the vulnerable and mysterious beauty of healing. Out of the hardness of their hearts they neglect justice and mercy and faithfulness.

As soon as I started playing basketball, I started spending more time with elder's daughter Leah. We'd attended fundamentalist sport camp together, now we shot hoops every spare minute, before and after school, at weekends. She and I, together with Jenny, travelled for a week with the headmaster and his wife as a prize for being the first members of the carpool patrol. When first I got to know her, she lived in a little house in the woods not far from Jenny's at the end of a long and winding driveway. Most of us lived a considerable distance from our church-school—perhaps a semiconscious show of our apathy for anything local—but Leah's family was furthest away. In traffic the drive to school took her mother at least an hour, sometimes more. For nearly all of us and especially through morning commuter congestion, every journey was a recommitment to leaving neighbours behind, to the coming out from far-off lands, the gathering together from all corners of the sprawling city up, up, up into our temple made with hands. All the more time to listen to Christian talk radio, made possible by the American Family Radio network, 91.5 Kingdom FM, Money Matters with Larry Burkett, James Dobson's daily advice spots. We moved seamlessly from messages about earthly prosperity—our certain reward for diligent obedience—to the hallowed halls of heaven on earth that contained our church-school. The further we drove to get there, the greater was our display of devotion to this one good church and school amongst all the churches and schools that our cars and their occupants rejected as we passed by. My internalisation of this ethos became evident to me one year in high school, when I was startled to realise I'd given someone the wrong directions to the church from the state highway, wrongly assuming that our daily journey there was northerly, and metaphorically towards heaven, rather than southerly, down towards the low places, toward all the land of the valley. Did we not look down from our holy height, from heaven gaze upon the earth?

In late October, 1990, the National Association of Evangelicals (NAE) met with President George Bush to discuss "the Administration's deteriorating relations with the evangelical community." Among the concerns of NAE director Dr. Robert Dugan, Jr., were rumours of discrimination against Christians working in the White House, of President Bush's support for gay activists and of his use of Federal grants to support art forms seen by the NAE as pornographic. Our church magazine ran an editorial

CHAPTER TWENTY-FOUR

covering this meeting, lamenting the ineptness and ineffectiveness of the Christian Right Establishment. "Alas, evangelical Christians ... are not playing such hardball, which is why they are losing, and losing bad."[99] Our pastor, on the other hand, a true believer, was in it to win it. In 1993, speaking at the Biblical Worldview and Christian Education Conference, he disparaged democracy as "mob rule," lauded the ideal dictatorship of a Christian state and declared religious pluralism a fantasy. "Nobody has the right to worship on this planet any other God than Jehovah. And therefore the state does not have the responsibility to defend anybody's pseudo-right to worship an idol."[100] Though not holding hands explicitly with every other movement that shared our goals, nevertheless, our pastor continued to attract members of these other movements, recruited them as teachers for our church-school, including the wife of Pat Gartland, chairman of the Georgia Christian Coalition. Setting aside our differences, we all trekked on towards the same vision, the reconstruction of the kingdom of God on earth, a tower whose top would reach into heaven and summon our Saviour again to earth, as soon as was humanly possible. By 1994, our church was celebrating what we saw as the successes of our efforts at claiming dominion in our surrounding community, the banning of homosexuality, the cutting off of arts funding and the removal of any financial backing for abortion in Cobb County, where our pastor and other church members lived. In March of that year, Dr. Stephen Hotze, a currently influential GOP donor who as of 2022 is being prosecuted for an election fraud probe,[101] delivered a plenary speech at American Vision's "Inner Circle" banquet, on the theme of "Restoring America's Christian Heritage" saying "[t]he only question is whose

---

[99] Lofton, J. (1991). 'The Blind Leading the Blind,' *The Counsel of Chalcedon*, Issue 3.
[100] Clarkson, F. (1994). Christian Reconstructionism. *Political Research Associates*, 1 March. Available at: https://politicalresearch.org/1994/03/01/christian-reconstructionismtheocratic-dominionism-gains-influence (accessed 20 January 2023).
[101] Boburg, S. (2022). GOP donor Steven F. Hotze described botched vote fraud probe in recording, prosecutors say. *The Washington Post*, 6 May. Available at: https://www.washingtonpost.com/investigations/2022/05/06/hotze-texas-recording-ballots/ (accessed 20 January 2023).

morality is going to be imposed on whom."[102] Our pastor too was as always crystal clear on his political philosophy. The purpose of civil government is "to terrorise evil doers!"[103]

While all that was going on out there, within the walls of our community we kids continued to taste the swift, severe retribution of home-grown, "godly terrorism."[104] After a while, Leah's family moved to a much larger home, a new build, carefully designed in the past-era style so sacred to our little commune, addicted as we were to the artifice of constructed nostalgia. This new home was even further outside the city, this was the house blessed ceremoniously by our pastor, the house whose side entrance greeted guests with the sight of an ornately carved wooden paddle hanging above an inner door, engraved with one of our community's most sacred texts. If memory serves me it was the words from Proverbs 13:24, "He who spares the rod hates his son." It was one of those verses that, when isolated, could be seamlessly resituated in service of smacking. I didn't study it closely enough to be sure. Each time I passed under this ritualistic implement of corporal punishment, my eyes would involuntarily move to the floor, I looked directly at it only once and didn't raise my eyes to it again, though this was not something I ever consciously reflected on. It hung over the door like a spectre, looming large as a semiotic lynchpin for everything our community stood for, all the obedience required of us, all the pits dug by the self-righteous to trap us, to terrorise we evil-doers, to send forth streams of tears from our eyes, for the law was not obeyed.

By this time, in addition to my ballet teacher's sadistic beatings, I had for many years frequently witnessed parents carrying crying children, even infants, out of the church service to a small room

---

102 Reeves, W. B. (1994). Hidden Agenda. The Influence of Religious Extremism on the Politics of Cobb. County, Georgia, Produced for *The Cobb Citizens Coalition*. https://radicalarchives.files.wordpress.com/2013/01/hidden-agenda-cobb-extremism1.pdf.

103 Christian Reconstructionism: Religious Right Gains Influence, Part Two, *The Public Eye*, 1994, Volume VIII, No. 2.

104 See Morecraft III, J. (2004). The Social Agenda of the Bush Administration. *Chalcedon Magazine*, 1 December. Available at: https://chalcedon.edu/magazine/the-social-agenda-of-the-bush-administration (accessed 20 January 2023).

behind the sanctuary for the sin of making any noise, moving even an inch. This tiny cry-room, as we called it (an unintended double entendre), had a large, soundproof glass window facing the pulpit and a speaker system that allowed its occupants to watch, listen and dutifully participate in the service without their disobedient babies and toddlers disturbing anyone, also without any privacy, the window working both ways. Some babies were hauled out to be hit by their mothers—it was mostly mothers—up to ten times in a single service, until they learned never to show any sign at all that they might need attention, that they might need food, that they might need to be held or given a toy, that what they needed mattered at all in the presence of the almighty god. Little Lord Jesus, no crying he makes.

This disdain for bodily needs made itself manifest in a similarly flippant attitude to mothers themselves. There was an implicit expectation that a new mother would be in church the first Sunday after she'd given birth, floating in on angel wings, in defiance of earthly exhaustion and carnal pain, of swollen breasts, of the feminal gushing of blood. One mother gave birth in the morning and arrived in all her maternal glory in time for Sunday evening service, newborn in tow. One church leader's wife carried a large, floral cushion into the church sanctuary one Sunday evening to ease her labour pains – she'd watch and pray so she'd not fall into temptation, her spirit was willing but her womanly flesh was weak, it counted for nothing. Newlyweds also frequently attended Sunday morning worship the day after their wedding. They might be excused from mid-week meetings during their honeymoon, but attending any other church, being away from us for even one Sabbath, was far from ideal. All pain, all sickness, all hunger, all longing, all love, all we subsumed beneath our disembodied Sunday worship.

Despite being so far away from the church-school building, Leah's house was a social centre for our church, buzzing with weddings, baby showers, parties and various houseguests who lived in their basement apartment for sometimes months at a time. Leah's parents commissioned a large family portrait of their likewise large family to hang in their formal living room, and a photograph of their family was also featured in our church's magazine, with this caption: "Biblical Family Planning." I often joined Leah's Biblical™ family for Sunday lunch, and some Sunday evenings a group of us would go there after church for games and snacks or a film.

My mother deemed Leah's company so suitable that she allowed me to attend a musical with her family on a school night and stay for a sleepover afterwards. I wore my blue velvet dress and dreamed that night of becoming an opera singer. The possibility of a woman in some occupation outside my closed community seemed suddenly more tangible, though I had no talent for singing. This is what some of we girls sometimes did, when, completely uneducated in the practical workings of identifying and pursuing a career, any futuristic thoughts apart from marriage settled on fantasy. We'll become an internationally known novelist, a botanist in the jungles of South America, we'll play professionally in the women's NBA, we'll work on a kangaroo preserve in Australia, a horse farm in Brazil, we'll discover the hidden caves of the ocean, we'll live on the moon, we'll walk faithfully with God, we'll be no more, because God took us away.

Leah's house was always busy, people coming and going and often showing up unexpectedly. It seemed their doors swung open and shut all hours of the day and night. The inner doors too seemed to frown upon any boundaries, most especially the en-suite bathrooms' sliding doors that I could never latch properly. Anyone could come in at any time – I was interrupted there more than once and took to using only the guest bathroom downstairs which had a proper door that locked. But what I remember most of Leah's house are the smells and sounds of her many sisters, her aunts, her mother, so many women and all their shampoos, aerosol deodorants, drugstore perfumes, hairspray and makeup, that hot and heady scent of the hairdryer, all mixed up and mingling. The noise and fragrance of getting ready, of washing off the day, of bickering and borrowing, the everyday life of women. To this day, a certain brand of shampoo,

CHAPTER TWENTY-FOUR

another of facial cleanser, the scent carries me back to those rituals, in those rooms, with those women, I buy them now sometimes to make that journey, though this odour-evoked trip is always tinged with grief.

Of all my church-school friendships, I remained in contact with Leah the longest. Our shared interest in sport was of course a factor but there were related reasons. For years, outside of church services and school both of us could be found almost exclusively in athletic shorts and t-shirts, always kitted out for a quick pick-up game of whatever sport was available. One time, required to wear our Sunday best to the school sports banquet, she and I threw off our shoes and ruined our stockings playing a free-throw game with a group of boys in the parking lot. In this, with her, I for some time enjoyed a sense of communal rebellion against the lace collars, the floral dresses, the dainty shoes, the strait jacket of a woman's gender conformity, the uniform of our fragility. The reality of she, an elder's daughter, doing this with me, this even got my own mother off my back, concerned as she constantly was that I dressed and behaved too much like a boy, too risk-taking, too brash, too competitive, too many appearances in low-rise jeans and baggy shirts. It's taken me a lifetime to feel comfortable in anything culturally marked as feminine, however fluid all such marking most certainly is. Any hint of biblical-womanhood-wardrobe I for so long associated with weakness, with being governed, gazed upon, looked at, calcified, deposited into a glass case, a neglected closet. We women decorated and decorating ourselves like fine china dolls, brought out on special occasion, kept otherwise under lock and key. I like to believe I dress as I please now, finally! wearing whatever suits me in the moment, carrying clothing beyond all rigid rules and narrow-minded binaries to the endless horizon of expressive possibility. And it's true, I've come so far in this, I have. Yet attending an ecclesiastical meeting as part of my academic research only a few years ago, I again worried over my choices, am I choosing this suit because I like it, because I want to wear it? Or are my preferences still borne out by residual rebellion against the cloak of respectability and acceptability? Perhaps the truth is somewhere in the murky middle, as it always seems to be, between the myth of fully free will and the dangers of determinism.[105]

Still, even as Leah and I enjoyed certain freedoms together, as an elder's daughter she seemed sometimes to think of me as her protégée and would rebuke me regularly for this and that unladylike infraction, sometimes modelling for me the necessary deference due to boys. On a few occasions she abandoned my company as soon as a certain boy showed up at her family's house. Times like these I'd end up sleeping in one of her sister's rooms for the night, better than going home. Over time, however, something pricked her conscience, she got the message hammered into us all over the years, that the best place for any of us to find a spouse was in the safety of our miniscule circle. One day she told me that she'd confessed to her dad that she'd gone too far physically with a boy she liked, there is so much we girls still have to learn about our own ignorant desires to conform to the world, Valerie. After this, Leah devoted herself even more to chastity and submission to men, she channelled all her strength into this commitment, and was admired and respected for it by most of our peer group.

---

[105] Cave, S. (2016, June). There's No Such Thing as Free Will: But we're better off believing in it anyway. *The Atlantic*. https://www.theatlantic.com/magazine/archive/2016/06/theres-no-such-thing-as-free-will/480750/

25

Women tend to find Arminianism more emotionally appealing than the "cold" precision of classic Reformed orthodoxy. Consequently, since "girlie-men" pastors want to appeal to women, the most vocal and influential members of the church, they preach sermons with all the spiritual nourishment of a pixie stix (remember that colored sugar candy in a straw?).

— Brian Abshire, "'Girlie-Men in the Pulpit or, the Feminization of the American Clergy, in Feminism in Family, Church and Culture, Chalcedon Magazine, 1 February 1998.

I often advise young brides who are traveling during their first weeks or months of marriage to start "homemaking" in a hotel, even if they are there for only a night, rather than groaning about having to "wait so long to have a home". How?... Your own cloth, your own candlestick, just one rose or daffodil is enough to make a difference... You will be surprised how much difference it makes to have done something to make a room your home, even for one night.

— Edith Schaeffer. [106]

---

106 Schaeffer, E. (1971). The Hidden Art of Homemaking. Tyndale House Publishers.

Women who are truly devoted to patriarchal authority, part and parcel as it is to Christian Dominionism, might surprise some with how consistent they can be in the demands they place on themselves and the men in their lives. Even at cost to themselves, they will defend a man's position as leader and, if he fails in his duty, they will often be the first to criticise him. For those who have not spent much time in such a community, the reality of women's frankness in this misogynist context can be unexpected. Some of this "no nonsense" style is driven by self-loathing, since, in such a community, certain expressions of emotion—grief, for instance—are considered ostentatiously feminine, a sign of gendered weakness. One woman from my church-school once rebuked her husband for crying during a period of self-doubt. "Be a man," she reminded him thus of his place, an act he expressed gratitude for, what was he thinking, being so open and so vulnerable. Who was he, a woman? Other women I know have bluntly asked men who've initiated a casual conversation with them to state their intentions. Well, do you want to marry me or not? If so, like a man state it clearly and now, so we can get on with What We're Here For. Otherwise, no point in standing here talking, move along, nothing to see or do here.

For a while, my friend Leah developed an interest in the eldest of two brothers who attended our school, sons of another local pastor. I try to remember when they made their entrance, but I can't say exactly, only that the first time I saw them was in our catechism class, and that when they came, our headmaster commented on the name of the younger son, pay attention everyone to the meaning of his name, God is indeed with us. The two brothers were close in age, the eldest in Leah's class above mine and the youngest in my tiny year group. They were a bit mysterious to us, first because their parents had immigrated from Europe, and they all spoke to each other in a language foreign to us. And second, because their parents had them so occupied with various activities during the week that we rarely saw them outside of school.

There was also the fact of their alien behaviour. At times they even

CHAPTER TWENTY-FIVE

seemed to be poking fun at us, though without any malice. The eldest brother, Leo, delivered a lengthy tongue-in-cheek monologue to our speech class about the benefits of regular swimming, including a lengthy argument in favour of the magnificent speedo, its hydrodynamic appeal and don't forget, ladies, it's also easy on the eyes. At this point, he gave us all a quick wink. When one of our Bible teachers erected a camera on top of a tripod, then switched it on without our knowledge to record our every movement, Leo chose the desk at the back of the class, directly in the camera's line of vision. On the day, none of us observed what he got up to in class while the teacher was out of the room, he kept it to himself. It was only later, when the teacher turned on the video he'd secretly recorded, prepared to surprise and humiliate us, that there was Leo, centre screen, flexing each bicep one by one then kissing it, disrupting and redirecting our teacher's bitter, humiliating intentions into a comedy act. We students laughed and clapped, and Leo took a bow, while the teacher wryly switched it off and told us all to be quiet, will you just hush.

And then there was the book report Leo's younger brother Alexander delivered in front of our English class. This was a time when a lot of we girls were reading Christian historical romance novels, stories of young and virginal Puritan women, pioneers or Victorians, all whose beauty and unparalleled modesty and chastity eventually shamed and tamed some rogue of a man, all set against the golden backdrop of a more noble era when men and women, masters and slaves, all knew their place. Fundamentalist porn, that genre that more than one scholar has identified as one of the greatest ironies existing among a people who claim to desire the absolute outlawing of all pornography. Texts whose climb to "climax with overtaking of the prone, vulnerable, and usually female body," women under tutelage, women in non-consensual bondage, a succession of "moments of enthrallment" and revelation, whose excessive and intense spirituality and visual imagery evokes so much implied sexual energy.[107] Alexander elected to choose

---

[107] Ulanowicz, A. (2015). Chick Tracks, Monstrosity, and Pornography. *Image Text Journal*, 8(1). https://imagetextjournal.com/chick-tracts-monstrosity-and-pornography/

one of these for his oral book report, complete with a dramatic reading of one of the most erotically tense passages in the book. The class descended into total chaos, I laughed so hard I could no longer see through my tears, finally the teacher told him to stop, that's enough, Alexander, we get the idea.

Alexander spun other minutiae of my life in other likewise memorable ways. I'd for some years now been fighting bitterly with my mother about my clothing, my hair, my pastimes, and in the most recent clash she'd vetoed my choice of school shoes, a pair of clunky black Doc Martens, and instead bought for me a pair of black ankle boots. The first day I wore them to school, very reluctantly, Alexander declared them the best shoes he'd ever seen and began asking me to wear them every day. He called them my 'mini-boots' and often said before we parted ways at the end of the day, "Wear those boots again tomorrow, Valerie, won't you?" I had no idea what to make of this barbless admiration from a boy – by then I suspected all such compliments and requests of having some ulterior motive, which I tended to perceive only when it was too late. Yet with Alexander there was none of that. His comments, his conversation, any physical interaction we had never invaded nor escalated. He seemed content enough in himself and interested only in sharing this, in acknowledging and shoring up my own contentedness. I'm happy so why shouldn't you be happy too? I feel good about myself, why shouldn't you? There's enough in this world for us both, and then some.

In this and many ways, these two brothers had a unique talent for being friends with nearly everyone. There were plenty among us who tried to level them, especially some of the boys tried at various points to put them in their place, to bait them somehow, sometimes by mocking them for some superficial thing. But none of these petty quarrels registered. Whatever flippant thing anyone said or did seemed to roll off their backs like water. I sensed they were swimming through their days with us effortlessly, their eyes on some spectacular future horizon, while the rest of us splashed

CHAPTER TWENTY-FIVE

and floundered about uselessly, pushing each other down in our desperation to avoid drowning.

It's no wonder then, that for quite a while, Leah set her sights on Leo, she liked the looks of his strong European jawline, she told me. She even went so far as to write him a letter stating her acknowledgement of his good qualities and asking him what his intentions might be, indirectly that is, so as not to challenge his own manly initiative. A bold move nonetheless and one I wouldn't have dared. Leah asked me to drop some hints with Leo here and there to see what I could find out, as well. By this time, Leo and his brother had learned about my first formal after-school job—a market research centre where I'd been working for nearly a year by then—and they joined me there. The pay wasn't anything to call home about, but we got regular bonuses under the table from our corrupt manager, who handed us wads of cash in exchange for completing surveys of all sorts. Whenever it came time to tell our boss which hours we could work, the brothers would scribble their names next to every available hour. In the summer and during other school holidays they worked full-time, even over-time when they could get away with it, though never on Sundays. One day a week, like me they set aside all fraud and embezzlement, all our naïve participation in organised crime.

Before I'd secured this job, I'd applied unsuccessfully for an entry-level position at several other places of business. Finally, I'd been offered this particular job as I'd shrugged nonchalantly when the lecherous older man who'd interviewed me on the spot asked me how I'd handle being rudely insulted by the general public, then proceeded to give me a graphic demonstration of what that might be like. I wasn't fazed. I'd been around predators subtler than he most of my life, and there was something oddly comforting about how explicitly corrupt he and his workmates were, how obvious and unabashed their deviance. Accustomed as I was to so much hypocrisy, the transparency of my co-workers' criminality and the absence of any invocation of God from their lips, all these I found refreshing. And so gradually, after the brothers joined me, I too increased my own hours, eager to spend more time in their company in this altogether different space, puzzling over its ease, wondering what these brothers were working towards, what possible future they had glimpsed, while here I was only working for petty cash and to satisfy my parents, who would allow me to get a driver's license only on the understanding I'd also secure a regular job. And so I began to get to know the brothers beyond the boundaries of our school.

Perhaps on the privilege of all this time together, I managed to convince the brothers to come to a party one afternoon after school, a casual get-together that some of us had organised. "There'll be a pool," I said slyly, knowing Leo would find that impossible to resist. He couldn't, and for several hours that one time only, a small group of us assembled at the gigantic mansion of a certain unpopular and awkward boy in the class below us. His house not only had a pool, it also had an elevator and numerous, lavishly decorated rooms for a mere family of three. The brothers arrived and swam the length of the pool over and over in their speedos, we all laughed together and snacked on whatever we found in the pristine, marble kitchen, we watched a film in the basement cinema and toured the many rooms. By the time the sun went down, someone had activated the house's impressive sound system, some lively music started up in the cavernous living room, Alexander took my hand with a wide grin, and for some unknown amount of time we danced and we danced and we danced. As soon as a song ended I'd stop to catch my breath, then the music began again and Alexander would reach for my hand. And so it went the rest of the night until late, I laughed, I smiled and moved in the refuge of his company, a security I'd not know again truly until a long time later, a shelter I would only ever be able to appreciate again, even to recognise, only because of Alexander.

As it happened, Leo wasn't interested in Leah—perhaps it was more he wasn't interested in any permanent link to our community—and somehow communicated this to her. Yet I remember his words were such that he didn't humiliate her or even

CHAPTER TWENTY-FIVE

make her feel she'd been let down. She was disappointed but without a break in fellowship. Then, before we knew it, it was the end of the school year, Alexander's parents arranged for him to graduate early, the same year as his brother, a year ahead of me. The day of their leaving they waved me into the church's cry room, where they stood waiting in their blue robes. "Come take a picture with us, Valerie," they coaxed me. Afterwards, some of us were congregating downstairs in the school's central room, that space where I'd played endless games of chess all those years ago, where my ballet teacher had beaten us all into submission, where Luke had bitten my earlobe, where on occasion our pastor had emerged from his office to rebuke someone's language, someone's volume, someone else's tone. On some impulse Alexander asked if I wanted to swing around as we'd done a few times before. He offered his hands, "One last time?" I held out my own, we grasped hold of each other's wrists, he spun me around the room, around and around, higher and higher, the room tilted and blurred, the building disintegrated as I circled, we laughed together one last time, this his final act of transformation. And that was that. The brothers were off.

That next year, after Leah had started university locally, I noticed one Sunday she was dressed much more stylishly than usual. I commented on this, and she took me outside to tell me what she wasn't ready for others to hear, that a certain well-respected young man at our church, already graduated from university and stably employed, had asked her father for permission to court her. His first edict as her husband-in-waiting had been to insist that she immediately purchase an entirely new wardrobe using his credit card. By the end, with the explicit approval of her parents, she spent close to $3,000 on trousers, dresses, blouses and shoes to satisfy her seemingly more sophisticated suitor. Also at his request, she wore these clothes to church, on dates, at any social occasion, she remade herself according to his requirements. I told her I was happy for her, I tried to feign excitement about her new style, this man throwing all that money at her feet, yet I was empty and anxious. It seemed my friend no longer stood in front of me, someone else was here in her place. It was not the clothes themselves, but where and how they'd come about, the claim they represented not just on her body but even mine, the signal they sent of the unacceptability of women's choices for ourselves, the necessity of yet more Man-policing, Man-dictation, Man-preference, Man-tuition.

All this Leah embraced, and in all this, we turned our faces opposite ways, she reaching eagerly beyond this particular courtship, which didn't last, to the next. This time with a younger man closely connected to our church, from a family as large as her own, a courtship which did finally end in a wedding the summer before my senior year of university, marriage marking the demise of many relationships among us. I attended her wedding by myself. Going alone seemed right to me, a sort of subtle objection. I would navigate on my own, I would set apart other aspects of my life away from their watching eyes. Leo and Alexander attended too, though I didn't see them till afterwards. They arrived together as they always seemed to do and left quickly at the end, a seamless and fluid passing through, carrying no residue of our trouble as they left. We said hello to each other on the pavement outside the church, the two brothers and me. I remember their sunglasses, their relaxed smiles and then their exit, all so uncomplicated.

FIRE

*There are three things that will not be satisfied,
Four that will not say, "Enough":
fire…"*

Proverbs 30:15-16

26

In place of the socialistic education advocated by John Dewey, your parents have educated you according to the new covenant in Jesus Christ. Instead of endeavouring a theology of pessimism, your pastors and teachers have sought to instil a victory-orientation in you that sees this physical world not as the domain of Satan but as the playing field upon which King Jesus will be victorious in history.

– Rev. Chris Strevel, 'A Graduate's Reaffirmation of Faith in God,' T he Counsel of Chalcedon, 2000, Issue 4.

Covenant firmly believes that students must be educated to understand life and the liberal arts in light of Jesus Christ which pushes the student to become a "world" Christian by seeking to integrate their faith with all of life and by seeking to transform culture physically, emotionally, socially and spiritually."

– 'Break on Impact,' Covenant Online, 1996, Vol. 2, No. 2.

I am a person who was not allowed to leave and now leaves, has left, has moved on. Yet my mind was mapped from infancy to navigate threat, to live amongst warring wolves, to expect their bite. Every act that resembled love was infused with transaction, with the take, take, taking. This is what I knew, this is what knew me.

In the early days of my initial exodus, when I went off to

CHAPTER TWENTY-SIX

university, I begged my parents to return home, this new freedom was frightening, wouldn't it be better for me to go back to Egypt, if only I'd died by the Lord's hand, surely even death there is better than this desert of uncertainty, all this unknown. The months, the years, even the decades after a person physically leaves an abusive community, a workplace, a relationship, a family, a marriage – these are times we are perhaps more vulnerable than ever. We have left, but what we left hasn't left us. It lingers in our genetic makeup, it traverses our veins, it tracks our thoughts, our movements, it will not let us go. We disentangle, we rewire, we rewrite ourselves, but this is a life's work. No, it is a life's rest.

On a "missions trip"—to the hometown of Mrs. Pastor's Wife—only weeks after my high school graduation, our church youth leader Mark expressed interest in dating me exclusively. We were walking away from a campsite through the woods to the van, then, it was pitch black and I couldn't see his face as he made his request known, I saw no form, there was only his voice. A few weeks prior, he'd sat on the front row for my high school valedictorian speech, in that manliest of manspreading poses, one ankle on top of the opposite knee, arm casually across the back of the chair next to him, eyes focused steadily, studying the scope of my potential.

Mrs. Pastor's Wife had forced—yes, forced—elder's daughter Jenny and me to sing Psalm 1 at this event, her last push in our training regime. "No thank you, I don't want to do it," I said politely, then again I insisted, "No, this really isn't for me, I'm not a very good singer." But she wasn't having it, and what was I going to do – make a scene? "Young lady, there is no saying no. You are doing it." The night of our leaving, Jenny and I took to the stage and sang of trees established by rivers of water, to a tune written by Mrs. Pastor's Wife or perhaps it was her sister, a point noted prominently in the printed order of the ceremony. Afterwards, Mrs. Pastor's Wife took the time to give us our only feedback. "You were a bit flat." She gifted me with a small vinyl-bound copy of *Spurgeon's Morning and Evening*, the third copy she'd given me in as many years, the one copy I have to this day. Now, as then, she took it upon herself to open her instructional present to me, lest I open it improperly, lest I fail her in the mechanics of this ritual gifting. She read aloud the inscription, I must receive also as she dictated, as she delivered, "with gratitude, for your faithfulness, vigorous and joyous testimony." Words, words, words, accumulated piles of pretension.

Youth leader Mark, on the other hand, didn't speak to me afterwards or much at all really. But I'd noticed him nearby on occasion before this, detected a particular energy there, wondered what it might mean. I'd asked Leah's mother about it, as he'd begun living in their basement apartment. She said only that he was a nice Christian man, any girl would be lucky to be connected to him. He was the second youth leader to be so appointed, studying as he was for the pulpit ministry under the sole tutelage of our pastor. The first had since married the daughter of one of our most dynamic duos, her father an elder, her mother one of our church-school teachers, and this young man had moved on to pastor his own church in our micro-denomination. After that we had pastor's protégée Mark. On one occasion, Mark had given me a lift home from somewhere and remarked on what a high achieving family I seemed to come from. "What are your parents doing so right?" he asked, another question seeking no particular answer, the kind that men ask aloud of themselves in the presence of women.

I was by now at peak annoying to all my peers and nearly every church-school parent. It had become something of a running joke at each annual school awards assembly. This year's Mathematics prize goes to Our Resident Overachiever. And this year's Science prize. Bible prize. English prize. Sport. The one who will represent our school at this year's district spelling bee. Highest overall average. While she's up here, let's get them all done. The times when someone else's child won something, the room erupted in relieved applause, finally a break in our tedious honour of this one girl. As for me, every year I was petrified of losing these contrived competitions, of what my losing would mean, every meaningless award faded away straight after I received it, it was always the next one that mattered, the one after that.

I know Leah too felt that fear of bounded attainment, though neither of us could've named it – she once cried over a 97 on a chemistry exam, cut down over those crucial 3 points that separated a brief boost of confidence from the threatening chasm of women's confinement. She and I had a saying we recited to each other to capture this sentiment we shared, mostly we said it when playing basketball, from a popular song, "So close yet so far away." We didn't truly know what we were saying, but then again, we did know, we knew, in that inexplicable way that all women do know, that gnawing knowledge we stuff down. Over the years I've seen other women express this same dejected crumpling at the sight of near perfect and therefore crushing results, particularly in women from communities ruled by men who significantly restrict our liberties. I recognise that particular trigger of their tears. I too have tasted and seen that sense of desperation. This is what we girls have, it is one of the only things we can safely take, the only achievement set out before us, the only way to win. But to win what?

My impulse was always to climb and climb, higher and higher, perhaps I'd ascend this mountain of men up and out, where no greedy hands could grab me, before my time in the façade of classroom equality ran out. If I fell, I could be sure of their satisfaction – Look how she didn't last. Look how women cannot endure. Look how much stronger, how much more intelligent we are than they. They would pursue my honour as the wind, I would plummet, they would eat me alive, all my prosperity would pass away as a cloud. Only books, only the mechanics of cognition, only accumulation of facts and figures, only aggressive arguments and achievements certified onto slips of thick paper by the officious scribbles of men, only these could lead me up and out. With each prize I proved myself, I declared, I was not born for this, I am more than this, I am more than a woman, I. Am. More.

At 17, I won a prize for writing a short story about an old man whose deepest wish is to fly away into the sky with a flock of birds, an extended metaphor for death, figurative language the only means to declare the condition of my crumbling inner self. Recently, my kids found this story in a box of my old things and were startled by its sadness. "Why did you write that, mummy?" they ask. "If I employed both a man and a woman in the same position, I'd always pay the man more," our Bible teacher told us all one day in class, in one of his many side lectures on the significance of (Man-head) "breadwinning" in the kingdom coming (note that the word "man" is always silent in that word's articulation). I babysat his kids once, I sat in the living room after they were asleep and watched as five, eight, eleven hamsters darted across the room, burrowing behind bureaus and bookcases. "They escaped and we can't catch them," the kids told me. "So we've given up." "What a shame she's so smart," my cousin overheard an elder say after my high school graduation speech. "Oh well, at least she'll make a good pastor's wife."

My high school graduation marked the start of the summer when our pastor stepped into the role of State Chairman for Howard Phillips's U.S. Taxpayer's Party, later renamed the Constitution Party. At their 1995 convention just one year prior, Matthew Trewhella, leader of domestic terrorist group Missionaries to the Preborn, had addressed the crowd with these words: "This Christmas I want you to do the most loving thing and I want you to buy each of your children an SKS rifle and 500 rounds of ammunition."[108] Our church-school pastor and Phillips were by this time frequently sharing the stage with fellow Reconstructionists at annual Confederate heritage conferences, Steve Wilkins, Douglas Wilson, Otto Scott, George Grant. And who could forget their final speaker, Larry Pratt, a gun rights zealot and former co-chairman of Pat Buchanan's 1996 presidential campaign, a man forced to resign because of links to white supremacist organisations and right-wing militia leaders.[109]

---

108 Blumenthal, M. (2009). *Republican Gomorrah: Inside the Movement That Shattered the Party*. Bold Type Books.
109 Berke, R. L. (1996, February 16). Politics: The Staff; Buchanan Co-leader Quits Under Fire – The New York Times. *The New York Times*. https://www.nytimes.com/1996/02/16/us/politics-the-staff-buchanan-co-leader-quits-under-fire.html

CHAPTER TWENTY-SIX

Around the same time, also in the mid 1990's, our church-school magazine published a piece bemoaning Anita Hill's statements about being assaulted by Clarence Thomas. This is a "black cloud over the name of Associate Justice Thomas," the author wrote, subtly deracing Judge Thomas in his summons of the threat of Black skin, paving the way then for full-throated misogynoir. Anita Hill was "Salome who danced before the Senate committee." "This time," our magazine announced with immense relief, "Herodias did not have her way. Thomas's head was not delivered."[110] In the years following, our pastor and his wife would share the stage with such abusive characters as the now infamous Duggar family from TLC reality television fame and the equally fraught with sexual predation Willis Clan.[111] Our pastor would co-author an introductory study course on law and government with Chief Justice Roy Moore and Doug Phillips, son of Howard Phillips, men both accused of sexual assault of a minor.[112] Judge Moore had won the loyal respect of our pastor because of his refusal to remove the 10 Commandments from his courthouse steps. Allegations of assault against such a principled man like him, just as against Judge Thomas, these must therefore be lies, our pastor insisted. One chapter in their co-authored book argued that women should not run for office, that Christians have a moral obligation not to vote for any woman that defies this ethic. No mention was made of the failed congressional candidacy of my pastor's dear friend Kathy McDonald, the dogmatism of his moral policies as slippery as ever on his own tongue.

In the year leading to my high school graduation, I'd applied to a small Presbyterian college, the one safe step beyond my church-school that satisfied my parents. The materials I received

---

110 Schlei, S. (1994). 'Sexual Harassment: A Trojan Horse for the Media,' *The Counsel of Chalcedon*, Issue 6.
111 *Family Covenant Ministries – Past Speakers*. (2015). http://web.archive.org/web/20211212070449/http://www.familycovenantministries.com/index.php?option=com_content&view=article&id=14%3Apast-speakers&catid=1%3A25th-annual-christian-home-educators-fellowship
112 Phillips, D., Morecraft, J. C., Moore, R., & Jehle, P. (2011). *Law and Government: An Introductory Study Course*. The Vision Forum.

emphasized the importance of a coherent and convincing expression of faith: *What does it mean to you to live as a Christian.* This requirement, this question I considered carefully, broke down into its composite pieces, agonised over. Was my faith coherent? What personal meaning did I attach to the act of living as a Christian? What patterns of behaviour did I recognise as Christian? Could I prove I was a legitimate recipient of salvation? I was a jumble of contradictions, the only Christian life I knew was marked by violence and hypocrisy, power plays and being played. But could I be convincing? This was a time when all prospective students were also required to complete a telephone interview. And, to add insult to injury, I would have to submit a church reference, written by someone who could testify—once again, not about the person and work of Jesus Christ—but about my spiritual life, growth and character. These requirements filled me with no small amount of dread. Surely they'd see straight through me, they'd know instantly who I truly was, the fakest of fakers, the chief of sinners, the most unworthy among the worthless, the liar, the hypocrite. When the call came through, I spun an elaborate story of all the evangelistic community work I thought other girls in other schools might be doing, leading a Young Life group, a club somewhere. I was ashamed and afraid of bringing up my stint in the church office, my servitude to Mrs. Pastor's Wife, all that harassment from smarmy humans of all ages that I—still then—endured in church, in school, in my after-school job every week. All the devastating details of my woman's place. What did it mean to me to live as a Christian? I tapped into my many false selves, the lives I thought she should be leading, the good works she should be doing to earn her crown. My phone performance was a success, I even later won a prestigious scholarship, news I heard while participating in embezzlement at my after-school job. I had no idea afterward whether what facts I'd fabricated secured these outcomes. And there was still the matter of the reference.

As soon as my pastor learned that I was interested in this particular college, that I needed a church reference, he asked me to come into his office one afternoon after school, without my parents. He wanted me to know several things. First, that there wouldn't be any good churches in the city where I was going. Second, that he had been invited to speak at the college once but hadn't been received well, so what chance did someone like me have. And finally, that I'd need to watch out for enemies of the faith on staff there, it would be like going into hostile territory, he absolutely did not recommend I go there, here he paused and waited for me to feel the full weight of his fully informed opinion, for some sign my thoughts had succumbed to the gravitational pull of his words. I stood still, between the rock of his will and the hard place of my conflicted desire to leave. Standing there I said nothing. But if your parents insist on this particular path, he added, I hope you'll keep me updated on what you hear there. So I was to be a spy.

An elder in the church approached me the Sunday after that and told me to look up his nephew David who was already a student where I was headed. A teacher at our school told me her younger sister was also attending there, a year ahead of me. And then I learned my first roommate would be the daughter of the editor of a prominent Christian news organization, another friend of my pastor's. I wondered if my pastor or his wife had arranged this, their hungry, interfering fingers always probing their way into so many details of my life. My roommate-to-be got in touch, then called me on the phone one day, asked me if I had a boyfriend, how many boyfriends had I had, did I want to hear about her boyfriend. So this was how it was going to be.

As it happened, my assigned future roommate had caught me in the briefest of windows when I did actually have a boyfriend – or something approximating that. A few weeks prior, when youth leader Mark—five years older than I—asked me on our mission trip if I was interested in dating him, I'd said yes too quickly, maybe to get it over with. I learned then he'd approached my father first, who, being pleased to be asked such a question Man-to-Man, immediately said "Sure" in our driveway one afternoon before returning to whatever task he was doing. Immediately after my assent to the honour of this relationship I felt a muddled mixture of relief and horror. I was now a mouse in a trap with a single square of quite questionable cheese. The fear of being owned and consumed again ascended, carrying burning bile through my oesophagus and into my mouth. I swallowed it down, I instinctively shrank from my new boyfriend in the days following, hardly spoke to him or even met his gaze, pretended not to hear him when he spoke, I was thinking, sifting, probing the alien planet of my own wishes, did I want this or didn't I? Frustrated by my mixed messages (why can't women just make up their minds?), he pulled the church van onto the side of the road near an overlook. "Valerie, can we talk for a minute?" We got out. The faces of the youth group stared at us greedily through the windows of the van, straining for a glimpse of their possible future. I tried to articulate the facts of my fear to my sudden boyfriend but I lacked the language. I had only the inadmissible evidence of my feelings.

"I feel somehow like you're asking something of me I'm not sure I can give yet."

"Oh, is that all? Don't worry. I know what I'm doing."

Did you get that? Men know what they're doing, and what they are doing is women, implied object, never subject. Women can be, we can be acted upon, but we cannot do, we cannot act. "I know what I'm doing." I heard these words again, verbatim, only a few years ago, when working with a Christian academic. The project he'd asked me to join seemed undefined as of yet. I couldn't understand my place in it, something again was off.

"Why am I here?" I asked. "I feel unsure of what exactly I'm contributing to this project."

"Don't worry. I know what I'm doing."

CHAPTER TWENTY-SIX

Again, this was presumed to be enough, his knowing, his perceiving, his contemplating, his decision to do or not to do, since a woman's knowing, also her un-knowing, these mean nothing, matter not at all. Again, I, passive object woman, was knowing and doing nothing. I was an item to be closely studied, claimed, handled, passed around, fought over, retrieved from the cupboard for ceremonial purposes.

One of the most difficult acts is leaving, in believing that I can go, I can exercise choice, free will. I too can act. It takes an act of enormous courage to discard the lie that I need these people, that person, that Man, the falsehood that without them I will be lost, that apart from them I should care that my roommate will think less of me, that without a man I will surely die. Now in the first week of my freshman year at university, I was talking on the phone to my youth group leader boyfriend. Mark mentioned he'd consulted our pastor about problems he was seeing with our fledgling relationship, failures he'd never brought up with me till now. This too was familiar territory and again I felt invisible, immaterial, uninvolved in my own life, un-doing, un-acting, drifting along in a current whose direction I could not choose. My only previous boyfriend, elder's son Joel, a similarly brief relationship in high school, had done the same. In his case he'd confessed to the church session that we had kissed, we had touched, we had briefly broken free in his car. He'd despaired that in this *He'd* gone too far, *He'd* stolen something from me, from my future husband, so *He* thought, and who else should *He* repent to except to a room of Men? Who else should debate and decide *His* forgiveness and *my* ensuing shame and worthlessness but Men? Joel soberly reported this piece of news to me after the fact, in one of the Sunday school classrooms before church, he pulled out a kindergarten photo of me, this was the picture of me he'd asked for and now kept in his wallet, he said "I've violated this little girl," I think he even cried at the thought. "Forgive me," he pleaded. "Slap me if I try this again. I give you permission to punch me."

I wasn't ashamed of what we'd done, what I had done. He had

behaved badly in some ways, details of which now rose to the surface of my cognition. I remembered he'd recited some line about how we were more mature than others our age, in some cultures people married very young, even at 13, he said. All this was manipulative, predatory, and I involuntarily shuddered at the sight of Joel's character filling out its fuller shape as he spoke. But I wasn't uninformed, I was no muppet. Despite my many desperate choices, I'd chosen to set Joel's stupid comments aside, I had consented, I had participated, I had for the first time in my life felt something of the possible lives lying dormant in my flesh, in my spirit. It was this beauty he was robbing me of now, in his hoisting of disgrace upon what I had considered holy, in his insistence that his own sexist guilt reign supreme in the portrait of our intimacy, in his recruitment of our Man-leaders to desecrate, to debase, to ruin my moment of hallowed hope. Now, in asking for my pardon, he sought my participation in my own undoing. This was unforgiveable. He disgusted me now, I found him repulsive and I told him so. I ended our relationship abruptly, and he despised me.

Now here I was, fielding the youth group leader's complaint, again passed through the sanctifying filter of the pastor's ear. Mark's beef was this, that in the first week of our relationship, I'd defied his casual order as we were helping a church member with some landscaping. I'd put a rock here rather than there, for no concrete reason except for something I'd heard in his voice. This he took to our pastor, concerned I was showing signs of being "un-submissive." Code for a woman acting without a man's approval, a woman presuming to know what she was doing and then doing it. He'd also reported how I'd said I was trying to love him, but that it took some effort. "He agrees with me, that all this is concerning," my so-called boyfriend said. "Well, maybe we should just break up then," I replied quickly. "Yes, probably so," was his reply. With this, I hung up.

That same night I panicked. On the one hand, this overbearing relationship had brought me only misery. In the few months we'd been dating, my now ex-boyfriend had wasted no time in asking me

CHAPTER TWENTY-SIX

to join a small group, led by Leah's parents, discussing a marriage book which advised a woman with a cheating husband to wait at home quietly, preparing his favourite meals. Entice him back with your appeal. Dress up in your most flattering outfit, make his home all clean and pretty, and he will come, he won't be able to resist the allure of home, it's what every man wants. Mark also had a horrid habit of blowing in my mouth unexpectedly while we were kissing, I the dry bones and he the breath of the spirit of life. This was hilarious to him and I'd said nothing, I'd let him do it, I'd sat there, silent as the grave. Then there were the times he had taken me out to dinner and hummed loudly over the bill, taking pains to make sure I knew that he'd not always be able to afford such extravagance. What an expense I was, he really couldn't carry on like this for much longer. The fact he'd selected the details of this date, that he'd ordered more food than I had, none of this seemed relevant. He knew what he was doing, it somehow followed that his feelings of failure were my fault. Another time we went to an outlet mall, a leather briefcase caught his fancy, and I stood for at least 15 minutes by the payphone while he argued with a customer service representative for an extension on his credit.

This unpleasant contact was nevertheless a link back to a hell I understood, I knew the rules, I had a sense of myself there. Who was I here, away from home, unattached? Who did I think I was? What did I think I was doing? I didn't yet know. Maybe it hadn't been so bad. Maybe I'd exaggerated his flaws. I started remembering some of the good times we'd had. He'd made me laugh occasionally. His parents seemed nice. Oh God. He was my only known anchor, holding me to the only territory whose terrain I had fully mapped. If I let go, I would spin off, into what I didn't know. I had left home, finally, yet I could envision nothing ahead of me, I had no sense of what any woman did apart from her family, apart from the people who refereed her life. I'd never met any such woman, I couldn't picture her in my mind, I couldn't locate even a mustard seed of faith in her existence.

I began calling Mark's pager, calling, calling, calling. I dialled again and again, he didn't answer, didn't ring me back, why should he, what obligation did he have to me anymore now, what does any man owe a woman he is no longer chasing. Yes, I was spinning away, I was out of control, I couldn't breathe. I lay on the floor of the bathroom all night, an empty shell. I walked around spiritless for days, sequestered myself in my room during all the freshman orientation events, scanned the pages of the books I'd brought to locate myself in more familiar worlds, while everyone else eagerly formed shiny new connections, found their people, leaned in eagerly. One evening my mom called to say she'd found a notebook of this ex-boyfriend's, left accidentally in the church kitchen, pages and pages of furious prayers. "Please help me not to hate her so much."

27

Christian Reconstruction means the reordering of every area of life and thought in terms of the whole word of God. Postmillennialism is the application of the biblical premise of victory. We are promised victory that the kingdoms of this world shall become the kingdoms of our Lord… Christians are going to exercise dominion in every sphere of life and thought. The church is not the only place for us to be Christian. We are to be Christians in every sphere and to bring every area of life and thought into captivity to Christ.

— *An Interview with R. J. Rushdoony,* The Counsel of Chalcedon, *1988, Issue 2.*

In this explosive book, Francis Schaeffer shows why morality and freedom have crumbled in our society. He calls for a massive movement- in government, law, and all of life – to re-establish our Judeo-Christian foundation and turn the tide of moral decadence and loss of freedom. A Christian Manifesto is literally a call for Christians to change the course of history – by returning to biblical Truth and by allowing Christ to be Lord in all of life.

— *'Publisher's Description,* A Christian Manifesto *by Francis Schaeffer, 1981.*

Within the first few months of my freshman year at Christian university, one of my fellow incomers left the campus permanently after hitting his girlfriend. We heard this only through whispers, no public announcement was made, no opportunities were signposted for education or counselling on intimate partner violence, its various forms. I didn't have the expectation of any of this support, mind you, but thought only, this is a place where these things also happen, girls are harmed here too. After this, I began to see more of the same patterns and people I thought I'd left at home and I worried about my slowly widening world. During certain times in the week, men and women students were permitted to mix in each other's single-gendered dorms. These set hours on weekends we called Open Dorms, a phenomenon fairly common across religious higher education in the United States. Some took this quite literally. One night, early in that first semester, I was in bed, reading, I fell asleep and awoke to a boy I hardly knew sitting in my desk chair next to my bed, staring at me. He'd broken no rules, technically speaking, as far as I knew he'd followed proper procedure – the dorms were open. He liked watching me sleep, he said, he hoped we could talk now I was awake, get to know one another.

So this was the behaviour of certain students. Then there were certain professors. As part of the scholarship I was awarded towards tuition, I was required to take leadership classes alongside 11 others, half of us women, a show of faux equality that also permeated the rest of the campus. The first semester of these classes was led in part by Henry Krabbendam, a minister in the Orthodox Presbyterian Church who had signed the Coalition on Revival Manifesto alongside my pastor in 1986. In one session with us future leaders he spoke at length about the importance of women accepting the necessarily long absences of their leader husbands, whose crucial work would by necessity cost us and our future children, a sad but nevertheless entirely necessary price. That semester, we were reading the biography *Malcolm X*, and Krabbendam pointed us to Betty Shabazz's example, in this way

CHAPTER TWENTY-SEVEN

clarifying his interpretation of this book's takeaway for us women. "You are present when you are away," Shabazz is known to have said, of her history-making husband.[113]

I was the one who wanted to be away. I was by then rushing out of the room after every class to avoid the gathering storm cloud of a certain small set of man-boys on our liberal arts campus who'd spotted in me something they could commandeer in the service of their ambitions. I was doing well in certain classes by all appearances, I came from certain stock, and as always this constituted a target on my back. In one Biblical languages class full of future seminary students, our professor moved along each row, calling out our names, signalling us to read out our translations one line of text at a time. This was a painful exercise which involved skipping over the majority since they hadn't done the work. I realized after a short time that some of these low-achieving pastors-in-training had somehow learned which church I'd come from. They materialised and circulated, orbited around the pull of my gravity, sized up the seize.

One particular man, a senior, asked me to come round to his off-campus trailer for "a little get-together of people in our class." I stupidly went along, keen to make more friends, I suppose. He and his brother and three other man-friends—ardent fans of theologian Meredith Kline—quizzed me for several hours about my childhood church and my beliefs, which hymn book was I accustomed to using and why, what did I think of this or that theological movement, had I heard of this and that Man, this Man said this, that Man said that, what do you make of all the Many things Men say. They even tried to send me home with books to read, Man's ultimate intellectual squash. At least I managed to refuse the volumes they piled in front of me on the table, a meal of Man-words I hadn't asked for and didn't want. I felt these books and all their questions again shoving me down as I'd been so many

---

113 Rickford, R. J. (2003). *Betty Shabazz, Surviving Malcolm X: A Remarkable Story of Survival and Faith Before and After Malcolm X.* Sourcebooks, Inc. (p. 111).

times before, then on a bed, then in a car, now here in a chair, trapped in this trailer, one of them my only ride back up to campus. At one point, one of my classmates pulled a packet of mints from his pocket, took one and broke it in half, then offered it to me, isn't that what girls like, a portion of pleasure, never the whole.

About a month later, one of this band of brothers—a man-boy minister-in-training who was notorious for walking out of chapel in protest whenever there was a woman speaker—called my room and abruptly asked me to go to the Christmas formal. Refusing outright was still not a safe possibility in my mind, but neither did I want to go anywhere with a man like him. I lied quickly and easily, saying thank you so much for asking me, but I'm going with someone else already, so sorry I already have a date. When I passed him on campus after that, his pale and sensitive face turned bright red, he rushed by, he seemed lost for words, he never again opened his mouth to me after that, what else could he possibly have to say, what conversation can be exchanged with any woman who isn't a prospect, an opportunity to take, to confiscate, comMandeer. Poor man. He'd have looked so good and felt even better with me around, and my refusal to perform as willing prop had utterly shamed him. The singular pane in the window of my perceived usefulness had shattered, and he left me alone after that.

Where my Reconstructionist pedigree seemed to attract some, it appeared to repel others. Another man-student two years above me walked over to me in the dining hall one day, asked me if I was from *that* church, then pumped his fist aggressively in response after I said, simply, "Yes?" I learned then he was from a church in California, in Rushdoony country, from a community who disavowed Reconstructionism yet behaved in ways that seemed to me nearly indistinguishable from it, organising public demonstrations against same-sex marriage, working to initiate what they saw as moral reform, their aim the redemption of the city, then the country, perhaps the world. I began to perceive, then, two factions who seemed to despise each other. On the one side were the hard-core triumphalists I could easily spot, working to rebuild some Old

Testament version of a theocracy. And on the other, the soft-core culture warriors, ambassadors, influencers, that more dominant strand on our college campus, those who would infiltrate and impact every corner of the world, transforming it for heaven's pleasure. The means for this was not law but rather some concept of grace embedded in cultural activity. Through such divinely blessed human enterprise, led by the most gifted among us, they would mend nature's brokenness, amass a God-honouring empire.

I began to see this play out in many of my classes, especially in one set of freshman classes called Self in Society, taught by several different professors who each brought their own flavour to the subject. I knew enough to stay away from the sections taught by the Reconstructionists on campus – also I hoped to hear something different than the same old something. Yet what I found seemed in the end more of the familiar, with different branding. My section was taught by a man related to the college president, who told us his qualifications were simply these: That he had been "heavily" and "deeply" involved in many "spheres of influence," and that he'd given all this cultural engagement stuff "a great deal of thought." In his class, we were pushed to examine how every activity here and now, every future task ahead of each one of us, all was to be infused with the aroma of redemption and sanctification. By means of this Theology of Work, we would bring health, we would bring wholeness, we would make things right. What's more, our work would—so long as it was kingdom-work™—be eternal, permanent. Are you "called" to be a mathematician, an artist, a journalist, a teacher, a plumber? Whatever plumbing you do, do your plumbing as unto the Lord, and he will establish your pipes, your toilets, your sinks, yea even your dishwashers and washing machines, both now and forevermore. Plunge the world's toilets for Christ! It's not enough to do your job well. Take every square inch of pipework captive for him, expand and brand, employ the finest plumbers in the land, by this shall Christian credibility and influence be restored in Western society. What's more, in this class, we were no longer Christians—he discouraged us from using this word—we were to be culture combat soldiers on a transformative mission. Our teacher encouraged us to come up with alternative labelling, some clever marketing of our Mandate, he particularly liked one keen student's suggestion. Followers of The Way. The promise of God saving our best and brightest output for the new heavens and earth would spur us on. I wondered, then, as I'd wondered so many times before, what work would be preserved and which would be burned away, what of the handiwork of those who could do little more than scratch their daily survival from the dust. And what of me, what of my many unmemorable recitations of all the slanted history I'd memorised, perfect scores on pointless exams, each essay an account of what my teachers wanted to hear, all those meaningless words bubbling up out of my scramble for survival, my angry and unsettled heart.

For this class, we were required to write several critically "reflective" essays exposing our problematic family patterns, since, after all, Christian culture wars begin in the home. Perhaps some of my classmates embraced this honestly – as for me, I was reluctant to talk so openly with any man, especially one I barely knew. More than this, I had not the slightest idea where to begin dissecting the layers of my upbringing, so my essays for our self-credentialed man-professor were nothing more than further pure performance. So convincing was I that our professor took me aside one day and asked if I'd consider helping him home-school his kids, an offer I immediately declined. For our final group assignment, which extended our redemptive vision to the wider society, I chose a project exploring environmental concerns in the surrounding city. Two man-classmates asked me if they could join me, okay, fine, I thought, don't be so cynical, I said to myself, give them a chance. One never materialised to do any of the work, the other likewise leaned heavily on my labour, he was more of an "ideas man," he said. I stayed up all night the evening before the deadline, finalising our video, I cursed myself into the early hours, wading through the muck of

CHAPTER TWENTY-SEVEN

the exploitative dynamic I had fallen into once again, one I was completely weary of. Was the whole world to be like this?

Carrying the weight of the ever-heavier responsibility of Taking Dominion, delegated by yet more patriarchal overlords—young men who were later hand-selected for special mentoring by our self-credentialed Brofessor—I continued to keep to myself, I stayed close to a few friends on the margins, with them I sensed the security of limited attention. Matthew drove up on the pretence of visiting me a few times, insisting we attend a basketball game, or some other similarly public event, presumably so he could spy out this new territory for his uses. This was part of an existing pattern all too familiar to me. At my high school job, on occasion he'd show up for a quick hello and a scan of the premises for any new womanly faces he hadn't seen on his last visit, well, who is this, you'll have to introduce me, Valerie. Then one day, my old high school friend Alexander called my campus switchboard, was connected to the phone extension in my room, he asked if I'd like to meet him and Leo at the two-dollar movie theatre halfway between our two campuses. By this time, Alexander had been writing me for some time, regularly, as soon as I'd arrived on campus. I bring this up as an afterthought because it has only just occurred to me, the fact of all those letters that even then barely registered. Though each one reached my campus mailbox, though I felt a sense of comfort at the sight of every envelope's arrival, though I read them all carefully, keeping every page carefully in a shoebox, Alexander's words made no lasting impression on my unreachable consciousness. My eyes scanned the pages, but it was as if I were reading something written in an unfamiliar foreign language, a tongue in which I had no proficiency, no schemata onto which Alexander's words could fix themselves, incorporate into. I could notice only what I expected to see, I was unable to see what I had never noticed.

Still, there is something a great deal more potent in the messages communicated by physical presence than in mere text. So when Alexander called, I said yes, of course, I was eager to see the two brothers, let's catch up, tell me all about what you've been doing. That night when I pulled my car in to the theatre parking lot, I saw not just the brothers waiting there but someone else they'd brought along. "Valerie, this is my girlfriend," Alexander said happily, proudly, gesturing to the figure next to him. "Good for him," I remember thinking, nothing else of substance, we watched a film, I can't remember which one, we drove our separate ways. Hope that never rises cannot fall.

28

Two of my friends suffered nervous breakdowns from the stress and persecution stemming from our activities [on the Birch Society]. Another became an anti-Semite. Still another went down to an alcoholic's grave. The great majority of the conservatives did survive this warfare, however, by becoming "serious Christians." Our anti-Christian enemies first took away our reputations, and then, not satisfied, they destroyed our careers... The movement is marching toward Biblical law, the home school movement, the Christian Coalition, the Promise Keepers, and other parachurch endeavors. We are winning and will continue to win, because we are willing to die for our cause.

– Ellsworth McIntyre, 'Oh, Say Can You See,' *Chalcedon Magazine*, 1 January 1998.

I observed a Promise Keepers conference that began with the sound of a trumpet assembling corporate worship, and the 10,000 men packed in the arena shouted out at the top of their lungs in response to Jehovah's call. It was a great victorious roar claiming the crowned rights of King Jesus and His justice over that arena and that city. Such a call should have been followed with "A Mighty Fortress" or "Christ Shall Have Dominion."

– Stephen R. Turley, 'Worship and Warfare: Recovering the Dominion Mandate in Worship Music,' *Chalcedon Magazine*, 1 May 2004

In October of 1997, the deeply divided school board of Ft. Myers in Lee County, Florida voted to adopt a Bible-as-history curriculum, covering the Old and New Testaments, developed by the *National Council on Bible Curriculum in Public Schools*. Among this council's board members was Howard Phillips of the U.S. Taxpayer's Party, close friend of my pastor.[114] Providing foundation for this manoeuvre, James Dobson's *Focus on the Family* had, in the year prior, distributed a curriculum folder recommending the explicit teaching of Bible as fact in state schools. So, for many in the Christian Right, this seemed a significant win.

Still, all was not well among the dominion-seekers. The Right was fracturing, and Phillips and some of his die-hard cronies had fallen out, following his break with the Republican party. Even some of the most conservative leaders in groups like the Christian Coalition were expressing willingness to support a pro-abortion candidate for the presidency, a compromise too far for Phillips and Dobson, who united briefly in protest. James Dobson went so far as to cast a protest vote for Howard Phillips, against Bob Dole in the 1996 US presidential election, which won him some praise from my pastor. But this partnership wouldn't last. The Republicans managed to persuade Dobson back into their fold in 1998, promising him that Christian conservative concerns would once again be top of the priority list.[115] Together with Phillips, our pastor and his hard-core Reconstructionist pals held their moral line. That year, *Reason* magazine documented some of the movement's internal quarrels, quoting from radical Reconstructionist George Grant's book *Changing of the Guard*:

> But it is dominion that we are after. Not just a voice. It is dominion we are after. Not just influence. It is dominion we are after. Not just equal time. It is dominion we are after.

---

114 *Florida Citizens Challenge Unconstitutional "Bible History" Classes | American Civil Liberties Union*. (1998, February 2). ACLU. https://www.aclu.org/other/florida-citizens-challenge-unconstitutional-bible-history-classes

115 Goodstein, L. (1998, March 23). Religious Right, Frustrated, Trying New Tactic on G.O.P. *The New York Times*. https://www.nytimes.com/1998/03/23/us/religious-right-frustrated-trying-new-tactic-on-gop.html

CHAPTER TWENTY-EIGHT

> World conquest. That's what Christ has commissioned us to accomplish (p. 50).[116]

This was my second year at university, and I was still doing well in my classes, finding my way, the classroom being one place I'd always known how to navigate. A model Christian pupil, I memorised ideas, terms, filled my head with arguments without any idea of their meaning in the wider world, I studied my professors' interests, I followed the lines of their reasoning and I set down certain concepts on paper in such a way as to fill them with confidence in the effectiveness of their teaching. What was the point of all this beyond self-preservation I couldn't have told you then. The close of each week of classes seemed an acceptable resolution, the completion of each exam its own end, each notebook I filled with urgent shorthand, each assessment returned to me with praise, I piled these up in stacks, a barricade of self-determination against looming kingdom comMandeering. For while Christian leaders on the national stages quarrelled and set their sights on the reclamation of land they considered theirs by divine right, the men in my life carried on seeking more immediate dominion over me. And not just me, of course not. Close to 800,000 men of the Promise Keepers movement gathered in a mass spectacle in 1997 at the National Mall in Washington, D.C. to freeze-frame Biblical™ manhood, to reclaim it, to urge each man to sit down with his wife, to repent of the mistake of allowing her to lead their family and to take charge. I'm not telling you to ask, I'm urging you to take, PK leader Tony Evans declared.[117] "We're in a war, men," wrote his compatriot Bill McCartney, "whether we acknowledge it or not. The enemy is real, and he doesn't like to see men of God take a stand for Jesus Christ and contest his lies."[118]

---

116 Olson, W. (1998, November). Reasonable Doubts: Invitation to a Stoning. *Reason*. https://reason.com/1998/11/01/invitation-to-a-stoning/

117 Spalding, J. D. (1996, March 6). Bonding in the Bleachers: A Visit to the Promise Keepers – Religion Online. *The Christian Century*, 260–265. https://www.religion-online.org/article/bonding-in-the-bleachers-a-visit-to-the-promise-keepers/

118 McCartney, B. (1996). 'Seeking God's Favor,' *Seven Promises of a Promise Keeper*, p. ix-x.

On my college campus, the stairwells of my residence hall building were among the spaces where certain men set up shop, strumming their guitars and crooning to any passing woman, their voices echoing up and down the five floors of the building where I lived, sirens on the stairs. One night, I was up late studying alone in the hallway so as not to disturb my sleeping roommates. A band of boys, eight or ten of them, all in masks, appeared through the door to the stairwell and motioned for me to be quiet, one told me to wake up a particular girl. The sight of them, the sound of their words soldered my flesh to the floor. Any thoughts of saying no, yelling, even just running to my room, none of these even entered my consciousness as possibilities, perhaps I thought I'd go in and ask their target what she wanted me to do, perhaps not even that, my mind seemed empty of thoughts. I know for sure only that eventually I got up, I opened their victim's door and called her name, in so doing I made myself their accomplice, a witless weapon of white male supremacy. They pushed past me, they rushed in to carry out their aggressive assault on a woman who'd somehow offended them, claiming later it was nothing more than a harmless prank and anyway, Valerie opened the door.

Things were about to go from bad to worse. That boy from my church-school, Luke, having become a man, now again he followed me, enrolled in the college I'd been attending, he ingratiated himself to my friends, pushed his way back into my life, extended the boundaries of home, redrawing the borders so as to encompass whatever small steps I was taking towards independence. Luke brought with him the latest news, he wasted no time in telling me, that my ex-boyfriend, youth pastor Mark, was now dating a woman attending another church in our micro-denomination, they'd been set up by our pastor's brother-in-law, it's serious, Valerie. When I heard this, I set my face like flint then casually excused myself to the bathroom and cried wildly, tears of fear, sadness, rage, so many emotions tangled up and pouring out of me like battery acid, they burned my eyes, they stung my face. How quickly men move on,

CHAPTER TWENTY-EIGHT

how far behind I was in understanding what any of this meant. I stared at my stricken self in the mirror, I composed myself, I sealed myself off again. "I'm going to marry Valerie," Luke told his roommate, this I later learned. Many years after, this roommate would tell me his reply, words whose revelatory, revolutionary meaning I am only just now, as I'm writing, finally catching sight of. "But does she know that?"

I didn't know that. I didn't want that. In high school, with Matthew I'd tagged along at times to places like Luke's mother's apartment. She was a kind and altogether refreshingly odd woman who didn't seem to fit in anywhere. I witnessed how Luke blamed her for his father's affair, was openly cruel to her, took offense at her strangeness that threatened to sully his social position. This was how he signalled to everyone he was nothing like her, unlike her he was worthy of inner circle attention, the further he moved from his mother the closer his redemption from the sin of being born to such a weird, unwanted woman. One afternoon we'd all gone round to watch a film, she brought in a glass dish of chilled prawns and cocktail sauce, an extravagant snack. "No one wants your food," Luke said cruelly, rolling his eyes. He too had absorbed this tenet, that all earth's problems are somehow rooted in women.

At university, Luke began fostering an especially close relationship with one of my best friends. He told me he was going to buy her an expensive piece of camping equipment for her birthday, some kind of compression sleeping sack. I tried to warn her then, watch out, I said, with Luke any gift like this is a carrot on a string, tempting you toward places you'll regret going. But she didn't understand, she found what I said strange and interfering, it's just a piece of kit, Valerie. Luke flirted with my roommate also, he asked her all manner of personal questions when he rang our room before eventually asking for me, so much so that she began to think he was interested in her, that he was asking to speak to me only as a courtesy, the empty privilege of old friends and whatnot. She asked me to mention her reciprocating feelings to him, see if he was genuinely interested. In this way, Luke subtly separated me from my women friends, placing his gifts, his compliments, his body between me and them, creating conflicts and situations I found difficult to cope with. I soon learned from a man-classmate that Luke was telling all his friends I was off limits, I'd been marked, he'd called first dibs. A group of us were chatting about this and that in the lobby one afternoon, and Luke mentioned offhand that people who grew up outside of our church-school couldn't really understand people like him, people like me, people like us, we the people, "That's why most of us, that's why we will likely marry someone from our church." Luke enrolled in some of the same classes as me, asked me to help him study for quizzes, for tests, I began selecting my classes almost solely on the basis of escaping him, no easy task at a tiny liberal arts college where all majors shared certain core subjects. On a campus such as ours, set on a hill, there was no escaping a stalker. And going home to my other microcosm for weekends, holidays, seeing any school friends meant seeing him again too. Around these familiar friends, Luke was especially confident, having seized a social rung he considered superior to mine, now he would hang over me, lord over me from his higher position, prepare for the pounce.

Once, when giving me a lift home, he smirked and murmured intimately, perversely, "Ah, I could kidnap you now, you know." One New Year's Eve, we were all together, our pastor's two sons, the eldest's girlfriend Sarah, Matthew, Luke, Luke's ex-girlfriend Anna. And me. Matthew had brought along an expensive bottle of champagne his father had given us all to share, as he often did. "Who knows what might happen now," Luke laughed, trying to catch my eye. How uncomfortable could he make me, how overtly could he dangle secrets of our certain future together in front of me, hinting at them, teasing and torturing me, never saying too much lest I be able to name and dismiss his plans. He knew exactly what he was doing. From the reactions of our friends, it seemed clear our group spoke about all this when I wasn't there. That same Christmas holiday, he casually announced that he'd dreamt about me the night

CHAPTER TWENTY-EIGHT

before. "I was putting you to bed, Valerie, tucking you in. What do you think it means?" Everyone laughed at my discomfort. Poor Valerie, she has no idea, does she? When summer came Luke asked my father for a job – my father ignored my wishes, my pleas, and promptly hired him. "I can't make important decisions based on your whims," he said.

I sensed again the world was shrinking, my life was closing in on me, I daily felt that familiar yet still unwelcome tactile sensation, the pressure of my entire body being crammed through a tiny crack in the wall, in the floor, concentrating in my tongue. It often kept me up at night, I couldn't shake it, I rarely slept more than an hour or two at a time. Finally, one evening we were all in the campus dining hall for some social occasion, a residence hall concert as I recall. I sat with my friends, and Luke sought me out and joined us, behaving in his usual odd ways, with a subtle possessiveness, always indirectly. When one friend offered to get me a drink, he said, "No, it's better if I get it." Another friend reminded me of a shared joke, something Luke immediately felt compelled to outdo, to redirect my view of the past towards something from earlier times, when only he'd been there. It was all too much. I confronted him then, demanded his honesty, no more of this thinly concealed, strategic flirting, these innuendoes which I was constantly prevented from looking straight in the eye, information I was denied the privilege to access let alone dismiss. "What do you think is going on here?" I asked. "I want you to say the words." He was startled, unprepared for my initiative. "Not here," he said. "Not here. Come to my room tomorrow and we'll talk."

It was the weekend, open dorms again. I had been to Luke's room only once before, when he'd moved in. This second time now, I didn't look around the room, I didn't make myself comfortable, I worried I might catch sight of some picture, some object of mine he'd somehow collected, some personal artefact that linked me and him. I'd have to ask for the item's return or torture myself later wondering whether he still kept it around. Staring straight ahead at him, interrupting his chit chat, I immediately moved to the only item on the meeting's agenda. "Well? What do you have to say?" I sat expectantly. Reluctantly, begrudgingly, then, Luke mapped out his hidden route for the two of us, It's all rather awkward your forcing it out into the open, Valerie. But okay, you've made me say it now. I thought we'd be friends, over time we'd grow closer, then all of the sudden, we'll realize, quite naturally, maybe even without saying anything, we'll find ourselves in love. See how it's already happened this way with two of our friends, they agree it'll be the same for us. The whole time he was talking, I sat still in the chair, expressionless, I didn't lean forward to show interest or backward to signal any sign of relaxation, I curled my fingers around the seat, I waited for a pause signalling he might be finished. When finally, he seemed to have said his piece, I responded immediately. I was clearer and crueller than ever I'd been in my life.

"No, never, I'm not interested in you that way. I have no respect for you, Luke, that's why. I only spend time with you when I'm completely bored, when I'm lonely and have no one else around."

This last set of digs I added after, hearing my first words, his face shaped itself into complete disbelief, he was incredulous, he gasped and even choked a bit as I began speaking, as I gained momentum in my short speech, what were these impossible words coming out of her mouth, was this some kind of joke. Who was this woman speaking so plainly, what inner world of thoughts and wishes dares to exist separate to mine? I left quickly afterwards, there was nothing more to say. Yet that night he called my room, to check again he'd heard me correctly, surely I couldn't have said what he thought I'd said, he must've misheard me. I dismissed him with one final and completely fabricated barb, the last defence I had in my arsenal, a weapon entirely beneath any semblance of dignity, yet one I was expert at using, the native language of our childhood: "My dad says I shouldn't date you."

One weekend a month or so later, Matthew drove up to visit with

CHAPTER TWENTY-EIGHT

some of our old crowd, said he'd heard I'd upset Luke, asked me what had gone wrong. Having taken hold of clarity in conversation with Luke, it was now growing more familiar to me. I picked it up again with conviction. I would be heard. He would hear me. "I will never love him," I said. "I will never marry him." "Don't be so sure," Matthew rebuked me, knowingly, sovereignly, in what, dawning suddenly on me, was nothing more than his typical way of talking down to me, of shoring up what Men know, what Men do on the basis of such knowing, of dismissing my certainty on any matter, waving it away like some pesky mosquito buzzing in his ear. I was enraged. But why the hell shouldn't I be sure about my own life, my own decisions, my own future? At that exact moment, another plinth propping up my faltering faith in our shared past cracked and shattered. I didn't know what might happen to me next, I still had no idea of possible future worlds, but I had never been more confident about what would absolutely not happen, not ever, not even over my dead body. I knew for sure I'd rather die than go back to any semblance of our shared past. I had never been so certain in my life, and this I held on to, my own knowing, the only substance of my hope. This was my beginning, and in the beginning, there began to be a little light.

That summer, I declined an invitation to the eldest pastor's son's engagement party on a boat owned by some of our wealthier church members, then I agreed to go to the beach on a childminding job rather than attend his wedding. I feared what Luke might do in either setting. Finally, in desperation, I feigned interest in a semester abroad. When Luke made arrangements to go as well, I stalled, I even at his request went to far as to give him a picture of myself to take with him—yes I'm still looking into studying abroad, yes, I'm still serious—then I backed out at the last minute, knowing his plans were too fixed to alter. Still, even from such a distance he tried to hold me down, sent strange and threatening e-mails certain nights after he'd clearly had too much to drink. My roommates conspired with me to avoid his persistent phone calls. "No, she's still not here. No, I don't know where she is. No, she can't call you back." With me they walked in falsehood, my foot hastened again after desperate deceit.

29

Sin and Eve have the penchant "to take over" in common... Just as was the case with her husband, what constituted Eve's sin in Paradise becomes a tendency with which the woman has to fight all of her life, the perennial propensity to take unilateral action and so to dominate. Against this backdrop Adam is charged not to yield to this tendency, but to resist it. Under no circumstances may God's authority structure be turned upside down. God gave him the authoritative rule in Paradise as a creation ordinance, and this ordinance does and must stand. Adam may not let himself be dominated, and in the process become a "weathervane," a "follower." He may never surrender his leadership responsibility. He must rule!

— Henry Krabbendam, A Biblical Pattern of Preparation for Marriage (Lookout Mountain, GA: Covenant College, 2000), p. 46.

During Luke's semester abroad, the world seemed to open up again. My roommate from my freshman year had gone on an extended trip overseas, and so I seized the opportunity to move into another room with two women with similarly introverted sensibilities. I settled again into the rhythm of my studies, I returned to cycling, this time with two other new friends, on our bikes we trekked every trail around the campus, we talked little and rode hard, only the terrain prompted any conversation, it was all so straightforward. One dry day we rode down a particularly steep and rocky hill, I came off my bike and gashed my leg open badly. We sat for a while there, I pressed down on the wound with a piece of cloth one of my fellow riders had torn off the hem of his shirt, and as soon as the blood began to clump and clot, we set off again, no one made a fuss, we carried on as we always did.

At the end of our ride, two of us made our way back into the dorm, having said our goodbyes to our companion who lived elsewhere. And where sometimes we carried our bikes up the stairs, this time we decided on the elevator, spying it waiting at ground floor unoccupied, a rare occasion as it was often broken or otherwise occupied. "Hold the door!" we heard a voice cry, and my friend pressed the button to let the caller in. A boy in our college's soccer team jersey stepped in alongside us and immediately eyed up my weeping leg. "Wow, what do you get up to?" he said. My friend looked sideways at me and then smiled toward the floor, at the stupidity of such a question, would you look at this fool.

This fool was John. I realized after that first meeting that I had a class with him, only because when next it met, after I pounded the table in frustration at a classmate's particular interpretation of whatever text we were reading, John leaned forward and tried to read my notes over my shoulder, then whispered something about how he found me interesting. This imposition my friend next to me attempted to disrupt with icy glares. "Stop stealing our ideas," she warned him. "Just who are you?" he asked me after class.

Yes, just who did I think I was? I was someone still looking for an exit sign, feeling around in the murk for an escape hatch, a way out. I was hunting for it, yet I didn't know what it might look like, I hoped I'd know it when I saw it. And as it happened, John appeared around the same time that one of my professors offered us students extra credit for taking his evening and weekend mini-course, Biblical Preparation for Marriage, and, after the conclusion of his lecture series, writing a lengthy response paper. I attended the course alone, same as I attended the rest of my classes, though at least half of the audience comprised the many already engaged-to-be-married college

CHAPTER TWENTY-NINE

couples, many of the remainder of us presumed to be in the marriage market. Over several long sessions, our professor spoke about the joys of the hetero-marital union, then veered into his true passions, the danger of women's domination, the importance of home-cooked meals on the table every evening—the family that eats together, lives at peace together—the necessity of children, he argued vehemently against oral contraception, what he called women's desire to "poison" ourselves with "those pills." The guilt got to me, fertile ground as I was. I was by then considering going on oral contraceptives to ease my unbearable monthly periods, the bouts of vomiting and pain that left me unable even to sit upright in a chair. I'd had to leave an exam halfway through, during one particular painful menstrual cycle, the muscle contractions were so severe. Not long after, our instructor having emphasized that birth control kills babies, I sat in the office of my gynaecologist and, against her advice, said I'd keep trying other methods of pain relief for now. My main lesson, though, from all this intensive marriage preparation, was that my being in that class sent another unintended signal. One evening, I was leaving the dining hall, a boy also attending saw me heading out and yelled out, "Hey, Valerie, wait and I'll walk with you. Let's go prepare for marriage!" Another fellow student asked if he could read my essay for the mini-course assessment after I completed it, "to see if we might be compatible." Then, not long after, one Friday my biking friend asked if he could tag along home with me that weekend and see my church-school pastor in action, Wow I didn't know you went to *That* church, Valerie. With these words, the figure of my friend morphed into Man, his request crushed me, not this again. Again, I was an access point. Again, a person in proximity to a site of perceived power. So it happened, that in my haste to put a warm body between me and all this, between me and Luke, between me and anyone else in invisible pursuit, in all this haste I stumbled into yet another trap. Here's how it happened.

John was in the year above mine, headed for theological seminary, like so many men among us. He was one of those man-boys who, lacking all confidence in his ability to be and do what Men were presumed to be and do, oozed nothing but. This was his pull, that he was loud and always laughing, he was fun and very funny, everyone knew when he was there yet none seemed to know him, he kept himself always available, courting everyone's attention while being simultaneously completely unavailable to any person. This was a dynamic I knew well, I'd dealt with before, and without being able fully to articulate why, I felt drawn to its familiarity. Yes, this is something I know. I can work with this, I can live with this. When first he came onto my radar, I noticed him sometimes having whispered conversations with a girl I didn't much know. "That's Heather, they recently broke up," a friend told me.

In all the time I knew him, John was entirely unreliable. I rarely knew when he might call or appear, he seemed perpetually threatened by the idea of giving any woman the privilege of counting on him. He swung between showering me with compliments and the magnanimous gift of his time and wallowing in insecurity about this or that, often disappearing for several days. Yet typically and predictably, he derived much of his energy from being around me and would eventually reappear. One weekend, when I was home, my mom found a picture of him, which one of my roommates had spotted in the discarded photos pile in the yearbook office. "You're welcome," my friend had said to me, handing it over. "Wow, he's so good-looking," was my mom's reaction. And then the supreme question, the only one she asked: "Is He interested in you?"

In the early weeks of our connection, John had the idea to run a marathon in my home city, a two-hour drive from the college, and so we started running together several times a week and then signed up for a few races as part of our training. When we met up for a casual run, we tended to go alone, just the two of us. He wanted to hear the story of my life, he said, yet he spent more time commenting than I did on talking, filling the space between us with words and more words, anything I said prompted some story of some noteworthy person he'd met, some special guy he knew, some deep reflection or question he puzzled over. I remember one particularly lengthy segment on his feelings of unworthiness in partaking of the Eucharist. But when it came to organised races, faced with such unmoveable scheduled activities, John nearly always invited someone else along, sometimes completely random people, a subtle reminder that if he absolutely had to be anywhere, it would never be solely because of any commitment to me, I must never get the idea either that he was there for me, nor that any absence could be interpreted as him letting me down personally.

One night close to the marathon, I heard a bang on my dorm room door. Someone had attached an elaborate, archaic notice written in curly Renaissance-style lettering, four men requested the honour of my presence at a performance the following evening in the campus auditorium. John's name was there, alongside three others of his friends, one of them the son of a Bible professor. I learned after that, that three other women had received similarly showy notices. We reported for spectator duty as requested, the four men appeared on stage in all their glory, performed some enigmatic script I can't now recall but which gave them endless amusement, finally together as one voice they simultaneously asked the four of us to attend the upcoming Christmas banquet with them. We noted they were careful to avoid any use of names, "We would like to invite you ladiesssss." It was up to us to infer, to presume which one of them was inviting which one of us. "I guess we're stuck together now," one of the other women said drily, on our way out.

Hiding in a crowd. Diffusing every interaction across multiple bodies. This method of John's was sorely tested for the marathon, as he couldn't drum up any interest from any other friends to join us, no matter how hard he tried. Even the week before, as we were sitting in the college dining hall, he stopped another girl walking past, "Hey, you like running, don't you? You interested in running a marathon with us?" On the day of the race, John's anxiety at the snare he'd set for himself was palpable. During our nearly four-hour run that Thanksgiving morning, he could bear to stay close to me for no more than five- or ten-minute increments. As he jogged alongside, I could see his eyes darting, eventually he'd vanish, perhaps he was in front of me, perhaps behind me, I didn't see him, I didn't look for him, I said nothing, I kept my regular pace, after a while he'd come back and crash into me with his presence once again, he like the ball on an elastic string, I the paddle he was hopelessly attached to, bolting out then springing back. Thunk, boing, thunk, boing, thunk, boiiiing. This is how it went.

On the evening of the Christmas formal, the Man-unit comprising John and his three friends waited together for us women—now an indivisible woman-unit—outside the banquet hall. We walked in together and awkwardly sat next to each man who had invited-not-invited us. If I'd thought ahead, if I'd dared, I would've invented some subtle disruption, sat beside the wrong man, oh I'm sorry, I thought you were my date not him, silly old me. Doing any such a thing, though, turning this Man-power play inside out so explicitly and forcefully on our dates, I wouldn't have dared to go as far as they. I knew the rules instinctually. Any semblance of equality between men and women on our campus was merely a pretence, and in some ways, this thin veneer of egalitarianism was worse than the overtly sexist hierarchy of my childhood. We could all attend the same classes, we all seemed to have the same opportunities, there were no explicitly gendered rules apart from the aforementioned closed and open dorms. Anyone could point to that and say, see? What more do you want? Still, there we were, doing this awkwardly contrived dance of dominance and submission, of ruler and subordinate, of hero and damsel, of kingdom-maker and kingdom-follower.

One semester, one of the women who'd been stuck together with me in the woman-unit ambitiously organised a women's evening discussion group in one of the classrooms. She invited one of the few women on faculty, and the agenda of the evening was something like this: An open discussion of what it's like being a woman on campus. I enjoyed the event, the mere fact of the meeting stirred something useful in me, though I recall little of what anyone said,

CHAPTER TWENTY-NINE

probably anything meaningful went over my head. But what I do remember is a certain group of uneasy man-students, who, set on edge by the exclusion of their man-bodies, paced the paths around the building, circled, fanned out, came back together, perhaps attempting by some supernaturally authorised osmosis to permeate the building's brick walls with their masculine aura. One man-friend was even openly sarcastic about the event to me. What do you women need to talk about anyway, all by yourselves? I shrugged. Why do you need to know?

Back now to the Christmas formal. The Man-unit had Manufactured the evening so that there would be no personalised contact, lest we get any ideas, lest we consider ourselves personally important in any way. The night was therefore completely uneventful – I remember only that the poor student receiving minimum wage to serve us replications of Renaissance recipes banged my head with a huge platter, yet in doing so gifted us with about 15 whole minutes of easy conversation. Can you believe what just happened? Poor woman, she must be feeling stupid now. Is your head ok? Are you sure? I once got hit in the head by something or other. Let me tell you about that time. Oh yes me too, here's my story about a related injury.

After the marathon and the Christmas formal, it took John several weeks to recover from these shows of possible commitment, to rebuild his fragile independence after such a blow, and I saw him little and heard from him not at all. One evening as a few of us sat talking in the residence hall lobby, a member of the banquet Man-unit laughed and told us shamelessly that he'd invited my friend to the banquet because she was his back-up girl, and "Back-ups sometimes need a little topping up." The Christmas break was coming closer, and so was Luke's impending re-entry to the country. A group of friends organised an evening out to the local theatre, to see the Nutcracker ballet. "Why not ask John," one of them said to me. Yes, why not see what the state of things was? By the time I called his room, John must've recovered a sufficient enough sense of manhood because to my surprise, he agreed. The evening of the event, though, again he acted strangely, over the course of the performance looking for some reason to be annoyed at me, when I didn't want to walk to the front and look down at the musicians during the intermission, he scoffed at my reasons. "They won't even notice us, they're used to people staring at them," he said.

After that, for the remaining days left in the semester, John completely ghosted me. I was of course by then used to him disappearing even for a few weeks at a time, but this was new. I could see he was actively avoiding me; I even saw him dash out of our dorm's lobby one afternoon as I entered. At some point before we were due to break up for Christmas, one of my friends confronted him without my knowing, forcing him by ultimatum to own up to me his true feelings. "I'll tell her if you won't," she said, deferring to him and to their secret shared knowledge, even in her intended loyalty to me. He rang me on the phone the afternoon of the day we were all due to leave for the Christmas holiday, asked if we could talk in the lobby. "I'm already down here, can we talk for a minute?" "Ok," I said, the meaning of his choice of meeting place registering inch by inch, as I stepped down the stairs, one by one. Why did I agree? Why did I subject myself to this? I was still in pursuit of my own knowing, I knew only that I'd rather face him than stay in this space of not-knowing.

I arrived in the lobby, we sat opposite one another on sofas next to the celebratory Christmas tree, lights and decorations, a joyous scene of one of our most sacred festivities. "I have to tell you something," he began. "I hoped I wouldn't have to, but I guess I don't want you to get the wrong idea. I just figured that you'd eventually get the message, that I wouldn't have to say it." He spoke so quietly and quickly I had to strain to hear him, I missed words, sentences, perhaps too my ears were blocking it out. Students bustled all around us, coming in and out, carrying bags and boxes, exchanging last minute Christmas presents, waving and hugging and calling goodbye across the room, Merry Christmas,

CHAPTER TWENTY-NINE

see you soon. Such a loud and public space, such was his selfishness that he'd situate such an intimate and painful, such a humiliating conversation in this crowd of witnesses, a cushion to shield him from any possible unpleasantness, any potential feminine outburst. What could I do except stare blankly, once again will myself to withhold any expression of objectionable womanly emotion? I mumbled something about how this was all fine, it's all fine, I don't care, whatever, I don't even know what you're talking about, I can barely hear you, blah blah blah. Just then, one of our classmates, someone we both knew well, saw us talking and jumped over from behind the sofa to sit next to John. "What are we talking about?" he said enthusiastically. I saw then the relief on John's face. Here was his hedge. "Nothing much," I said. "I've got to go."

That night my roommate confessed she'd known what was coming. She told me about her ultimatum, though she hadn't known when or how he'd handle things, but she'd seen me headed downstairs and realised that's what it was about, she'd thought this rejection would be better coming from John. All the human connections of my life were again in these ways debated and decided, Man-euvered in a closed court, outside my lowly jurisdiction. I was a tool, one in a set of many, fashioned, tested, tried, used at whim. I felt again that sense of internal vacancy, where would I go now, what would I do next, the future seemed again to me a blank wall, an empty room. Over the holidays, I didn't tell anyone at home what had happened, I wrote out a pile of separate letters to John, all the things I should've said but hadn't. But couldn't.

How dare you trample on my feelings in order to figure out your own.
How dare you presume I was so fragile as to expect immediate commitment.
Who do you think you are, thinking me incapable of sensing your rejection.
Only a selfish coward would risk leaving a friend so confused.
You speak as if I'm not clever enough to get your implied messages.

I see straight through you.
You aren't my friend.
You only want to use me.
You would've thrown me away without even bothering to tell me.
I hate you.
Fuck you, you fucking asshole.

I wrote each letter out, I held them in a bundle, I destroyed them, one by one. By the end of the two-week holiday, I'd decided to do what I did best. He'd never see how much he'd hurt me. I would cover my face, I would hide in secret places he could not see, surely the shadows would hide me and the light would again become night around me.

30

As to the unconscious way in which Dominionists "are there" in the world, how they habitually comport themselves, put aside for the moment authoritarianism, about which enough has already been said. Instead, let us focus on an element often overlooked by social scientists, namely, the heroic impulse.

— James Aho, Christian Dominionism and Violence, Oxford Research Encyclopedia of Religion, 2021.

I thought we were not going to talk about guys anymore – isn't there a better topic. Not for us who are just here for our MRS degree. I know it's important to have a social life, but is getting an education important to anyone on this hall? Ya, an education on how to get your MRS. This is the marriage mill on the hill.

— Statement by the Women of Third South, The Tartan, Covenant College Yearbook, 1994.

In 1998, our church magazine set forth the "rich heritage of Southern Presbyterianism," lamenting the progressing decline of the Presbyterian Church in America, most particularly its seminary president's willingness to accept broader interpretations of the creation narrative in Genesis 1. "There is one denomination that self-consciously seeks to hold to a strict subscription of the Westminster Standards," our church elder wrote, naming of course, our micro-denomination, singular bastion of faithfulness.[119] As my pastor very well knew, I was attending the college connected to the condemned Christian church denomination du jour. One weekend when I was home, he mentioned my college by name from the pulpit, his eyes scanned the congregation and met my gaze then, directly. Look what reprobates you're messing with, child. Look, little girl, at whose teaching is corrupting you. Everyone, observe how our daughter is defiled, see how she betrays us. The weight of Matthew's enrolment at a state university was seemingly undetectable on our pastor's scales of righteousness, disproportionately calibrated as they were by the sins of women. Still, I felt fully the sharp edge of his judgement, I was ashamed, I was still so far away from being able to shrug it off.

In the same issue of our church-magazine, another author announced the founding of a new seminary, Greenville Presbyterian Theological Seminary, and the installation of its first president, Joseph Pipa, whose son was also a student at my college. This young man was among those who attended the exclusive off-campus parties of the smugly rebellious, which I deliberately dodged. I can't claim any pure motives for this, likely I still thought myself superior, but also it seemed to me that the women of that world, even in their insurrection, were just as led here and there by the whims of men as those of us who bowed and scraped in submission. And here was the real meat of it for me, that they alone bore any social consequences, we passed their names around the campus eagerly like freshly minted money, did you hear about Jo's late night massages, did you hear about what Hannah does when she drinks, here again is the name of this and that individual woman and what she has done, repeated many times over until we couldn't think of one without the other. In all our talk, the looks we shared, the general atmosphere on campus involved treating certain women as aberrant beasts among

---

119 Otis, J. (1998). 'The Rise and Fall of Southern Presbyterianism,' The Counsel of Chalcedon, Issue 3.

CHAPTER THIRTY

a host of ethereal maidens. As for the men, these same desires for the thrill of transgression were unmarked and unremarkable, excusable, what they did was nothing more than nature. I sometimes heard men talking together after the latest revelry, I saw how they too disregarded their own actions, how they held up their hands, gesturing their bemused un-involvement, it's these wild women and their appetites, look what they involve us in.

What mattered more among men was what they believed. Among Joseph Pipa, Sr.'s desirable qualities was his commitment to a strictly literal interpretation of the creation narrative in Genesis 1 but likewise his affirmation of a belief close to the heart of my pastor and his pals, the propensity in women to be more easily deceived than men, and, as a result, the need for her to stick to domestic duties.[120]

> GPTS, with its staunch commitment to Old School Theology, stands as a beacon on the vast landscape of American seminaries. All those who identify themselves with Reformed Theology should enthusiastically support the work of this seminary.[121]

Meanwhile, on the larger stages of the Christian Right in the United States, various leaders were likewise self-identifying as faithful traditionalists. James Dobson, president of *Focus on the Family*, was the closing speaker at the Southern Baptist Convention in Salt Lake City, which that year amended its statement of essential beliefs to include a definition of the proper biblical family. This prescribed a woman's gracious submission to her husband, she having "the God-given responsibility to respect her husband and to serve as his helper in managing their household and nurturing the next generation."[122] The names on the committee proposal, which was soundly approved, included mostly men and two women, the latter identified principally

---

120 'Faith and Practice with Dr. Joseph Pipa,' Faith and Practice podcast, 12 February 2020. https://www.sermonaudio.com/solo/gpts/sermons/2142015184229/
121 Auton, L. (1998). 'Rebirth of the Old School,' *The Counsel of Chalcedon*, Issue 3.
122 Southern Baptist Commission. (1998, June 9). *1998 Report of the Committee on the Baptist Faith and Message*. https://www.utm.edu/staff/caldwell/bfm/1963-1998/report1998.html

as "homemaker," where the men's brief biography contained only their leadership roles.

As these movers and shakers moved and shook, in the microcosm of my existence, things with John turned out better than I could've hoped, though my hopes were hardly a measure of what was good or healthy. When first I came across John again on campus, I could quickly see he was shocked by my nonchalance, my casual and vaguely friendly greeting, as if nothing much had happened, Why yes, I had a wonderful Christmas break, the happiest really, what classes are you taking, I've got to go now. I hurried away. I didn't signal my plans for any future meeting, I didn't say "See you later," I didn't do anything beyond what I'd said and done to any other person on campus to which I was acquainted but mostly disconnected. John's surprise at this made me feel safe again, the walls I had constructed were sturdy, my camouflage complete. Only something else happened next, something that I should've seen by now, really I should have seen it coming.

John had expected me to be clingy, heartbroken, depressed, perhaps to plead with him, he'd anticipated feeling the satisfaction of all that, see how women want me, need me, see how desirable I am to them, see how again I have taken the reins of rejection, mastered, ruled. See what a winner I am. In the absence of all that, his interest in me was almost immediately rekindled. What does she know that I don't? By that point, Luke had returned to campus from his semester overseas, and he called me one evening, full of fresh one-upmanship about what life was like over the ocean, altogether different from everything you've ever known, you'd have had to be there to understand, Valerie, what a shame you weren't. Then to the point. He said he'd heard I was somehow involved with John. "Do you love him?" he asked directly, feeling in himself some god-given right to demand access to my emotions, my decisions, my intent. But I too could be direct, and I faced him head on. "Yes," I said, without a second's hesitation, the question of whether or not what I felt was love meant absolutely nothing to me, this solution to the seemingly

CHAPTER THIRTY

unsolvable problem of Luke rolled off my tongue effortlessly. "Oh. Are you sure?" "Yes," I said again. "Yes." "Well, he's a good guy," Luke said then, though he knew nothing really about John at all beyond a certain set of superficial social traits.

From this I knew he'd leave me alone, at least for a while. Luke had once told me about a certain guy's code, a pact that he and his "brothers" on his residence hall had apparently formed, that they'd not get in the way of any of their fellow hero's intentions towards any woman. What's more, they'd let no other man so much as glance in her direction. "Any girl any one of us is interested in is totally off limits." At the time, he'd dropped this detail ever so casually. I was meant to know this group of popular guys on campus all recognised his claim on me, he intended me to marvel at this stamp of legitimacy, but also to feel the weight of the veiled threat therein, to see there was no way out, no one else would have me, I would be with him or I would be alone. Only now, here I was with my spanner, unexpectedly clogging up the gears of his cunning contraption. As I placed the phone back on its receiver, with it I laid down all that pressure, all the burden of Luke disappeared into the dial tone along with his voice, down the cord of the phone, into the wall, out into the street and into the night. I breathed out endlessly, I leaned back in the chair, I sat silently and still before the substance of all that freedom, fleeting as it was.

After that, the dysfunction between John and me multiplied. Recent weeks had taught me that I had some leverage here. The more nonchalant I appeared, the more he would want me, and the further away Luke would remain. John began again to circle me, to sniff and to spy, to call my room and then occasionally to disappear. I held my nerve, I showed not the least amount of expectation, I pretended not to recognise his voice on the phone, I acted as if I didn't see him in any room I entered, unless he came over to me I pretended he didn't exist. I could see all this only increased the strength of my magnetism, he grew more and more desperate to see me interested again, to see me subdued to his disinterest. One evening he showed up unexpectedly at the door of my room during open dorms, the first time he'd ever done so. One of my roommates was standing out of the line of his sight as I opened the door, she silently beamed and made all kinds of happy gestures that only I could see, Valerie, just look what a well-favoured boy has graced you with his presence.

That night, as it happened, one of my marked essays for a Bible class—a core requirement for every student's degree—was on my desk, the professor's praise in red pen across the top. As John walked around the room, he glanced down. "I've never had that kind of feedback before," he said simply. "I think that professor just likes girls better." The next day he caught me casually in passing in the lobby, suggesting we play tennis. I was happy to join in anything physical like that, though I had little skill for this particular sport. So that afternoon we made our way to the college courts, I with my borrowed racket, he with his need to recover manly ground. I'd prepared for a friendly game, but I saw quickly he was there to win – not just win but show me up. He celebrated each point against me to the point of cruelty, he laughed at my clumsiness, he hit the ball harder than was required, he gleamed with pride and satisfaction. He would see me suffer.

In the weeks that followed he upped the ante, he talked to me often about another of his particular talents, water-skiing, correcting my attempts to join in the conversation, my enthusiasm about my mom's expert ability to ski on one ski instead of two. "That's slalom skiing, don't you know that?" he mocked and laughed at me in my ignorance, incredulously, triumphantly, his smirks and taunts smacked against me, another round of the bloody knuckles I'd played in high school. Who would wince first? I was already faltering and he knew it, but I carried on, by my endurance I would gain my own life. What did I tell myself in all this? I had said no to other men, I assumed in myself a sense of personal choice, the overt act of choosing John, of considering and weighing up our shared interests and giving him time to grow up. In this way, I hid my misery even from myself. Maybe it was worse, likely my unhappiness was simply

CHAPTER THIRTY

irrelevant, like a putrid smell so common my nose could no longer detect it. That entire spring semester, our connection proceeded in this way, with no understanding between us except what was entirely unspoken, that occasionally we would spend time together, that most of the time we wouldn't, that he would keep taking from me until he was tired, that eventually he would again tire of what he could take.

That semester, we were in the same creative writing class. One evening our professor read aloud a poem he'd written about his late wife, chronicling the measure of his despair that he'd poisoned his marriage by persisting in his worry that he loved her more than she loved him, he'd always felt insecure around her, maybe she'd abandon him, he'd fixated on the fear that she was always on the edge of leaving, he'd clung to her to keep her close, to keep her from going away. Now she had gone. She had left. The classroom was mostly full of minimally rebellious creative types eager to prove their worth, they debated the rhythm of the piece, the parallelism of the lines, "I'm curious about your use of metaphor here," they said, "This is interesting word play in this line." I was sitting in the back, against the wall, John to my right. The words my professor read, his cadence in reading them, these sent up a flare I recognised, there it was in the room, all alight and approaching, it was spiralling towards me, it sunk into my gut, burning there against my flesh, I would be consumed. Help, help! I fought back tears of despair, I didn't cry but neither could I keep my face from falling, the dam was breaking, I hadn't prepared for this, I hadn't known it was coming.

The next day or a few after, our professor happened to cross paths with me in the library. John and I were both there, his favourite public study place.

"Are you okay, Valerie? I noticed you had a particular reaction to my poem in the last class."

I couldn't answer in front of John, of course I couldn't. Maybe I was even glad he was there to prevent my feelings from crystallizing into thoughts, into words. "Yes, it was a powerful poem. I understood it, that's the thing," I managed to squeeze this language out of my mouth without also weeping, a feat of mammoth emotional strength. He looked at me – my professor looked. And in that look I saw something I couldn't recall ever seeing before, that unique and altogether rare look of someone who sees. The face of a witness. A single kind and knowing expression can, in a mere moment, reach into the depths of a sad heart. This is done only by the sight of one's spirit, that incredible work of the inner eye, a vision that cannot be attained by any simple, step-by-step process, it cannot materialise at will, cannot be manufactured, faked, cannot be attained by violence. I'd carried on waiting for the meaning of my life in secret presents, a clear blue sky, that magnificent rhythm of bending my bike back and forth up a hill. Now here was another little thing, this momentary glance that carried with it every gift in the world.

About ten years ago, I wrote a trusted minister, asked him for advice, I'd been starting to work through the past, and I was particularly worried about the mental health of one of my peers from our church-school. How could I begin to make sense of all this, with this hurting person, about all these things I'd shut away? The Man-Minister forwarded my entire e-mail without warning to another Churchy Man I didn't know. Please can you advise this woman. She has moved on from it all. She has gotten over what happened in that Reconstructionist church. But this other person in her life is stuck, still angry, how sad she can't just let it go. I'd not said any of this, I saw in his words a statement of what I too was meant to do according to him, what I'd already been doing, what I'd been getting so very wrong. Just let it go. Why can't you let it go.

What does a person do when she has witnessed so much cruelty and despair, yet never been asked or allowed to speak about it, to recall it, to try to understand, to learn, even to heal from it? What becomes of a person when almost no one asks what this place and this people did to her and to her family and friends, when no one

CHAPTER THIRTY

thinks to question what the outcome is of such a place? What fruit grew from this, from you? These are the things about which almost no one inquires. Denied permission to record in the public memory what we have witnessed, we carry the stones of memorial in our bodies, documenting all we've suffered as a matter of historical record, an archive of the minutes of torment written into our very blood. The modalities of our memory are these: migraines, rashes and other skin disorders, digestive disorders, dental cavities, depression, insomnia, anxiety, allergies, cancer. When our voices are silent, when we cannot find the words, our bodies cry out, communicate in their own language that brutal history which our tongues have been forbidden from telling. In this way, on the evidence of all the layers of familiar bodily sensation, that deep cognizance of the gut, on the evidence of these two or three witnesses, they who hurt us will surely be condemned. Until then, some of us may even resist medical treatment, therapy, other forms of help, in this way we protest the erasure of the voice of our body, our only witness to that principal pre-existing condition that is the patriarchy. I tell you, if we become silent, our flesh will cry out. On the strength of all our corporeal testimony a matter shall be confirmed.

In graduate school, the symptoms of my lifelong chronic illness suddenly became much worse. Where I'd had episodes of sometimes severe symptoms here and there for as long as I could remember, I was now violently sick every few weeks, doubled over in pain and vomiting for hours. At my husband's insistence, I finally booked an appointment to seek some answers. The doctor who came into the examination room to see me, all those years later, did something only one other person, a previous college professor of mine, had done before. After ruling out cancer and other immediately life-threatening disease, after diagnosing me with a chronic autoimmune condition, this doctor now tended to my soul. Her words still ring in my ears: "A woman of your age shouldn't have these kinds of severe symptoms, this kind of debilitating disorder. What has happened to you, dear child? Who has done this to you?"

31

She shows her love for him, not only in sweet tokens of physical affection, but also in endearing practical ways as well. She tries to be sensitive to his moods, knowing that soft words turn away wrath. She provides what he needs both in health and sickness, and she cares for him diligently and tenderly when anything troubles him.

— Rev. Joseph Morecraft, 'A Full Length Portrait of a Virtuous Woman,' *The Counsel of Chalcedon*, 1999, Issue 1.

Racism exists on campus; racism is swept under the rug.

— David Yleah, 'Students Speak out on Diversity,' *The Bagpipe*, 1998, Volume XLIII, Issue 12.

Every patriarchal community establishes for itself a certain amount of formal education they consider acceptable for women. This can fall anywhere from zero schooling to so much as a postgraduate degree or elite professional qualification. But what does not vary is the primary purpose of a woman's education: to fulfil her duties of hearth and home and ultimately, to serve men, to attract and engage her husband, to hold his attention, to present herself as a shining trophy for him to carry about as he carries out his all-important work. And this shall be a sign unto all men that, having subdued their women, such men are kings, consummate governing authorities, fit to subdue

CHAPTER THIRTY-ONE

and rule the world. So it is that a woman raised by the patriarchy who dares to step beyond the bounds of acceptable education will inevitably schlep along with her the unwieldy baggage of false guilt and fear. She may pursue a degree but always with an internalised anxiety. She may get a paid job and secure her own financial independence but always with an eye towards the door. This is the internal push and pull that a woman must grapple with within herself, even if she has already physically removed herself from a place of control and harm. Even when she has set her face forward, there will always be someone and something pulling her back into the cage she was groomed for.

Even now, this dynamic still hunts me down, though it has at times taken on a slightly different flavour. A man-minister cruelly tells me on the phone that the feelings I'm facing, having returned to paid work after having a baby, what I name to him as a tangle of false guilt and postpartum depression, filling my pockets like stones, he says no, my anguish is rooted in a healthy "female" conscience whose longing is for home. I know this isn't true, I'm angry, but he's kicked at the very wound I brought to him for healing, he's commended the vulnerability I was so desperate to shore up. For the despairing woman, there would be no kindness from her friend. I had picked up the phone in hope; I now put it down with reinforced grief. On another occasion, when I talk about how a certain book helped me, as a teenager, to disavow the idea that women owe men obedience, a certain woman family member tells me that I should guard against un-submissiveness. A Christian research partner says to me how relieved he is to see my face, how tiring everyone else is, they tire me out, they don't understand, Valerie, can you say something to make me feel better. Another narcissistic man at church sighs happily at the sight of me. "I could hug you," he says. They love the sense of a thinking woman's presence, and they will do what they can to keep me close. I am a woman with degrees, market value, I am there for their ego, a suitable sounding board, worthy witness for their prowess. I am a drug that needy and self-important and insecure men are hooked on. In my presence they spy a strength they can steal, slurp, extract, suckle, inject, a potent potion, fuel for slaying the world's dragons. No woman and especially no thinking woman can exist without weathering the constant threat of being abducted, commandeered, dismantled, absorbed. Unless what we bring to the table serves such men, unless weaponised women witness us likewise surrendering ourselves in entirety over to Man-Purpose, they all will despise and erase us, they will utterly blot out our memory under heaven.

On my undergraduate college campus, we women were regularly reminded of this our principal duty, not least in the many jokes about getting our M.r.s. degree, that kind of joke we laughed about in order to mask our participation. It was all so funny, wasn't it, how little our education really mattered? Each year on campus we all talked about, rolled our eyes towards and nevertheless eagerly joined in with the most recent round of Spring Fever, the sudden urgency with which Christian men, close to graduation, begin to scramble for a suitable wife to prop up their next stage of life. Marriage mill on the hill. Ring by spring. (Divorce in due course.) This was particularly oppressive for the few Black students on campus – more than once, I heard a woman who lived on my residence hall talk about being sick to death of people assuming she would end up in a relationship with one of the handful of Black men on campus, why wasn't she dating him yet or what about that other one.

Some heterosexual couples among us awkwardly attempted some cobbled together version of formal courtship, made difficult by the fact neither party was living under the immediate eye of the woman's patriarch father. Some sought out a proxy, a local pastor or other Man-figure who could be trusted to keep a close watch on their interactions. Some men and women got married the day of graduation, to save extended family members an extra journey, while you're here let's just get it done and dusted, two for the price of one. Some got married while they were still studying, then moved off-campus into some version of couples housing while they completed their studies. Some wives became almost immediately pregnant, some dropped out. One man a few years

CHAPTER THIRTY-ONE

older than his fiancée, having graduated first, promised her they'd live near campus until she finished her degree. He wasn't the only man I knew to break this promise, overruled as it eventually was presumed to be by the wife's commitment at the altar to obey her husband in everything. A few married women attended classes while pregnant, including a daughter-in-law of the college president. One particular interdisciplinary studies professor, yet another known Reconstructionist who had worked alongside my pastor in various ventures, was student advisor to one of my roommates and told her in no uncertain terms that she should focus on one thing and one thing only: finding a husband.

None of this was unusual, none of this was unexpected, and none of this would abate after my time at college in the late 1990s. Nearly two decades after I began my undergraduate degree, sociologist Stacy George surveyed 2,500 undergraduate students across the 15 colleges that belong to the Council for Christian Colleges and Universities. Over eighty percent recalled hearing conversations at college about pressure, at least occasionally, to get married.[123] Such pressure polluted all our studies as women. We must simultaneously make sense of a subject area whilst spying out a spouse. From this way of thinking, talking, behaving, there seemed to be no relief. Keen to be seen, women among us publicized their marriage potential by baking cookies, cakes and brownies for men's residence halls in their spare time, bringing local children they babysat into the dining hall in a parade of motherly potential. See me feeding them, you, see me as a mother, see me as your wife. I lost count of how many bridal showers I was invited to as the semesters rolled by, the occasional lingerie shower, sexy trappings to transform her into an object of desire for that special night, then came the baby showers. I sat awkwardly to the side as women took turns guessing the baby's birth weight – skipping over those of us who lacked the relevant knowledge. At another shower—this one pre-wedding—the host directed us to take it in

---

[123] George, S. K. (2019). *Ring by Spring: Dating and Relationship Cultures at Christian Colleges.* Wipf and Stock Publishers.

turns to pray that our friend's first baby would be a boy and that he would be "called" to the mission field.

Back home, in and amongst the never-ending stream of numerous pyramid scheme parties, my church-school had of course already celebrated several weddings among my peers. A deacon's daughter, who had, during several years of courtship in high school, prepared her boyfriend's school lunches, finally moved her meal-making to their shared kitchen. His school lunches became work lunches. Her mother-in-law, wife to a church elder, had already instructed her in the specifics of his food preparation, he likes his sandwiches just so, make a tiny slice in his fruit to save him the frustration of peeling. One weekend I hosted a wedding shower for a friend. Her fiancé—a man who once told me that praying with girls turned him on—showed up briefly before the party to crack a few jokes about how he was looking forward to having a woman do his laundry, before leaving us women to ooh and aah over various home goods gifted to the lucky housewife-to-be by her friends.

I'd already experienced senior scrambling from the moment I arrived on campus, and so far I'd managed to wade my way through. But what did I have to show for it? I'd taken a few memorable classes which had pushed me in helpfully critical ways. I'd met some good friends. Yet little of what baggage I had carried with me to campus had been unsettled in any substantial way. My arrival there marked the radical introduction to my experience of a woman with a PhD, yet I witnessed her and the other women on academic staff being treated the same as I'd come to think women would always be treated. Denied leadership positions. Absent from certain subject areas. Most likely to be part-time. At a production of *Much Ado about Nothing*, I arrived early with one of my roommates to get a seat near the front. A residence hall of man-boys shortly piled in with their privilege, they insisted we move, their friend was playing a lead role, how dare we occupy the space theirs by right of brotherly association. Not wanting to sit amongst such hostility, my friend and I moved towards the back. Just as the play was about to begin, one of the few women on faculty arrived, she an older woman, the only seats remaining in the far back corner. I stared through the space of all those painful minutes as she walked past the row of boys, even stumbled on a step in the dimmed lights, each second like liquid amassing in a swelling blister, her eyes looking for a seat, her searching ignored by the brotherhood near the stage, until a woman student waved her in, gave up her spot, then took her place on the aisle floor, side-lined, where women seem always to end up.

In campus life, many of us kept up the pretence of our empowerment, we voiced our opinions in class, at times we even pounded the desks to demonstrate the passion of our points, we enjoyed certain limited freedoms that more fundamentalist colleges would've denied us. We had made it to higher education, indeed we were there. Yet the very oxygen we breathed was nevertheless infused with the same stench of domination and subordination. My freshman year, some girlfriends and I worried together about the blatant aggression and racism of a certain white student towards his Black girlfriend, a woman on our residence hall. He made his cruel "jokes" boldly in groups of us, at parties, his man-friends laughed with him, we talked to her about it a few times, we were unsettled, we could've reported it, maybe we should have, but to whom? Our patriarchal professors, with their partial procedures and their mid-lecture jokes about which students might marry, Valerie and Marty, I see you've both scored well in this week's set work, will it be wedding bells next? Yes, who would've listened to our misgivings – our residence hall advisors? Involved as they were in fuelling the prank wars that gave men license to commit violence by proxy on our most private spaces? One group of man-students smeared foul-smelling cheese into the carpets where women socialised, they invaded our rooms, every year one group of guys rummaged through women's drawers during classes, inserting their Man-bodies inside our dresses, our shirts, our shorts, our bras, parading into the dining hall all decked out in dominance, a pack of wolves as in that famous fairy tale, who don the clothes of the women they've recently consumed.

One morning close to Christmas, one of we women woke to discover the frozen carcass of a raccoon, wearing a stolen pair of her panties, positioned festively in a poinsettia outside her door. At a campus-wide talent night, a group of guys made another show of their white male supremacy by wordlessly setting up a circle of folding chairs on the stage, then sitting there chatting to each other about this and that for a quarter of an hour, commandeering our attention simply by virtue of their gender. One of these campus captains for a time had a destructive relationship with one of my roommates – a woman related to a now infamous Christian apologist. Her so-called boyfriend regularly belittled her, she talked often about this, courageously confiding in us how worthless he made her feel. Over a meal one evening, this boyfriend declared as she and I sat side by side that he'd be interested in me if he weren't already involved with her, he pointed at us each in turn to signal our interchangeability, what do you say to that, Valerie. Most nights he called our room in the early hours, waking us all up, pleading with her to come to his house off-campus.

And now here I was, in the midst of all this mess, ending my junior year, walking around without defined purpose, uncertain of my future usefulness, appearing dangerously available for direction. Or was I. John was still holding me on the tether of his conflicting feelings, desire vs. distaste, interest vs. hate, pride vs. resentment, fear vs. envy, all woven together and lashing out at me randomly without warning. Today he would be endearing and funny. Tomorrow he would cut me down to size. He surprised me with a gift, a collection of Disney soundtrack CDs, yet more infantilising garbage, expensive enough to cast doubt on discarding it. He made promises and broke them, said he would show up at this time or that and then fail to appear. I too still held him at some length—did I hold him though, was I actively holding—in order to keep him around. Luke still loomed large, though by now he was acting oddly around another woman on campus. This other woman approached me one day to try to make sense of it, he always talks about you in strange ways,

CHAPTER THIRTY-ONE

Valerie, then he'll ask me my opinions about parenting and other various and sundry things related to marriage and children and theology. I told her my advice in the bluntest of terms: that guy is bad news. Go with your gut and get away. I learned from this that this man of war was still imagining himself hovering around me as if in a holding pattern, still firmly fixed in his flight path, yet spying out other opportunities should he be forced to attempt an emergency landing elsewhere.

Purity culture was in full swing in conservative evangelical Christian churches, schools and campuses across the United States. None of this was new to me, of course it wasn't. All this was typical. It was casual. It was mundane. Even in its most violent forms, it was so common as to be mostly invisible, rarely spoken of, when on rare occasions its exposure loomed, it was quickly hidden and hushed up. I'd heard, I'd lived an advanced version of all this and much worse for as long as I could remember. Still, it emptied me out of all feeling to realise nothing much had changed since childhood, nothing but the simple matter of geography. An audio tape made the rounds that year among the student body, from Man-head to woman-feet, forty-five minutes of musings from some Christian relationship guru, I can't recall his name now. John asked me to listen to it one afternoon, he and his guy friends had learned so much from it, he said. I rode a stationary bike in the gym for the recording's full duration, my legs spinning faster and faster, all while this Man's voice in my ear proclaimed the existence of some masculine brain switch that, when tripped, signals the point of no return in physical intimacy, past that sudden mechanical flip he is unable to stop, he cannot be blamed for anything that happens after that. Basic biology. Women, he warned, don't dress too attractively but also don't be too frumpy, be friendly but not flirty, men instinctively crave "something soft," so don't be hard, an assertive woman is undesirable. All this and more is what goes through a Man's Mind when we see a woman we find sexy, he said. We can't help ourselves. You women are the cause of our lust and marriage God's only solution.

In this way, we absorbed message after message to hate our bodies and the bodies of others, to fear physical contact and yet to long for it. Whether someone had a ring on their finger changed this very little. One married woman I knew hesitated to tell her parents she was pregnant. Now they'd know—for certain they'd now know—she'd had sex. Friends grappled with the guilt and shame of kissing their boyfriends, being touched and touching, the fear that others might find out, that they might join the unofficial campus list of "loose women" which as I've mentioned already of course had no Man-equivalent. We could be angels or whores only, our bodies would lead either to life or total destruction, but which were we? Jezebel or the Virgin Mary? We were caught between poles, a toxic soup of sexism internalised and externalised wherever we went. David, my church elder's nephew, having already graduated, rung me up one day to sing my praises on this account. A friend still on campus had told him we'd stayed up late one night talking and, amazingly, to his shock and admiration, we'd had no physical contact, we hadn't even kissed! Nothing had happened!

"Nothing happened." Yes, this is how he put it, how I've so often heard it put, since anything between men and women except sexual interaction is nothing at all. "Nothing happened" is also what a friend's husband told her, when she confronted him about his office flirting, his sexting. If we don't kiss, if we don't touch, if the empirically measurable molecules of our bodies do not bend towards our sexual attraction, it's as if we never met, our meeting is of zero substance, zero connection, it doesn't matter. Nothing has happened. Nothing at all.

But what these men saw as nothing was so often so much of my something. I'd thought, at the time, that this friend of David's and I were having a pleasant evening, a meeting of the minds, a lengthy conversation about things that mattered. Yes, this was something of substance. I'd met this guy for the first time before I came to campus my freshman year, during a scholarship competition weekend, as he too was a scholarship holder, a so-called future leader. We'd had a

CHAPTER THIRTY-ONE

good conversation then and connected here and there in the years following. This recent time we'd stayed up late in the night talking about doubt and other complexities of life. Now I wondered, were all these minutes of dialogue merely vacant spaces between touches, between kisses, between flesh pressed against flesh? Was I nothing except for this, my genitalia, my reproductive capability? Nothing had happened. I'd passed some repulsive purity test with this conversation partner, now he and David respected me so much. David said as much on the phone, "Stay gold, Valerie," this was how he always ended our calls, how he too set me atop a lonely pedestal, commanded me there to remain, positioned for eventual taking. He hinted at this occasionally, used just enough ambiguous touch at certain times to stake his claim. David was by then in medical school and, on one visit back to campus, he asked to adjust my back as practice. His hands moved lower and lower, and as they did, under such intense felt pressure it was as if my body was no longer mine but his. I didn't want this to happen, yet neither could I move, turning to stone was my only instinctive resistance. Several of my friends were with us, and one interrupted David's bodily invasion by laughing, that wordless form of feminine disruption which nevertheless upset him deeply. "I wasn't doing anything," he said gruffly. Nothing at all.

"Stay gold, Valerie." John too talked to me at times in this language of otherworldly aspiration, of comparison, positioning me against other girls. Would I be a goddess or a slut? He talked about their behaviour and mine, their clothing and mine, he mentioned he'd talked with his sister about a trend they called "sexy pants"—what were in actual fact merely yoga pants—he was glad I didn't have any such item in my wardrobe, he was glad I was like this other girl but not that one, what did I think of her. More and more he argued with himself out loud, involving me in his assessment of me and of my womanhood, his expectation that, passively, I would sit by, still and silent while he ran the measuring tape of his Man-morality against my every molecule. It's so strange, how long this hangs on, decades later I feel a need to prove somehow that my children are indeed my husband's biological descendants, to point out to others how much they look like him, act like him. Such is my latent mistrust in the institution of marriage, in monogamy, even in love. I am no angel, after all, I think, I am only a woman. No, No, No, listen to me say it again to myself, I am a human being, as capable of complex choices as any.

Even so, when John asked me just before the end of the semester, right before his graduation, just before we were preparing to part ways for the summer, if he could have a "serious" talk with me, I expected to say yes to formalizing our relationship in some way. I also knew he'd likely have a set of disclaimers miles longer than any expression of affection. And so I steeled myself, I prepared myself, I knew no other way, I planned to state my own misgivings before he had a chance to whittle my expectations down to a mere nub. That afternoon, I listened while John talked briefly about how much he'd enjoyed spending time with me, how he had given all this serious thought, graced me with the privilege of entering the contemplations of his Man-mind, he'd taken a youth minister job at a wealthy church near the college for the next year, he was keen to stay near me during my senior year. He'd talked all this over with a friend—a woman whom we both knew had been burdened with unrequited love for him the past four years—she'd recommended he not say any of this to me, but he'd come to a decision, wasn't I impressed that he had disregarded her advice in my favour.

"We should date, Valerie. I'm saying I want us to be together."

These were the words I'd been waiting for. Is this what love was, was this how it began? I state this question clearly now, but at the time, it didn't enter my thoughts, so low was my bar, so far away was love from my experience. Such privilege was for the lives of other people perhaps. How could I have recognised it, this sentiment I hadn't seen, had never sensed? At the sound of John's words, his carefully prepared monologue of intention and desire, the mechanics

CHAPTER THIRTY-ONE

of his decisiveness intended to thrill me, to privilege me, to fill me with gratitude, I don't know what I'd expected to feel in response. I had no conscious concept of what it might be like to relax around a person I had some kind of romantic feelings for, to long for someone without fear of being used and discarded, to be at ease in the presence of another person, to be seen, to be prioritised, to be accepted and even longed for, simply because of who I am. I had none of that. Everything was still so awkward.

Still, John's words were my cue. I launched into a series of my own caveats. I wasn't entirely sure about our long-term compatibility, I wanted to take things slow, I didn't want him to get the wrong idea, let's take our time with this. Later, John would tell a mutual friend that I'd stolen the words from his mouth, I'd said the things he had planned to say, I'd pre-empted him, and he didn't much like that, no he did not. Again I'd played an unexpected hand in our cat and mouse courtship. No surprise then, that when his family came into town that following week for his graduation, he didn't invite me to the celebratory lunch. He could barely bring himself even to introduce me to them in the hall afterwards. "This is Valerie," he said, the resulting blankness of his mother's face suggesting I was nothing more than a new name, here is a random person who happens to have walked by, who by chance is standing here, my son has introduced her just to be polite. Meanwhile, Luke was graduating that day as well and expected me to join his family for lunch, though I had no memory of agreeing to that. He'd made these plans on my behalf or else perceived some hidden meaning in something I'd said. When I didn't appear, he rung me up, wondering where I was, why hadn't I joined them, he'd seen John and his family exit without me, see how quickly a woman separated is a woman sought, a woman stalked.

32

At the heart of mature femininity is a freeing disposition to affirm, receive, and nurture strength and leadership from worthy men in ways appropriate to a woman's differing relationships.

— *John Piper and Wayne Grudem, Recovering Biblical Manhood and Womanhood, 1991.*

I went home that summer, to a house to which my parents had moved after I'd left for university, my things moved to an upstairs room I'd never before occupied. My pastor wrote a lengthy two-part series on "The Heart of a Godly Man" in which he reaffirmed his model for manhood, rooted in his dualist theology. God the father of wrath of the Old Testament and god the son of his salvation of the New Testament, "between God and God manifested, between the God who afflicts him and the God who is on his side and will vindicate him."[124] God of wrath and confusion, god of antisemitism, god of western white men.

I got another summer job, this time at a supermarket. I waited for John to call in the evenings after work and he didn't. I waited for John to e-mail, and he mostly didn't. Every three or four days he sent something brief and matter-of-fact, vague and mostly meaningless,

---

124 Morecraft, J. (1999). 'The Heart of a Godly Man, Part 2', *The Counsel of Chalcedon*, Issue 3.

CHAPTER THIRTY-TWO

his usual style for risky modes of communication I might print out, might point to as concrete evidence, look here, the record is clear you cared about me. "Hey, Valerie, I started my youth group job, I'm taking the boys to a campsite now, hey, Valerie, I have to go here and there, no time to write anything." Even from such a distance, he was already pulling away, reminding me that while I must locate my usefulness in him, he would never truly need me in any way.

Within a short time of being home, my parents asked my sister and me to sit down in our living room. They reported to us that our brother had gotten married to someone we'd never met, that was that, all done and dusted. As soon as he heard of this scandal, our pastor was thrilled to announce the news hot off the press from the pulpit, eagerly sucking up all the gasps in the room like some hyper reformed Presbyterian dementor. I saw his face more fully then, it bulged out into the room and towards my chair, all that pride and self-satisfaction congealed and wobbling in his cheeks. I discerned things there I hadn't consciously seen before, my eternally troubled stomach linked hands with my clearing vision of our community, my eyes darted away from my pastor's face and towards the door, I even recall someone near me turning to look as well, what has she seen in the back of the room. When I got home I called John and left an urgent message, difficult family news, please call me back. He didn't ring back nor did I try again, that much seemed suddenly beneath my dignity. Something was happening to me. I let it lie, I left it, I left, I flexed again the slowly strengthening muscle of my leaving.

In the days that followed, one evening I was on the phone crying in conversation with a friend about all that was happening, when my father came into the room and said I'd better not be talking about family matters with anyone outside the family, hang up the phone now, we aren't in the business of airing our dirty laundry. Hearing such words, delivered in such a voice, I perceived then something else, the strangeness of the room I was in, the mismatch of myself within it. I sensed some impending catastrophe, some tragedy, something sinister was coming close, was already here, if I stayed here I felt suddenly certain I would die here. I determined there and then that night to do the only thing I was learning to do. To leave. In this I didn't think of John, I didn't think of him or any such man, I thought only of myself and the urgency of my escape. I had to get away. I wouldn't stop along the way, I wouldn't look back, lest I too turn to salt.

As it happened, my friend Emma had a spare room for the summer near our college campus. She had just graduated and moved in with two other recent graduates, one of whom had gone to Swiss L'Abri, where—she'd later tell us—she enjoyed long conversations with older, deeply troubled and sometimes married men.[125] So it was that within days of my decision, I quit my summer supermarket job, I left John a message that I was moving, I drove up and away with a packed car full of my belongings. I moved my things into the spare room. I got a job making sandwiches at a local business. I settled in, I sank into some relief, into my first ever summer of being away.

Days passed after my move, then a week, and John still hadn't returned my calls. I'd left one additional message for him after I'd arrived, suggesting we meet up. What a ridiculous thing to ask. I felt shamed by my own fingers dialling each digit, by the words that formed my fumbling message, how had I come to this point of stooping so low, chasing this boy, bowing before him seated on the throne of our relationship. Then came the weekend. Emma and I were at church and saw him sitting nearby. She made a face at him, and he sauntered over after the service, said something like, would it be ok if I stopped by this afternoon to talk, the language of formality, as if our last conversation just weeks before had never happened, as if we were mere acquaintances asking politely, when might be a good time, only if it's convenient, only if it's not too much trouble, are you sure. It was dark when he finally showed up. I heard him dragging his shoes on the gravel drive. Now he was sitting anxiously

---

125 Stone, R. M. (2013, April 1). Remembering Edith Schaeffer, the Evangelical in Pearls and Chanel No. 5. *Christianity Today*. https://www.christianitytoday.com/ct/2013/april-web-only/remembering-edith-schaeffer-evangelical-woman-in-pearls-and.html

CHAPTER THIRTY-TWO

in our small living room, the posture of someone who wanted to be anywhere but here. He talked a long time, so many words, words, words, though I can recall only a single set of syllables from his self-indulgent speech about my recent arrival. One word that dribbled cowardly out of his gaping mouth, putrefaction emitting in my direction from his self-satisfied face which I now found unbearably abhorrent. "Presumptuous." This is what he said, I'll never forget this word he pushed out of his mouth and flung towards me. This vile combination of sounds hovered about the room then, hanging over me, so ridiculous it seemed unreal, an apparition surely. Had I simply imagined that he'd rearranged the universe in such a way that all we like planets orbited around him, his athletic man's body, his glowing personality, his importance, his popularity, his manhood? Even the mountain where we lived and studied was apparently his territory, all its fullness and those who dwelled therein. What was beneath all his posturing but arrogance and insecurity, all mixed and mingling together in a nasty, narcissistic stew?

I laughed. That's all I could manage in the moment, all that seemed appropriate. I could only laugh. How else could I express all that had led to this moment, all that history that I carried on my back, written into the book of my flesh, with me to this room, this minute. It was inexplicable, he could never have comprehended any attempt I might make at laying it out. We'd be sitting there for days and what even would be the point. So I laughed. And yet of course this was absolutely everything he couldn't manage, how overwhelmingly unbearable for me to respond in such a way to something he'd said in all seriousness. When a certain kind of man speaks his mind, when he is serious about what he is saying and doing, there can be nothing more unacceptable than to be fodder for women's humour. "No, no, no," he started up then again. "You're misunderstanding me," now he was gesturing in desperation at the empty space, summoning... what? Who? The molecules of oxygen in the room? Some invisible allies he could conjure up by force of will? No, he said over and over, he didn't mean to say this or that, he meant it this way and that way, didn't I understand the goodness of his intentions, he meant well, he waved as if at other people, shared acquaintances who weren't there, they would surely side with him, they would support him here and now, they would affirm his interpretation, his meaning, if only they were here to relieve him, to agree how wrong I was and how very right was he. Look at this cloud of witnesses surrounding me, watch them coming to my defence.

I would not ease his suffering, and I did not. I no longer had it in me. He left then, no clarity between us except that word of all words and my emasculating laughter, still lingering in the room. Still, I had set something in motion. A few days after, a group of us met up to watch a film and order pizza, John hadn't invited me nor I him yet there we were, together again in the same room. Someone brought out a deck of 'Would You Rather' cards. John chose a spot on the floor in the corner opposite to me, anything other than the risk of even the most superficial physical contact with me on the sofa. "It's so sad, he can't even sit next to you," one of our friends said to me as we left. I shrugged then, what was this relationship but an enhanced form of separation, two people agreeing to push each other away. What had it ever been but that. What even was love from all these men I knew but special dispensation to treat one woman more cruelly than any other, mere proof of their worthiness in the church's masculine mission?

And then, finally—by accident, by divine intervention, by mere chance, somehow—John forwarded me an email thread between him and a man from his home church, a mentor. They were discussing John's feelings for me, his burgeoning interest in me but above all his reservations. His e-mail included this line, which caught in my eye like a fragment of broken glass, sparkling violently from the screen, cutting my cornea, searing my optic nerve. "I guess I've just always thought I'd end up with someone more attractive." Sat before this pile of syllables, I breathed in sharply, I felt the formation of that familiar and rapid internal vacuum, my spirit seemed to abandon me briefly then, I knew the hollow of its absence, another

CHAPTER THIRTY-TWO

destabilising moment of disassociation, another in such a long line of similar signals.

After reading the e-mail a few times, enough to be confident I'd not imagined what I'd seen, I deleted it. My vision was forever changed. This too was a secret gift, as harsh and painful as it was, here were heaven's small things revealing in full colour John's grotesque and startling figure, his hatred of me fully on display, concentrated in all its ugliness, its violence. I sensed God's voice again to me in all this, this time not a whisper but a shout. These men who set their sights on taming and saving the world, who desire women's bodies in service of their kingdoms, they fear and loathe their need of us, with force and severity they will always end up laying hold of our shape, butchering and tearing our flesh, dividing our earthly substance from our spirit, dominating, dissecting and consuming us. Upon our anatomy, they practice their cosmic pre-eminence. This is the only dynamic they know. How paradoxical it seems—absurd—even now, that the poisonous and degrading hate these Dominionist men confuse for love would, in the end, awaken in me a firmly rooted faith in the existence of and radical equality accomplished through God's wondrous, life-giving power which unsettles and dismantles all human empires. In this happy place of peace, the first are now last and the last first, a revolutionary rebalancing of all unjust scales. Naively, so many over the years have believed they could absorb me into their Man-Wars. I leave all their loathing behind, empowered.

33

Isaiah 3:1-5, 12 the inevitable judgment of God is announced. Chaos will prevail. The infrastructure of society will collapse. T he authority structure will break down. Children will exercise tyrannical control in the home, and women will rule the roost. Male irresponsibility is matched by female domination. Isaiah 3:16ff, further, lists the characteristics of such dominating women. They call people's attention to themselves. They do so by the way they walk. They do so by the way they dress. They do so by the way they deck themselves with ornaments. The list of these ornaments seems endless.

– Henry Krabbendam, A Biblical Pattern of Preparation for Marriage (Lookout Mountain, GA: Covenant College, 2000), p. 48.

In 1999, sensing his life would soon be drawing to a close, Rousas Rushdoony delivered his final audio message to his supporters.[126] "Chalcedon is not going to stand still after I am gone," he promised. "Chalcedon must continue to do its work and increase its scope, because we are living in very troubled and difficult times, when the world is facing the wrath of God for its departure from him and his word." That same year, the *New York Times* reported that

---

[126] Rushdoony, R. J. (1999, October 22). *A Personal Message from R. J. Rushdoony*. The Chalcedon Foundation. https://chalcedon.edu/resources/audio/a-personal-message-from-r-j-rushdoony

powerful political lobbying group, the Christian Coalition, was now in financial and leadership turmoil.[127] A few short years later, Pat Robertson would resign from the group he helped found, and hard-core and soft-core Dominionists alike would continue to rally themselves, the world isn't ready for us yet, we must continue to work and to wait, to bide our time in faithfulness, until God rewards us. As one member of the Oklahoma House of Representatives would put it, "the Religious Right can't save America. However, God can and Christians are His soldiers."[128]

The United States was gearing up for the next presidential election, and white evangelical Christians wanted Bill Clinton out. Where the Christian Right, including my own pastor, had dismissed allegations of sexual harassment brought by women like Anita Hill against men they considered allies, now they would use Paula Jones' similar accusations against President Clinton as a platform from which to disrupt the Democratic Party's control of the White House. Pat Robertson, Operation Rescue's Patrick Mahoney and Liberty University founder Jerry Falwell assisted Jones in publicizing her story and creating a legal defence fund. Clinton eventually settled the case out of court, and in November, 1999, attorney and founder of conservative legal organisation the Rutherford Institute, John Whitehead, published his account of defending Paula Jones in court. By this time, Whitehead had distanced himself publicly from his friend and Rutherford Institute founding board member Rousas Rushdoony, claiming to have moved on from his early Reconstructionist views. Still, more than one scholar has pointed out that Whitehead's representation of Paula Jones fit neatly within the ambitions of the Christian Right, to repossess the Christian country they believed had been stolen by an irreligious state.[129]

---

127 Goodstein, L. (1999, August 2). Coalition's Woes May Hinder Goals of Christian Right. *The New York Times*. https://www.nytimes.com/1999/08/02/us/coalition-s-woes-may-hinder-goals-of-christian-right.html
128 Graves, W. D. (2002, March 1). Cal Thomas, Religion, and Politics. *Chalcedon Magazine*. https://chalcedon.edu/magazine/cal-thomas-religion-and-politics
129 Moore, R. J. (2007). *Suing for America's Soul: John Whitehead, the Rutherford Institute, and Conservative Christians in the Courts*. Wm. B. Eerdmans Publishing.

And Whitehead, ever the opportunist, would go on to hold hands again with the Reconstructionists when it suited.[130] The woman Paula Jones herself was largely irrelevant, then, she was primarily a tool, a means to an end, as women so often are.

I left John then, I didn't tell him about the e-mail I'd seen, I simply stopped talking to him as he had to me. Neither would I sit around in my sadness. I sought out the company of another group of friends living nearby, and I started cycling again with one of them every day after work at the supermarket. So the summer went on easily after that. Again, I located some peace in a friend's company. So much so, that we decided to go on a biking trip together for the rest of the summer, staying with a family he knew in the northeast, the only obstacle my roommate's flippant joke to my mother on the phone that my biking friend had a drinking problem, which she received with all seriousness, forever mistaking ally for enemy and vice versa.

Predictably, though, when John heard of this trip from a mutual friend, when we returned weeks later and he showed up urgently and unannounced at my house, when I told him—as if it weren't obvious by now—that he and I were definitely through, after he learned that yes, I really was moving on, but oh it was worse, that I was enjoying the company of some other person, some other guy – back he came again, propelled by all the force of that whirlwind that is masculine rivalry. Why would any man seek out the company of any woman I've rejected, what does he know that I don't know, what might I gain by claiming her back. Some of these questions he posed to me directly that day, all indignant about someone new stepping in before he could get his head around it, what about the "guy code," inscribing all his outrage on the fabric of my presence, expecting the ever faithful feminine sounding board.

I wish I could say that was it, that having been trampled for so long, that I finally stood up in resolve to act only in that manner

---

130 See Macias, S., Schwartz, A. G., Selbrede, M. G., & Whitehead, J. (2019, April 1). *# 55 Do Christians Have a Responsibility to Check Government Overreach?* (guest John Whitehead). https://chalcedon.edu/resources/audio/do-christians-have-a-responsibility-to-check-government-overreach

CHAPTER THIRTY-THREE

which would, in my own opinion, constitute my happiness and my happiness alone, without reference to any such man, so deliberately disconnected, now so wholly unconnected to me. This is not how it works though. This is not how any of this works. And for the whole of the next year, my final year at college, John tortured me like he always had done, again and again attempting to fix me in the centre of all his self-love and self-loathing, like an insect mounted on a pin. My senior year at university was nearly unbearable because of this. I remember almost nothing of any class I took, I sat mostly silent in each one, yet I worked, I performed, somehow I kept my good grades, and in the end the main success I can report from that time is only this, that I kept showing up. I did what I knew how to do. I set myself in the seat, in the classroom, with pen and paper. I kept going, I didn't stop, despite all the manipulation, the belittling, the games, the questions I continued to face from friends and nosy acquaintances at home, do I have a Man in my life, when am I going to get Married, what do I think I am doing, what will I possibly do without a Man.

There is so much more I could say about all this, but then again, it was nothing but more of the same bombardment. Dominion-seeking man sees woman. Man wants woman. Man moves between controlling, belittling and love-bombing woman until she feels sufficiently lowly enough to submit to his will. Or, if she's lucky, to shield herself with whatever means she can get to hand. But it wasn't just John who tried again and again to take hold of me. One weekend in the fall of that final year at college, Matthew and Luke were passing through town on their way to some climbing location and asked to stay the night at my house. Emma and I invited a group of friends round that evening, a buffer of bodies against their presence. But Matthew and Luke dodged this, they set their terms, said they were going out with others and would come round in the early hours to sleep. By the time they arrived it was late, and Luke sprung a surprise when I pointed to the couches. He insisted on taking my bed, he wouldn't drop it, and I was by then so tired. He challenged me. "Are you really going to make a guest sleep on the sofa?" A last ditch attempt to re-establish some semblance of supremacy over me. Matthew showed no sign of supporting my outrage but simply stood there, waiting for us to sort it out. So I gave in. Whatever, sleep in my bed, I don't care. Luke took this and took it further, not only sleeping in my room, in my bed, between my sheets and on my pillow, but he even closed the door to the living room, shutting me out of my bedroom, leaving me to wonder what he was doing in my most private of spaces. Matthew and I talked a bit into the night, he on one couch and I on the other, about what I don't remember, then after several more long hours of anxious thoughts, I went to sleep, I pretended to be sleeping still when they got up early, I heard them whispering about whether or not to wake me, should we ask her to come with us. Finally, they left, and I felt the flutter of a note placed on top of the blanket. A number to call if I wanted to meet them. After I heard their car reach the end of the gravel drive, I got up, I checked my room for any signs that Luke had gone through my things, I bagged up all the assaulted bedding and threw it outside.

That New Year was the start of the new millennium. Sociological paranoia tinged with excitement spread through American fundamentalism, through the various branches of Dominionism. Was it all finally happening? Jerry Falwell – who had presided at my brother's wedding the summer prior – broadcasted his prophetic vision, "A Christian's Guide to the Millennium Bug," recorded on video for the masses, yours for the low, low price of $28. In the lead-up to the supposed crash of the world's banking systems, Reconstructionist Brian Abshire, recently declared a genius by our movement, recommended that we all begin stockpiling food, money, that we purchase a firearm, he personally recommended "a semi-automatic, 12-gauge shotgun," along with a "concealed carry permit," if possible.[131] Emma's mother, worried about our Y2K readiness, brought

---

[131] Abshire, B. M. (1998, November 1). Y2K and Disaster Preparedness: Some Thoughts on Survival and Security in An Unstable World. *Chalcedon Magazine*. https://chalcedon.edu/magazine/y2k-and-disaster-preparedness-some-thoughts-on-survival-and-security-in-an-unstable-world

CHAPTER THIRTY-THREE

round a massive rainwater barrel and stacks of canned food, reassuring my own worried mother who was herself stocking up. I learned later that, unbeknownst to me, Emma's Reconstructionist parents had given her a handgun, which she stored in our attic crawl space.

On the evening of the world's destruction, we hosted a party, and my church elder's nephew David drove up to celebrate with us, encouraged by a friend who was engaged to one of my housemates. These two men insisted on sleeping at our house. David had brought a sleeping bag and claimed his territory on the floor of my bedroom, joking about how it was just me and him at the end of the world. He pulled out a journal he'd brought and read out lengthy portions of it to me, a jumbled mix of reflections on the complexities and struggles of his wealthy white man life. After a while, we went to sleep. I woke up at some point and there he was in my narrow bed. In trying to drape my arm across his body, he'd stirred me awake. I mumbled something about having to use the bathroom and slept the rest of the night with Emma in her room. He said nothing about it the following morning, he left, and Emma told me afterwards he'd tried a similar stunt with her one weekend, when she had stayed at his apartment one night with a group of friends. Somehow he'd made his way to where she was sleeping, and she woke up to him holding her hand under the blanket. I don't know what happened after that. I didn't ask, and she didn't tell me. "He loves you, you know," David's friend told me. This is what they saw as love, the identification of a woman untouched and empty of other men, ready to be duly stuffed with their sex, ready or not here I come.

On and on, like this it went, until finally, graduation approached. Though I'd tried to close the door on our relationship again and again, John pressured me successfully to invite him to Senior Banquet. On the night, my mother expressed her regrets to him, "I'm so sorry to hear we won't be seeing much of you after this," which prompted yet another of his identity crises, another round of Manologues in my living room that very night. Before graduation, one of the men's residence halls on campus planted the head and entrails of an animal they had butchered on one of the women's halls, their latest homage to the sexual politics of meat in a long and rapidly escalating line of "pranks" they'd become known for. A few students were nominated to give departing speeches in the daily chapel service. One woman used the egalitarian veneer of her time at the podium to reinforce our call to go forth boldly and change the world. For our graduation ceremony, the speaker we selected from among us was a young man who would some years later appear in a Netflix documentary on the Fellowship, a right-wing Christian political organisation pervaded by what one journalist would refer to as "a stale whiff of viciously inadequate masculinity."[132] And then came the date of one particular afternoon, when one of my English professors asked me into his office and suggested I apply for a place at a linguistics summer school. You have promise, he said. You could do more. You should try.

These were words I'd rarely heard. Had I ever heard them? Certainly never from any others of my professors whose classes I'd dutifully attended and who'd marked my work as well done. I could do more than _____. I considered the ways I could fill in the blank my professor had left. I couldn't have done more than I'd done. I was the first person to graduate university in my family. I'd done this against so much opposition. And I was tired of doing, doing, doing, all this defiant doing. Yet there was another possible meaning here. I could do more <u>without the hindrance of these men and this place of men</u>. This professor helped me with my application, he was outraged when my Biblical languages professor refused to write me a letter of recommendation on the grounds that my priorities as a woman were grossly misplaced. Years later, when the possibility of a job at my old college came open, this same professor wrote to me and said, do not come back here. Do not apply. Yes, there it was again. You could do more. You could do better.

So, before college graduation, I applied to the linguistics summer

---

132 Seale, J. (2019, September 15). *The Family: Inside the sinister sect that has infected western democracy*. The Guardian. https://www.theguardian.com/tv-and-radio/2019/aug/15/the-family-netflix-powerful-sinister-christian-sect-trump

CHAPTER THIRTY-THREE

school, I got in, with this professor's help I even got a small scholarship. All this last-minute encouragement, this support, wholly and wonderfully disconnected from my usefulness to any one person and their puffed up plans, this boost meant that when John came round on the day of my departure, to dissuade me from going, I had the confidence to refuse him entry to the house, though I agreed to talk with him in his car. "What are you doing, Valerie?" he asked. "I don't want you to go. Not yet." Still riding the high of the exit my professor had pointed out to me, I dipped deep into my rationed reserves of confidence again. "I don't want to talk to you anymore," I said. "Do not call me. Do not write to me. I do not want to hear from you ever again." At this, John pulled my arm and began to cry and cry more, he repeated my name, he whimpered and wouldn't let me go, again I was stuck in some boy's car, in some Man-space, I jerked hard and harder, my arm was free, I forced the door open, I pulled my way out. He'd not hold me in. He'd not hold me back.

Epilogue

Sam Fife, a leading promoter of the Manifest Sons of God teaching, taught that the aging process had stopped for him and when asked his age, he would simply answer "I AM". He assured people that he would never die but was in the process of being changed into an incorruptible life.

– 'Kingdom Triumphalism,' Let Us Reason Ministries, 2009.

For Chalcedon, the work remains clear and unchanging. Although the times in which we live are changing, there is nothing we're facing that wasn't spelled out presciently in the teaching and writing of R. J. Rushdoony.

– 'Chalcedon Editorial, 'Christian Reconstruction vs. "Social Justice Warriors,"' Faith for All of Life, May/June, 2017, pp. 25-26.

"Come back to the people who love you," one church leader said to me recently, after I exercised my right to withdraw my membership, when I again said no to being treated like an appendage in service of the vision of a gaggle of talking masculine heads. My family and I had left our church of 16 years because of safeguarding concerns, because of the sexism that bared its fangs when I began pointing out these matters, because we'd tried and failed to bring about change. She is just confused, such people tell each other. She's led her husband astray. It's only a matter of time before her woman-feelings abate and she sees reason. Now wait for the energetically lobbed love bomb, that excessive attention, admiration, affection, that pretence of kindness that aims to distract you from the memory of harm, of discrimination, to plaster over the cracks of cruelty.

No. Again, no. This vision of love is not the only one possible, it isn't the love I want. It is no love at all. When someone is harming me, claiming me, seeking dominion over me, my every no is a yes to myself, a yes to the truth, it is a yes to everyone else who is also being exploited and otherwise harmed, it is a yes to Love, in which there is no fear. This form of radical love is often mistaken as selfishness and cowardice by people who don't know any better. At times, as the years have accumulated confidence, I've said no without fully understanding why, hung up the phone on someone by instinct, refused an in-person meeting on gut feeling, removed myself from some cruel enclosure even before I can name its features, before I can articulate any watertight argument to justify my exit. I am a sojourner, I am a sideliner, I am merely passing through, I have no allegiance to power-seeking spaces, these hungry dictators who cling to the night, the playbooks of kingdom warriors whose dwelling place is passing away. The strength of my impulse is sometimes enough. Choosing this is choosing dignity, tranquillity. I flee, I leave things behind, destructive relationships, belongings, professional connections, something is off, something has been off, has gone fully off, I sense and smell it. I won't go back there. Never again. If I keep saying it, maybe it'll be so.

It has taken decades of mistakes to learn to believe myself in this way, to act in ways that honour my body and my soul, that respect their dignity. One of the cruellest acts of vandalism in an abusive community is its defacement of love and the glorification of hate and violence that goes on in its place. So many times the internalisation of this twisted substitution I've acted out unconsciously, accepting and even seeking so many selfish and all-consuming relationships, using others and allowing myself to be used by them in this desperate scramble to reclaim the world and locate my relevance therein. I regret the racism I internalised and have inflicted on other human beings, the pride, the judgementalism, the endless striving after a certain version of aggressive excellence. I hate the lingering cargo I still carry of never being good enough, the false guilt that still lingers when I rest, when I enjoy seemingly useless pleasures frowned upon by people of evangelical authority, when I ask for help, when I stop, when I give up, when I move on, when I accept what's good enough for now. Months after we left our church, our elder contacted us again by e-mail, he said it was clear to him now that we really weren't coming back after all. Do you see how that works? Why can't she just get over it? We prayed for her healing. Why haven't her feelings subsided? Why can't she let it go? She must be bitter. What is wrong with her? She must be lost.

I'm still learning. I worry I will never learn. A few years ago, I attended an online meeting with a Christian academic who was interested in a collaboration. We'd e-mailed before, but this now was our first face to face conversation. I learn we are about the same age, though unlike me he's never held a permanent post in academia. We talk about our partnership. He emphasises that in our shared work he will be project lead in name only, that we'll never publish anything as collaborators without full agreement, that we'll split the work evenly. He's so excited that I'm interested in the project, finally he's found me. He talks about his advocacy, his concern for justice. It all sounds good. I'm enthusiastic too. We talk of next steps. Only then, somehow, our discussion pivots to books we've read—whatever slippery strategies he used to get where we went next I've now forgotten—and now he is holding up books to the screen for me to write down the titles. As he lifts each book towards his computer's camera, he turns his face to the side, pauses briefly, a gesture that says, I'll wait while you take this down. I'll sit and do nothing while you slip into the role of secretary, student, subordinate, servant. His actions signal I am expected to begin my ascent to the heights where he already sits.

This sudden shift startles me. I notice now the display of books behind him, how unlike me he's written nothing down during our meeting nor has he typed any notes. I am again the empty vessel, and he the filler. His grand design, like that of so many others like him, begins with my subjugation. This isn't right, it doesn't feel right, it doesn't feel good, it isn't good. I begin to calculate my exit. Still a hopeful fool, I persevere, for a time. Our project is more important than his personality. I tell this to myself, as if saying this lie will make it so, the mission is more than the man, isn't it? He's immature maybe, but he means well, his intentions are good, don't be so cynical. I say all this too. I can rise above his petty displays of dominance. This is just what certain Christian men do. This is just who they are. I repeat words to myself I've heard others say in times like these. At times I can't help myself in this, it's so deeply rooted, default. But when finally I have doled out every cheap grace beneath my dignity, when at last I have admitted to myself that I'm here again, here where I've said I'll never again go, not ever, finally I say no. I again exercise my agency of leaving. I say to him, "We will be equal partners, or we will part ways." This he would tweak for future audiences. "She made an ultimatum, so we let her go."

To be let go is not the same as leaving. Still, it's ambiguous enough to be useful when talking about an act of leaving that the person left behind experiences as rejection, since this phrase's meaning is in the eye of the beholder. To let a person go is sometimes to terminate them, to expel them legally from employment. It doesn't pack the punch of "You're fired" – that phrase is reserved for the worst offenders. "To let go" is strategically soft. By the authority vested in us, by and through us, we've decided you should leave and so you may leave. There's the door, you may now go to hell. You may. This company, this church, this organisation, this relationship, we no longer require the use of your services. Fill in the blanks however your imagination chooses. Buried in the 'may' is the 'must.'

Oh but that's not the meaning I intended, my former colleague might say, if pressed. What I mean to say is we allowed her to leave, we gave her permission to remove herself from our aims and objectives of her own accord. All better now? I go, I exercise my agency in going, but still, he declares this has happened on his authority. Not only he, but the collective-we on whose behalf he speaks, all we-plural who agree have released the latch, the righteous-we now against the unrighteous-me. Now I-by-myself am able to make my exit. Men sometimes say such things when they know they cannot force a woman to return, when they must talk in ways that signal that it was something that happened only because they permitted it. They speak as bosses, as directors, as rulers, as generals and judges, as the kings they imagine themselves to be. "We'll allow it." One example I've heard from time to time, "I allow my wife to work," falls from the lips of men who expect me to marvel at their permissiveness over their subjects. Look what I let her do, look where I grant her the authority to go.

But perhaps he won't allow it, perhaps he doesn't want to accept what her leaving means. If a person who leaves is perceived as still within reach, still vulnerable, still dependent, if a man still perceives his reputation for reigning to be dependent upon her staying, if he still wants her, wants to feel his power over her – he might show up unexpectedly at her new place of residence, he stalks her, becomes chummy with her friends, finds out her schedule. Luke continued to do this, even up until mere weeks before his own wedding to someone else from our church-school. I was then working at an insurance company, he somehow got hold of my work number and rang me, one final check to see if I'd reconsider, surely now she regrets the words of rejection she said to me all those years before, surely seeing me slipping away, she has seen sense. "How did you get this number," I asked him. "I never reveal my sources," was his reply, another of those flippant faux jokes that masks the Man-right to withhold information, to conceal Man-military strategy. I wasn't to know how he tracked me. Now as I'm writing I'm remembering more, that this carried on even beyond the state of his marital union, he travelled up without his wife one weekend to where I was living, he showed up at my church, another time he left messages on my home phone, here I am just putting some salmon on the grill, thinking of you. I left, but I could never leave the kingdom of his thoughts.

When there are children involved, where before a man was

uninvolved with his own kids, a mostly absent and disinterested father, now he might appear suddenly attentive, challenge their mother's parenting. He might virtually stalk her, troll her anonymously on social media, show up at her church, her place of work, let himself into the house they used to share, rearrange something in her kitchen, her bedroom, put something new in her garden, in her driveway, somehow materialise and make his presence known, slap her around. Some signal that sends this warning: You cannot leave except on my terms, only when I decide, when I feel settled in my own mind, when others' opinion of me is by no means dependent on my connection to you. It will get worse unless and until you come back or unless I let you go. It's up to me. Some women do not survive their leaving.

We tell such men to "let her go." When next I saw John after I returned from my summer of linguistics studies, he said, "I've decided to let you go." He told me some sad story about how our Professor Krabbendam had come across him all curled up and crying in the foetal position in a corner at the church where he worked as youth minister. You should let her go, our professor allegedly told him. Perhaps he meant this as a solution to John's internal anguish. She's already gone, now for your own sake you need to let her go. Still, this too doesn't seem right. His letting or not letting has nothing to do with it. No, the fact is this: I Left. Subject + verb + zero object. We women sometimes talk about leaving like this without stating whose actions prompted our exit. This way of claiming complete agency can be empowering. We occupy the position of actor. We mark ourselves as those who carry out the material process of the removal of our selves. A man's permission has no place in this equation. Our language lays down the facts of our liberation.

Language like this can also be an act of self-protection since to name something threatening is to open oneself up to punishment. When I left my colleague and our faux partnership, he challenged my reasons. "How could you say I disrespected you, how could you possibly say this about me, after all I've done for women?" Yes, of course, how dare I question the integrity of someone who's done so much for so many women other than me, how very dare I position myself as more important than these recipients of his salvific acts, how miniscule I am in comparison to the legions of my sisters he has supposedly helped, what right have I to speak against someone with so much significance, against such a Man on such a Messianic Mission. I had a hunch then how this might go, how this particular man would reframe my leaving in service of the façade of his identity as feminist advocate, so I sent a letter of resignation to the organisation overseeing our project. More than just leaving, I left on my own terms, I declared my reasons and my perspective before witnesses. I am leaving, but I am by no means leaving him to take advantage of any residual ambiguity. "I didn't know you were going to do that," my indignant colleague said to that. "I could've told them things about you, but I didn't." Here now was a veiled threat, "How dare you act without my foreknowledge. I did not grant you permission to act in this way. I did not authorise your action. I could punish you if I so chose." This too I neutralised. "Go ahead," I said. "Say anything you need or want to say, just as I've done." Unlike men like him, I carry no worries about my reputation among supposedly powerful people, I have left them behind too, I lose no sleep over my absence from and insignificance in their empires.

His next move was to limit anyone's ability either to witness my leaving or to listen to my account of my departure. Some of this was through silence. "Where did Valerie go?" another person in the organisation asked him, months after I'd left, having heard no news of my exit. My former colleague also began complimenting me to mutual friends and acquaintances, fortifying his friendships with them, creating a strategic dilemma for anyone who heard my version of events. "Oh, but he thinks so highly of you," one friend said. "He said such nice things about you. Look how generous he is in his description of you." This too was familiar to me. My childhood pastor also spoke well of me at times, so too other elders from my church-school. They occasionally took credit for things I accomplished. "I was one of her first teachers, you know." In this way, some men recruit others to cover their tracks, proxies to act in their interests, to assist them in leaving no trace, to promote collective rewriting and forgetting of all they've done wrong. We are so nice now. Whatever she says now, we were always so very nice. We got along so very well. It's inexplicable why she left, likely it was some personal difficulty, she was always so flighty, she who took flight.

And what about when power-hungry people leave, what are the ways they formulate the narrative of their own leaving? My childhood pastor was eventually challenged in an inevitable power play he'd modelled for years. By that time, he had already sold our hallowed church-school building, property prices in the area having sky-rocketed. He then also sold the dominion-seeking school itself without consulting the headmaster, his close friend and church elder, by the way you're now out of a job. Our original church-school was razed to the ground after that, a fitting end perhaps. A few years later, spying some vulnerability, some in my childhood church eventually rose up to shoot our pastor down, seemingly keen to take his place as pack leader. Our pastor played his final move, he declared the courts of his own kingdom illegitimate, he stormed out of the church he'd founded before anyone could question him. He left before any could make him leave.

His mentor R. J. Rushdoony had already died by then, in 2001, the year I started graduate school. A few months before his death, Rushdoony wrote a short treatise "On Death and Dying," which directed his followers to concern themselves not with heaven, not with life after death, not with the resurrection, not even with eternity but rather with God's commandments, the law.[133] "We live in a world of death because of sin and we have a duty to overcome sin and death through Jesus Christ," he declared. And who better equipped to instruct us in the way of these kingdom

---

133 Rushdoony, R. J. (2001, April 1). On Death and Dying. *Chalcedon Magazine*. https://chalcedon.edu/magazine/on-death-and-dying

commandments but Rush the Scribe, Rush the Prophet,[134] Rush the Champion.[135] "There is nothing we're facing that wasn't spelled out presciently in the teaching and writing of R. J. Rushdoony," his followers would later reassure themselves, in the unsettling aftermath of his leaving. There is nothing more important to Babel builders than being absolutely correct in their calculations, they refuse to take reproof, they make their faces harder than rock.

Some will resort to even more extreme measures to control the narrative of their leaving, to prolong their pre-eminence over the people they've left. "I'm just not going to leave," Trump told one aide, after losing the 2020 presidential election to Jo Biden. "We're never leaving," he said to another. "How can you leave when you won an election?"[136] Some set the goalposts of dominion so high that they defeat even death. In 1979, the same year my family left Alaska, Movement cult leader Sam Fife perished in a plane crash in Guatemala, along with three of five other passengers on board. He was 54. According to newspaper reports, Fife and his fellow travellers had just completed a visit to the Quiche Theological Institute in Totonicapan, and their plane had hit bad weather shortly after take-off.[137] Fife had for some time been manufacturing a myth about his immortality – as part of this he stopped revealing his age, even when directly asked. After his death, then, his followers faced a conundrum. How could they reconcile Fife's promise never to leave with the fact of his leaving? In the spirit of Fife's declaration that his divine body would never decay, the Movement cult's official line about his death was this, that "Sam had achieved such a level

---

134 Schlissel, S. M. (2001, April 1). *Rousas ha' Navi' Rousas The Prophet: A Funeral Message*. *Chalcedon Magazine*. https://chalcedon.edu/magazine/rousas-ha-navi-rousas-the-prophet-a-funeral-message

135 Sandlin, P. A. (2001, April 1). *R. J. Rushdoony: Champion of Faith and Liberty*. *Chalcedon Magazine*. https://chalcedon.edu/magazine/r-j-rushdoony-champion-of-faith-and-liberty

136 Cillizza, C. (2022, September 12). *Donald Trump almost didn't leave the White House. Because, of course*. *CNN – The Point with Chris Cillizza*. https://edition.cnn.com/2022/09/12/politics/trump-white-house-lost-election/index.html

137 *The Akron Beacon Journal*, Sat, Apr 28, 1979, p. 1

of perfection, he could no longer be on this earth."[138] So unworthy were Fife's followers, so unrighteous, so filthy, that Fife was forced to leave, to take his superiority elsewhere. It's his followers' fault he left. If only they, if only we had been deserving enough, holy enough, if only we'd claimed the cosmos quickly enough, he would have stayed.

Men from my college years have used a similar strategy, placing the blame for their leaving, which has taken such forms as secret visits to a sex worker, frequent flirtation with work colleagues, double lives, all such leaving, all they lay squarely on the shoulders of their wives. After all, each one, he is a king, and kings do not falter. If only she'd not been so weak, so uncommitted, so un-submissive, so unsupportive, so selfish, so unwomanly, so un-useful, if only she had proven to be all she had seemed.

The idea of Sam Fife's saintly status fuelled speculation among some, similar to conspiracy theories that circulated after the death of Larry McDonald, similar to held-out hopes that Trump that had actually won his second election, that Fife had not in fact died at all, but was living elsewhere, perhaps among a people as worthy as he, perhaps we too might one day go there, if only we are holy enough. Fife's successor was a man called Buddy Cobb, whose teaching affirmed and extended the goal of sinless perfection, total and complete obedience to God, by which we will achieve eternal life.[139] Though numbers have dwindled in the Movement, some of Fife's farms are still not only running but by some noticeable measures thriving. A rather sketchy convention centre and airport connected with the cult is still in operation in Georgia, USA, run by Darryl Cobb, Buddy's son.[140]

---

138 McPadden, M. (2019, April 3). Inside The Apocalyptic Cult That Performed Exorcisms & Saw A "Demon On Every Doorknob." *Investigation Discovery: Crimefeed.* http://web.archive.org/web/20190709192111/https://www.investigationdiscovery.com/crimefeed/id-shows/the-move-apocalyptic-cult-that-performed-exorcisms-saw-a-demon-on-every-doorknob

139 Cobb, B. (2001). *Dead to Sin.* http://web.archive.org/web/20120209161617/http://humlog.homestead.com/dead_to_sin.htm

140 *Contact Us | Bowen's Mill Christian Centre.* (n.d.). Retrieved January 27, 2023, from http://bowensmill.org/contact-us

EPILOGUE

But there has also been further scandal. Another of Fife's close associates, involved in the purchase of the land for settlement in Alaska, a man called Douglas McClain, along with his son by the same name, have over the years been exposed as career criminals, with currently more than $7.8 million in civil judgments against them.[141] Among the crimes they have been accused of are preying on terminally ill patients, some of them elderly, with promises of a miracle cure called Immunosyn—derived from goats' blood—for HIV, cancer, multiple sclerosis and other grave illnesses.[142] Five years into investigation into their dealings, their crimes attracted some attention worldwide since one of the McClains's blood drug co-conspirators, Stephen Ferrone, is—oddly enough—married to the actor Vince Vaughan's mother.[143] This was seemingly bizarre enough to reach my newsfeed in England. But what struck me, more than this celebrity link, was that during the period when this former friend of my parents, Doug McClain, was peddling his snake oil, the husband of one of my church-school friends died of cancer while waiting in desperate hope for a similar so-called miracle drug to be delivered. How enigmatic are these seeming coincidences, when our lives move in circles like this, the tides flow in and out, the sun rises and sets, on its circular course the wind returns, to the place where the rivers flow, there they flow again, taking us back to where we started, so there is nothing new under the sun.

In 2016, Buddy Cobb's granddaughter, Ang, confronted him on film about the abuse she and others had suffered as part of the Movement community.[144] She asked him why he hadn't done

---

141 United States Securities and Exchange Commission. (2011, August 1). *SEC Complaint: Stephen D. Ferrone, Douglas A. McClain, Jr., Douglas A. McClain, Sr., James T. Miceli, Immunosyn, Corporation, Argyll Biotechnologies, LLC, Argyll Equities, LLC, and Padmore, Holdings, Ltd.* https://www.sec.gov/litigation/complaints/2011/comp22057.pdf

142 Levy, A. (2014, January 23). Christian businessman indicted on theft charge in elder bilking case. *San Antonio Express-News.* https://www.expressnews.com/news/local/article/Christian-businessman-indicted-on-theft-charge-in-5169919.php?t=bf3319cbb3c550e514

143 Janssen, K. (2016, May 2). Vince Vaughn's stepfather liable in goat blood drug case, jury finds. *Chicago Tribune.* https://www.chicagotribune.com/business/ct-goats-blood-scam--0503-biz-20160502-story.html

144 Cobb, A. (2016, October 16). *Buddy Cobb.* YouTube. https://www.youtube.com/watch?v=LOS6E3_Zk4Q

anything to confront the people who harmed so many children. "What are you going to do about all the abuse? Why don't you get rid of the people that are abusing?" Cobb's reply, several times repeating himself, is one of immediate distancing, none of that there has anything to do with him here, and anyway, nothing happens except what is the will of God. His granddaughter presses him, "So everything that happened to those kids was God's will?" "Absolutely," he says, smiling, gesturing. "Everything is going according to the will of God. That's so they can see what evil is like when evil has its day." Do you see? Even their harming you is a lesson, allowed by God, that you might understand what consequences you face if you turn away, if you presume to know what's good for you, if you mark yourself as an ally of the enemy, if you let them down by leaving.

Why don't you just leave? Why didn't she leave? This is another way we talk about leaving, assuming complete liberty to go and come as we please. It's so easy, just pick up your things and go. I heard a religious leader make this flippant point publicly, at an academic conference on marital captivity in religious environments a few years ago. We were discussing women stuck in limbo in abusive marriages, able to get a civil divorce but unable to meet the legal-spiritual requirements of their religious community. "No problem, she should just leave her community then," the religious leader said. She can start a new life elsewhere. Change your name, change your address if you're afraid of brutal repercussions. So simple. As if we can glide effortlessly in and out of such controlling spaces, of the resulting trauma, as if we can erase and start over, as if we can ignore all the defensive instincts we've honed by being treated as those hunted, as if we can pretend we will be left alone after leaving. As if there are not those who refuse to let us go, those who catch the scent of our wounds, stalk us in pursuit of the taste of fresh meat, pull us down into the dust of their earthly ambition. As if what we have left behind leaves us. No matter when a woman leaves, she's left too early, she's left too late, after all this time, you're leaving now? Perhaps things weren't as bad as you said. You could've left but you didn't. Now you've left, you should've instead stayed, at least a little longer. Look what you've left behind. Look at the manner of your leaving. Look who you've deserted. All this leaving is on my mind, how so many of the men and women I've known have forbidden me and others from leaving, how when we leave, people condemn us, reclaim and reframe our departure. A pastor's wife once expressed gratitude to one of her daughters-in-law like this, "I'm so thankful that you stay home instead of abandoning your children to work." This is another kind of unauthorised leaving. To leave the gendered space of home, even temporarily, is to turn your back on your place in the kingdom of men, to reject your husband, to jilt your family, to blaspheme the name of god, to take the side of Satan. How dare you go out to visit the women of Shechem and jeopardize the second coming, predicated as it is on all our good work.

A friend reported a story of when she visited the church of my first youth leader, where he'd introduced himself to her with this single question, "So, do you work outside the home?" With all such words, they scan us women up and down, they prepare to approve or disapprove, they reel us in, they rebuke our unacceptable leaving from the centre of domesticity where we belong and serve, the launching pad of all their dominion.

So many people I know, my friends and family members even, have suffered through many dysfunctional relationships, sold to them under the guise of a woman's domestic purpose. So many of my childhood friends and acquaintances, church leaders and sons of church leaders, men I knew at college and at many other such places since, are torturing their wives with self-centred sex, marital rape, silencing our expressions of anger, controlling our access to money, deliberately sabotaging our relationships with other people, indulging in secret intimacies with our friends, flirting with anyone and everyone while withholding connection from the one they've vowed to love forever. More than a few are criminals. Some are stalkers. Some abuse animals. Some are physically violent. Some are rapists. Some women I know are also cold and abusive, normalising in their marriages, in motherhood, what they suffered during childhood, withholding medical treatment from their children, expecting immediate and unquestioning obedience, deliberately creating harsh home environments under some semblance of apocalyptic preparation, fostering that dependence that disguises itself as the victorious family. Andrea Dworkin, in her book Right-Wing Women, captures this dynamic insightfully.

> She conforms, in order to be as safe as she can be. Sometimes it is a lethargic conformity, in which case male demands slowly close in on her, as if she were a character buried alive in an Edgar Allan Poe story. Sometimes it is a militant conformity. She will save herself by proving that she is loyal, obedient, useful, even fanatic in the service of the men around her. She is the happy hooker, the happy homemaker, the exemplary Christian, the pure academic, the perfect comrade, the terrorist par excellence. Whatever the values, she will embody them with a perfect fidelity. The males rarely keep their part of the bargain as she understands it: protection from male violence against her person. But the militant conformist has given so much of herself—her labor, heart, soul, often her body, often children—that this betrayal is akin to nailing the coffin shut; the corpse is beyond caring.
>
> Women know, but must not acknowledge, that resisting male control or confronting male betrayal will lead to rape, battery, restitution, ostracization or exile, confinement in a mental institution or jail, or death.[145]

Yet it's worth saying again: in white male Christian supremacist movements like Dominionism, women are so often the most brutal betrayals of other women, keen as they are to resist violence by redirecting it towards others more vulnerable than they. They may rationalise it like this: The world is harder than I'll ever be, they say.

---

145 Dworkin, A. (1983). *Right-wing Women: The politics of domesticated females*. Women's Press. (pp. 14-15).

EPILOGUE

If I have to suffer in the name of righteousness, so must you. What's more, you'll thank me for it, praise God for it. Whatever cruelty you think you're enduring, I promise it can get worse, so suck it up, stop crying, go back to him, to them, come back to me, we're doing you a favour, you'll be sorry when you see the horrors awaiting you if you try to leave this community, this marriage, this relationship. The place of us woman is to sacrifice. Get up on your cross and follow me. By and by, such women persist in guiding their sisters to suffer in service of the empire they cling to and to loathe themselves in the process. Truly, there is no love among people of war. Some of us have left, have been left, are thinking about leaving, are desperate to leave, are putting away persistent thoughts of leaving. Some are in the long, painful process of leaving and going back and leaving again. Some stay for the children, for their parents, for fear of violent retribution, for fear of poverty, for fear of judgement, for fear of being labelled as 'them' against the righteous 'us,' for fear of God.

As I sit here today, I see clearly how extremely successful all those years of grooming were, and even in the face of so much violence, how vastly my compatriots' accounts of our youth differ from one another. There is my past, his and hers, ours, theirs. Some person I used to know will read my words and protest, No, it was never like that, she got that all wrong, it all went like this instead, we were happy, we loved one another. They cling to their hope like heaven. For some, these were the golden days, the best of all times, "such a blessing, if only our kids could have what we did." One church-school friend speaks this wish to me over Skype, her husband sitting nearly out of my line of vision, just enough Man-presence to intimidate both her and me. Under his eye. I watch my words for her sake. In this one utterance, in this one image, I see the state of their current lives, how deeper their descent into hell.

So many of us have chosen what's familiar, are still choosing only what's known, even when it harms us. We choose it over and over, we re-sacralise it, we pass it down to our children, our children's children, now it's typical, now we don't have to see it anymore, now we don't have to face the uproar of change, the risk of something new or different.

What a danger it is for warriors to be even a little bit wrong. I see others of us have given the appearance of leaving but merely been transferred to another abusive relationship, another cultish institution, another movement that offers fast-food answers, demanding payment via the same excesses and abuses. We are so eager to place our every decision into the hands of someone else. We pretend to prize liberty while we sit in a cold and joyless prison. In some minds, moving on to another anguished community is progress, finally a more ideal, more correct form of holy misery from the wholly inferior first attempt. If only those first fools had put it properly into practice. The problem of that past place was this uncommitted leader or that ignorant one – except for them, we'd all be slotted suitably in our cells by now. Every Man, woman, child in their correct place. Such people boast about peace, they walk in the stubbornness of their heart. The iniquity of fathers on the children and on the grandchildren to the third and fourth generations.

I want now to be honest with myself, to carry no shame about who I was then, or ten years ago, last year, yesterday. I've spent years weighed down with confusion and shame at my stupidity, my internalised misogyny and racism. I've been smitten with madness and with blindness and with bewilderment of heart, I've been oppressed and robbed continually, seemingly with none to save me. How could I join in all these acts of oppression, since I myself know the feelings of being oppressed, since I myself also have been oppressed? So many times I have sworn to myself I'd not go there again, I'd not allow myself to be put through that again, I'd not participate in harming anyone else.

But here's the real sting, not only that we embrace the hate that harms us but that we can also be ignorant of Love, deprived and unaware of it, unable to locate even our own longing for it. This is what all the arrogance, the chilling cruelty and violence, the endless accumulation of wealth and influence and power of each and every

Dominionist theology, what all this empire building ultimately robs us of – the stunning mystery of intimacy and connection, of gentleness and dignity, of complexity, of knowing and being known, of letting go, of revelling in beauty without calculating its kingdom purpose.

Perhaps more than all of this, the mind-set of war denies us the wonderful world of being a pilgrim, a wanderer, a wallflower, a guest, even a nobody.[146] All these are treasures deemed worthless in places where only certain expressions of power are prioritised. How heartbreaking, that we can be seen and loved and yet be fully unaware of what gifts of contentedness, what sensitivity and self-loving and self-sacrificial service lie within our reach when we sit off-centre, as people of the quiet spaces. How bleak that our eyes can scan a text written in the language of kindness, by those who seek simply to stand as witness to our humanity, those who invite us to bask in the perfect peace of love. How devastating that, lacking all proficiency in such a tongue, we can be untouched and unmoved by such unfamiliar and stunning tenderness.

What hope is there for us? What rest can be found for we who have made so many lives such a misery? As I am finishing this text, two men from my church-school have died, one an elder and the other a drug addict and criminal of my own generation. The elder's family have puffed up his life with praise, a man who

> pushed through pain and infirmity for years, rarely with any complaint… a man of rare and incandescent genius… character of utmost excellence, steadfast dedication, fervent enthusiasm, and unimpeachable integrity.[147]

---

146 "I'm a quiet soul. My favourite sound in the whole world is the sign of a teacup finding its place on a saucer… I need to express my identity through the metaphor of a nap." (Parry, M., & Olb, J. 2018. *Hannah Gadsby – Nanette*. Netflix. https://www.netflix.com/title/80233611)

147 *Dewey Harper Hodges Obituary*. (2022, January 31). Tribute Archive. https://www.tributearchive.com/obituaries/23875218/dewey-harper-hodges

Hundreds of comments have poured in to social media from people I used to know, this obituary has invigorated their faith in the kingdom that broke so many backs. What a life well-lived, they say. What a shining testament to our city of Men. No one speaks of the death of the boy who was filmed playing in the church-school parking lot for Bill Moyers' film about Christian Reconstructionism all those years ago, whose life – like mine – was poisoned by so many abominable demands. His death lingers in the shadows of our history, for so many an acceptable casualty, tolerable collateral damage in our endless brutal war.

I'm sick to death of so many empty and insecure expectations, the hasty promise that things will be fine, it'll all work out, we will all win, just stay positive, chin up, if we work hard enough, if we have enough faith, if we ourselves are enough, all the rushing past grief with the peace, peace, peace. Regardless of where I am now in my life, the joy and contentment I have located, the anger I have learned to accommodate, the rage that no longer rules over me, I want to sit awhile here in the sinking sand of so much suffering, in all our grief, in our every sadness, our affliction and our wandering, the bitterness and the gall. For this, I put on sackcloth. I lament and wail. In the face of so much enforced forgetting, I will hold onto the memory of all our devastation. I will meet its angry eye. I will not look away.